Effective Practice for Adolescents with Reading and Literacy Challenges

"*Effective Practice for Adolescents with Reading and Literacy Challenges* is an important book that addresses a critical problem—literacy instruction in high school—in a masterful, evidence-based manner. Written with teachers and administrators in mind, this book offers numerous instructional ideas for working with diverse groups of struggling learners. Importantly, the instructional ideas emanate from a solid research base, one that can benefit both struggling learners and their teachers. Kudos to the authors for tackling an important topic in such a competent and practical manner!"

Howard Margolis, author of *Reading Disabilities: Beating the Odds*

"Denti and Guerin have assembled a work that is an elegant mix of evidence-based practice, instructional leadership, and practical ideas and strategies. The book is broad in scope, written with great clarity, and very hands-on. Few edited works are ever able to achieve the 'Let's get practical!' theme of this text. Teachers, students and other professionals who read this book will appreciate its clarity but most of all, they will be able to put so much of what they read to use right away and begin 'changing students' lives on Monday.'"

Wayne A. Secord, author of *Clinical Evaluation of Language Fundamentals – Fourth Edition*

"*Effective Practice for Adolescents with Reading and Literacy Challenges* presents a wealth of evidence-based teacher and student strategies that will strengthen the practice of both general and special educators at the secondary level. The varying perspectives of the chapter authors adds to the richness of this text while reinforcing the book's theme: through intense, intentional intervention we can make a difference in the literacy of struggling secondary students."

Anita L. Archer, author of *Rewards Reading Excellence: Word Attack and Rate Development Strategies*

Lack of reading proficiency is a barrier to understanding the academic content of any discipline. *Effective Practice for Adolescents with Reading and Literacy Challenges* provides secondary teachers with the knowledge and the strategies they need to improve their students' reading skills.

Editors Denti and Guerin present a comprehensive collection of articles by a selection of prominent literacy and education researchers that provide practical approaches to improving literacy and offer accounts of successful evidence-based programs and practices that can be tailored to the needs of teachers working with struggling readers.

Each chapter includes questions for review, a list of web resources, and suggested small group activities, making this volume a valuable tool for all teachers, regardless of content area.

Lou Denti is the Lawton Love Distinguished Professor in Special Education, and Director of the Center for Reading Diagnosis and Instruction at California State University, Monterey Bay.

Gilbert Guerin is on the staff of the San Jose State University Foundation where he directs teacher preparation projects in literacy.

Effective Practice for Adolescents with Reading and Literacy Challenges

Edited by
Lou Denti and
Gilbert Guerin

Routledge
Taylor & Francis Group

NEW YORK AND LONDON

First published 2008
by Routledge
270 Madison Ave, New York, NY 10016

Simultaneously published in the UK
by Routledge
2 Park Square, Milton Park, Abingdon, Oxon OX14 4RN

Routledge is an imprint of the Taylor & Francis Group, an informa business

© 2008 Taylor & Francis

Typeset in Minion and Trade Gothic by
Florence Production Ltd, Stoodleigh, Devon
Printed and bound in the United States of America on acid-free paper by
Walsworth Publishing Company, Marceline, MO

Library of Congress Cataloging in Publication Data
Effective practice for adolescents with reading and literacy challenges/
    edited by Lou Denti and Gilbert Guerin.
        p. cm.
    Includes bibliographical references and index.
    1. Reading (Secondary) 2. Reading comprehension. 3. Reading
    —Remedial teaching. I. Denti, Lou. II. Guerin, Gilbert R.
    LB1632.E34 2008
    428.4071′2—dc22   2007021580

ISBN10: 0–415–95736–2 (hbk)
ISBN10: 0–415–95737–0 (pbk)
ISBN10: 0–203–93725–2 (ebk)

ISBN13: 978–0–415–95736–6 (hbk)
ISBN13: 978–0–415–95737–3 (pbk)
ISBN13: 978–0–203–93725–9 (ebk)

To all secondary teachers who care deeply for students who struggle to read. And to the students themselves who persevere.

Contents

About the Editors

Lou Denti, Ph.D. is Lawton Love Distinguished Professor in Special Education at California State University, Monterey Bay where he directs the Center for Reading Diagnosis and Instruction (see http://readingcenter. csumb.edu for an overview of center activities, conferences, and professional development opportunities). His research interests include struggling readers at the secondary level, education policy related to literacy instruction, differentiating instruction, and secondary level collaboration and inclusion. Dr. Denti recently co-edited a special series for *Reading and Writing Quarterly* entitled "Pointing the Way: Teaching Reading to Struggling Readers at the Secondary Level." His most recent book is entitled *New Ways of Looking at Learning Disabilities: Connections to Classroom Practice.* His new book of poetry, *Shadows and Moon,* published by Caddo Gap Press, delves into the feelings students experience when they just don't quite fit in.

Gilbert Guerin, Ph.D. is the author or co-author of the following books related to literacy: *Addressing Learning Disabilities and Differences, Bridges to Reading, Informal Assessment in Education, Improving Instruction for Youth at Risk,* and *Critical Steps in Curriculum Reform.* He is the co-author of recent articles entitled "Confronting the Problem of Poor Literacy: Recognition and Action" and "Plans, Predictions, and Frustrations in the Education of a Troubled Youth: A Case for Enhanced Early Literacy Efforts". He has developed an online instructional resource site for high school teachers of students who are at-risk of school failure located at http://alternativeed.sjsu.edu. Dr. Guerin's training module is entitled "Adolescent Reading Development".

Dr. Guerin is on the staff of the San Jose State University Foundation where he directs teacher preparation projects in literacy. Previously he held faculty positions in education and in psychology at San Jose State University, University of California at Berkeley, Hayward State University, and Dominican College at San Rafael. He holds state licensure as a psychologist and teaching credentials in elementary, secondary, and special education.

Contributors

Dr. Linda Carnine is Technical Assistance Provider for Western Region Reading First Technical Assistance Center, University of Oregon where she provides expertise in reading content, beginning reading assessments and reading interventions, program implementation, and reading coaches training and evaluation. Dr. Carnine has published numerous articles and books addressing strategies to promote reading and literacy instruction for students at risk of school failure and for students with mild to moderate disabilities. She is most noted for her DISTAR and Corrective Reading publications.

Dr. Mary E. Curtis is Professor of Education and Director of the Center for Special Education at Lesley University in Cambridge Massachusetts. She has written numerous articles on reading diagnosis and remediation, the role of vocabulary in comprehension, and reading skills of at-risk teenagers. Dr. Curtis served as Co-director of the Boys Town Reading Center where she oversaw research and development on *Reading is FAME*, a remedial curriculum shown to reverse reading failure in older adolescents.

Dr. Marcia Davidson is an Assistant Professor at the University of Maine in Special Education. She was Senior Research Associate at RMC Research Corporation, conducted two national randomized trial studies on early literacy curricula, and is currently the co-PI of a four year IES grant evaluating early literacy curricula. She is also Technical Assistance Provider to states for Reading First. Her research interests center around reading fluency, early and adolescent literacy, and teacher quality.

Dr. Lou Denti is Lawton Love Distinguished Professor in Special Education at California State University, Monterey Bay where he directs the Center for Reading Diagnosis and Instruction. His research interests and written works address struggling readers at the secondary level, education policy related to literacy instruction, differentiating instruction, and secondary level collaboration and inclusionary practices.

Dr. Kevin Feldman is Director of Reading and Intervention with the Sonoma County Office of Education (SCOE) and an independent educational consultant working with publishers, schools, and districts across the country. Dr. Feldman's primary focus is on improving academic literacy. His major contributions are in the areas of building vocabulary and academic English, assisting struggling readers, preventing early reading failure, differentiating instruction to meet the full range of learners, and accommodating and accelerating ELL/Special Education and other high risk students. As the Director of Reading and Intervention for SCOE he develops, organizes, and monitors programs related to PreK-12 literacy and the prevention/remediation of reading difficulties. To learn more about Dr. Feldman's work, please visit the SCOE web site (www.scoe.org/reading).

Dr. Bonnie Grossen specializes in school-wide implementation of research knowledge to guide low performing middle and high schools across the nation. She has over 50 scholarly publications and 30 reports of original research studies published in peer-reviewed journals. The thrust of her research is to help students with disabilities achieve rigorous academic standards in general classrooms at the secondary level.

Dr. Gilbert Guerin is former Chair of the Division of Special Education and Rehabilitative Services at San Jose State University. In his current position as Grant Writer through the Foundation at San Jose State University he has been successful in securing grants to prepare teachers in the area of elementary and secondary literacy. He has written books on curriculum, literacy, and informal assessment for at-risk youth as well as articles on correctional education. A psychologist and a special educator he has developed a grant supported web site, http://alternativeed.sjsu.edu, that provides instructional modules in alternative education.

Dr. Kate Kinsella is Teacher Educator in the Department of Secondary Education at San Francisco State University. She teaches coursework addressing academic language and literacy development in linguistically and culturally diverse classrooms. She has maintained secondary classroom involvement by teaching an academic literacy class for adolescent English learners through the University's Step to College Program. She publishes and provides consultancy and training nationally, focusing upon responsible instructional practices that provide second language learners and less proficient readers in grades 4 to 12 with the language and literacy skills vital to educational mobility. She is the program author for *Reading in the Content Areas: Strategies for Reading Success,* published by Pearson Learning and the lead program author for the 2002 and 2005 Prentice Hall secondary language arts program *Timeless Voices: Timeless Themes.*

Dr. Vicki Lord Larson, a respected scholar, is past President of the Wisconsin Speech-Language Pathology and Audiology Association, and has received the association's top award, Honors of the Association. She served as an American Speech-Language Hearing Association (ASHA) counselor. She was selected as an ASHA fellow, one of the highest honors given by the national association. She is a board-recognized Specialist in Child Language and a noted author in her field.

Dr. Ann Marie Longo is Associate Professor of Education at Goucher College. Prior to her current position Dr. Longo served as Co-director of the Boys Town Reading Center. She received her doctorate degree in Reading from the Harvard Graduate School of Education. Her research and teaching experiences have included students at the university, secondary, and elementary levels.

Dr. Louisa Moats has been a teacher, psychologist, researcher, graduate school faculty member, and author of many influential books and papers on the topics of reading, spelling, language, and teacher preparation. She has authored several books, including *Speech to Print: Language Essentials for Teachers* (Brookes Publishing); *Spelling: Development, Disability, and Instruction* (York Press); *Straight Talk About Reading* (with Susan Hall, Contemporary Books), and *Parenting a Struggling Reader* (with Susan Hall, Random House). She has also written numerous journal articles, chapters, and policy papers including the American Federation of Teachers' "Teaching Reading *is* Rocket Science" and the Learning First Alliance's *Every Child Reading: A Professional Development Guide.* Dr. Moats is currently Consultant Advisor to Sopris West Educational Services for Literacy Research and Professional Development. She is focusing on the improvement of teacher preparation and professional development through the design and dissemination of LETRS (Language Essentials for Teachers of Reading and Spelling), a series of modules for teachers. She serves on the National Board of the International Dyslexia Association.

Dr. Judy K. Montgomery, (CCC-SLP) is Professor of Special Education and Literacy at Chapman University, Orange, CA and a Board Recognized Specialist in Child Language. She worked for 24 years in public schools as a speech-language pathologist, Director of an AAC Center, Principal of a K-8 School, and Director of Special Education. Her interests include developing language and literacy for students with mild, moderate, and severe disabilities, and building professional collaborations with general educators, special educators, and reading specialists. She has also published in the areas of noise-induced hearing loss in children, inclusion, AAC, pre-school phonological disorders, and school administration. Dr. Montgomery served as President of the American Speech Language Hearing Association (ASHA), California Speech-Language-Hearing Association (CSHA), National Tri-Alliance, and the US Society for Augmentative and Alternative Communication (USSAAC). An ASHA Fellow, she has received the Honors of CSHA, and the Division of Communicative Disabilities and Deafness (DCDD).

Dr. Irene Nares-Guzicki is Associate Professor in Special Education at California State University, Monterey Bay. She is currently CSUMB's representative on the Chancellor's Faculty Advisory Committee for Literacy in California. Her expertise areas are in bilingual special education, assessment, literacy, and pedagogical practices. She plays a vital role in the California Association for Professors in Special Education and is also the President for the Council for Exceptional Children.

Dr. Edy Hammond Stoughton is Visiting Assistant Professor in Special Education at Indiana University, Indianapolis. She teaches both pre-service and in-service teachers in the Teacher Education Program. Her research interests include interconnections between academic and behavioral difficulties, holistic approaches to literacy learning that draw on cognitive, affective, and environmental factors, and the effects of teacher identity on building classroom relationships.

Editors' Thoughts

We wanted this book to be accessible for the classroom teacher. When we first asked contributors to think about writing a chapter we told them over the telephone or via email to try and put themselves in the middle of a classroom nowadays. How would you go about teaching to diverse adolescent learners who struggle to read? We wanted practical strategies and programs that a teacher would be able to use or share with district leaders. As we progressed, we noticed that we needed chapters on systemic change. We worried about the teacher with all these great ideas and methods with little support to implement the new concepts and strategies at the school or site level. So, we invited a few authors to shore up that end of the book—insightful ways for leaders in schools to incorporate new procedures and policies that have a solid research track record. It is our hope that the ideas in the book resonate for you and the book serves you and your students well, now and into the future.

Preface

Literacy is the cornerstone to improving school achievement. Reading, writing, and speaking are required in every academic subject and, while the context, symbols, and discourse vary by subject, literate understanding and fluency are the constant denominators of success. Advances in our understanding of literacy have increased our recognition that reading instruction should not end in elementary school and that a broader concept of literacy is needed at the high school.

The changing nature of high schools has led to recognition that instruction in reading, writing, and speaking needs to be embedded in classes outside the English department and should be a legitimate and vital part of all instruction. Schools today face radically changing student demographics, new demands that all students achieve content standards, expectations that all students will pass high school exit examinations, and pressures that graduates provide an educated workforce.

Teachers face enrollments that, increasingly, are second-language learners, are learners that in earlier years may have dropped out of school because of poor achievement, that are technologically but not academically literate, and that have, immediately available, an infinite variety of competing entertainment. On the positive side, teachers hold the space where students gather, teachers have the knowledge that students "need to know," and teachers provide passage to work or advanced education. When students have access to knowledge, when they are successful with that knowledge, when they are skillfully instructed and positively motivated, class can be the "best game in town."

In recent years interest in literacy, heretofore almost the exclusive domain of elementary schools, has intensified at the secondary school level.

National interest developed, in part, as a response to the school reform and accountability movement and to mandatory high school exit examinations. The federal legislation that created "No Child Left Behind" also increased pressure on the schools to reach and teach all students at all grade levels.

In recent years, corporate, foundation, and state support of secondary school literacy has resulted in new research, initiatives, programs, and conferences. The following are a few examples of these activities: "Schools for a New Society" (2000) by the Carnegie Corporation of New York, "Reading for Understanding" (2000) from WestEd and its Strategic Literacy Initiative, "Achieving State and National Literacy Goals, a Long Uphill Road" by the Rand Corporation (2005), and the "Secondary Literacy Summit VII" (2007), California Department of Education. The strands at the Summit conference covered the following range of literacy needs: "Intensive Intervention," "Strategic Intervention," "Advanced," "Benchmark," "Across the Content Areas," and "Literacy Leadership."

The need to improve high school literacy is urgent. Each year thousands of young people leave school without the literacy skills that are needed to advance in the workplace or lead full lives. This book provides concepts and strategies designed to assist professionals and others who have responsibility for teaching or supporting young people in their quest for skills in reading, writing, and communicating.

Structure of the Book

The editors believe that vocabulary is the gateway to fluency and comprehension for adolescents who struggle to read. The first section reinforces this notion centering on how best to teach vocabulary to all students effectively. The authors in this section create a theoretical foundation for their proposed methods and strategies and then give the reader cogent examples of how to use the techniques, not only to increase vocabulary acquisition, but also to increase reading skill. The reader can be assured that the authors have had plenty of "in the trenches" experiences and the suggested approaches are useable in real world classrooms. In the opening chapter Feldman and Kinsella contend that educators across disciplines and grade levels routinely confuse rigorous and robust academic vocabulary teaching with assigning an array of independent or collaborative vocabulary activities, and that what instruction does take place frequently lacks the foresight, planning, and efficacy to prepare students responsibly for the lexical demands of challenging curricula. The authors in this section tackle the lexical divide at secondary schools with powerful teaching and learning strategies based on evidence.

The authors in the second section peer into the hearts and minds of marginalized students in secondary schools. Sadly, if one has problems reading, writing, and spelling, navigating through halls of learning at any middle or high school presents a formidable challenge. Students at risk of school failure, whether identified or not, need teachers who not only instruct, but mentor with a deep sense of caring. The authors carefully construct a lens to look at the problem and then offer suggestions to assist students both academically and socially. The chapter by Vicki Lord Larson goes further to help educators understand that strategies for students with language disorders are very different from generic vocabulary strategies for students who may need an intervention to shore up their fluency or comprehension. The voices of the students sing out in this section. Their music and their message are loud and clear—don't give up on me!

The third section looks at program coordination issues and logistical roadblocks, i.e. scheduling that makes change irksome and most difficult at secondary schools. Without systemic change the suggestions and strategies advocated for in this book will end up moored on the shoals of good intention. The authors challenge the readers to roll up their sleeves and begin to tackle literacy and reading problems at their respective schools head on. Careful not to proselytize, the authors back up their change strategies with solid evidence, legal underpinning, and real school examples. This section is dedicated to helping middle and high school teachers change the way they provide literacy instruction based on research and best practice. The authors ask the reader to be forward thinking and not settle for the *status quo*.

The contributors to this book have generated a wellspring of ideas, strategies, and new directions for educators working with upper grade students who struggle to read. The editors hope that you will find their work compelling, insightful, and useful.

Vocabulary— The Gateway to Reading Fluency and Comprehension

In this section the authors address how best to teach vocabulary to secondary students who struggle to read. The strategies and suggestions offered are practical and useable in today's classrooms. **Kevin Feldman and Kate Kinsella**'s chapter "Narrowing the Language Gap: The Case for Explicit Vocabulary Instruction in Secondary Classrooms" presents a model for comprehensive vocabulary development which includes four essential elements: (1) reading volume, (2) direct teaching of individual words, (3) teaching word learning strategies, and (4) fostering word consciousness. The authors focus on direct teaching of individual words and couple it with new evidence-based strategies to ensure that students apply what they learn in both academic and writing contexts.

Judy Montgomery's chapter "Evidence-based Strategies for Vocabulary Instruction/Intervention" asks some very fundamental questions about how to enhance adolescent vocabulary and then proceeds to answer the questions in a clear and very direct manner. As Montgomery so poignantly states, "Adolescents will increase their vocabulary if they read and they will improve their reading if they recognize more words. That is how vocabulary grows. Reading matters." The big challenge is to get struggling readers to read. Montgomery meets the challenge head on with methods and approaches that definitely are teacher friendly. Every strategy or method espoused is backed by evidence-based statements so that the reader can review the literature to expand their thinking and knowledge base. A salient feature of Judy Montgomery's chapter addresses tier two words and their importance in secondary education. Montgomery indicates that tier two words are high-frequency words that show up in many academic classes and have multiple meanings: however, they are not often taught since they appear "common," but in fact, they are not well understood by many students.

Curtis and Longo's chapter "Teaching Academic Vocabulary to Adolescents to Improve Comprehension" reinforces the two other authors' research and ideas promulgated in this section. The instructional activities described in their chapter are appropriate for promoting vocabulary learning in any classroom—whether it be via the sort of "stand-alone" units they designed or through instruction integrated into a content area. Success in using the activities depends on following some general guidelines, however, which include introducing and activating word meanings, presenting words in a variety of contexts, providing multiple opportunities to learn words in active and generative ways, and providing ongoing assessment.

Louisa Moats challenges our taken for granted assumptions about spelling at the middle and high school level in her chapter "Can You Teach an Older Student to Spell?" Educators and lay people alike seem to think that spelling is for elementary school children and has little relevance for adolescents. The old adages, such as "I am a lousy speller," "I just use spell check," or "no need to spell correctly these days," though pervasive throughout society in general and in secondary schools is summarily challenged by Moats. She indicates that average and below average students can be taught how to think about words and what questions to ask when they do not know a word. She offers concrete strategies that make the reader want to include spelling instruction (the way she proposes) in content and remedial classes.

In summary, these four chapters clearly articulate that vocabulary instruction at the secondary level is the gateway to comprehension. After reading these chapters, educators will now have a "toolbox" filled with activities, strategies, methods, and websites to choose from when delivering instruction.

CHAPTER 1

Narrowing the Language Gap: The Case for Explicit Vocabulary Instruction in Secondary Classrooms

KEVIN FELDMAN AND KATE KINSELLA

The limits of my language are the limits of my mind.
All I know is what I have words for.

Ludwig Wittgenstein

Introduction

The Importance of Vocabulary for Secondary Students

There is a clear consensus among literacy researchers that accelerating vocabulary growth is a vital and often neglected component of a comprehensive reading program, especially for secondary students. (National Institute of Child Health Development Report of the National Reading Panel, 2000; Baumann and Kame'enui, 2004.) Numerous studies have documented the strong and reciprocal relationship between vocabulary knowledge and reading comprehension (Beck *et al.*, 1987; Stahl and Fairbanks, 1987; Baker *et al.*, 1995; Graves, 2000) as well as general reading ability (Stanovich *et al.*, 1984). Research focused on school age second-language learners similarly concludes that vocabulary knowledge is the single best predictor of their academic achievement across subject matter domains (Saville-Troike, 1984). As students move into secondary settings the academic vocabulary demands increase dramatically in terms of both text reading and classroom discourse. This becomes a significant challenge for older struggling readers presenting a major impediment in terms of listening and reading comprehension (Hirsch, 2003). Moreover, vocabulary knowledge is so strongly related to intelligence that noted psychologist and creator of the modern IQ test Louis Terman (1916) indicated that, if he were to use one factor to determine IQ, it would be vocabulary.

After clarifying the extent of the language challenge, this chapter will explore a series of research-supported and classroom-tested strategies secondary teachers can utilize to develop the impoverished lexical "toolkits" of their students. These strategies will address the three essential questions every teacher concerned with vocabulary inevitably encounters: (1) which words warrant direct teaching, (2) what is a "best evidence" approach to teaching a new term directly, one that will work with struggling students including English learners and students with disabilities, and (3) how can one ensure students utilize newly acquired vocabulary in their academic speaking and writing. The chapter concludes with a set of structure application activities that will assist practitioners in applying the ideas explicated herein to virtually any type of secondary educational setting from the mixed ability general education classroom to a literacy intervention program.

THE LANGUAGE GAP—WORD POVERTY

The recent nationwide efforts to improve early literacy indicate we have made commendable progress in teaching beginning readers to decode, including students from economically disadvantaged homes and second-language learners. However, Chall *et al.* (1990) documented a troubling national trend dubbed "the fourth grade slump": even after successfully learning to decode text in the primary grades, many low-income children (including English learners) begin to fall behind in reading comprehension at the fourth grade. Chall *et al.* clarified (1990) how the vocabulary demands, especially in content area reading, markedly expand at grade four, exposing the dire lexical needs of students who come from linguistically impoverished backgrounds. More recently, Hirsch (2003) posited that, after the primary grades, the much-heralded achievement gap between socioeconomic groups (National Assessment of Educational Progress, 2004) is in fact a language gap. Hirsch (2003) maintained, "instead of the term 'reading gap,' clarity would be better served by using a more descriptive term like 'language gap' or 'verbal gap'" (p. 10). Similarly, other researchers have demonstrated that the "language/vocabulary gap" is also at the center of the disturbing disparity in academic achievement between Anglo and Latino students across our country (e.g. Carlo *et al.*, 2004). Moats (2001) depicted this disparaging gap in vocabulary knowledge as word poverty. Word poverty has far-reaching and devastating consequences, for impoverished lexical skills impact not only on students' word-reading ability at the end of first grade, but also their reading comprehension in eleventh grade (Juel, 2004).

STRIKING LACK OF VOCABULARY INSTRUCTION

Given the pivotal role of vocabulary in virtually all aspects of academic competence, it is alarming that classroom research consistently reveals how relatively little focused academic vocabulary instruction actually occurs in the typical K-12 classroom. For example, Durkin (1979) found that upper-elementary teachers spent less than 1 percent of their overall reading instruction focused on vocabulary. More recently, Scott et al. (1997) documented the paucity of vocabulary instruction in 23 ethnically diverse upper-elementary classrooms, reporting that only 6 percent of school time was devoted to vocabulary, with only 1.4 percent allotted to content area vocabulary. Biemiller (2004) reached a similar conclusion, noting that there appears to be relatively little explicit vocabulary teaching in the elementary grades. The scarcity of systematic, intentional vocabulary and language teaching has also been documented in programs serving English learners (Scarcella, 1996; Gersten and Baker, 2000; Dutro and Moran, 2003). Dutro and Moran (2003) and Fillmore and Snow (2000) emphasized that simply exposing second-language students to English-language-rich, interactive classrooms is woefully insufficient; intensive instruction of academic vocabulary and related grammatical knowledge must be carefully orchestrated across the subject areas for language minority students to attain rigorous content standards.

Most classroom teachers serving developing readers across the subject areas would no doubt find incredible Beck et al.'s (2002) terse summary of K-12 vocabulary instruction in which the researchers conclude "there isn't much" (p. 2). Conscientious teachers who devote considerable class time to various vocabulary activities such as word sorts, crossword puzzles, and dictionary exercises will surely bristle at the assertion they are not addressing vocabulary. However, although there is certainly value to such activities, these practices do not represent what many experts would consider to be substantive vocabulary instruction. In conjunction with vocabulary scholars such as Beck (2002) and Marzano (2004), we contend that educators across disciplines and grade levels routinely confuse rigorous and robust academic vocabulary teaching with assigning an array of independent or collaborative vocabulary activities, and that what instruction does take place frequently lacks the foresight, planning, and efficacy to prepare students responsibly for the lexical demands of challenging curricula.

Drawing upon a wide body of empirical research in literacy education, the following text summarizes several broad conclusions about what "works" in vocabulary instruction.

Effective vocabulary instruction is more than simply implementing a recommend list, such as:

- looking up words in the dictionary
- using written context to figure out word meanings
- unplanned, extemporaneous vocabulary teaching
- wide reading of fiction and non-fiction texts
- direct teaching of important individual words
- teaching independent word learning strategies
- fostering "word consciousness."

Let us consider each of these points in greater detail.

What Does Not Work

Prior to detailing a research-informed process for both teaching and assessment, it is imperative to be mindful of the serious limitations inherent in the three most common vocabulary teaching practices in K-12 classrooms:

1. looking up words in the dictionary;
2. using written context to figure out word meanings;
3. unplanned, extemporaneous vocabulary teaching.

While each of these practices do have their place within a comprehensive literacy program, they lack the efficacy and dependability required to serve as core tools to help educators aggressively narrow the lexical divide. In the section that follows, we will briefly examine the inevitable shortcomings of each of these ubiquitous practices.

Assigning Words for Students to Look Up in the Dictionary

Considerable evidence indicates most children struggle when attempting to derive meaning from conventional dictionary definitions (Scott and Nagy, 1997; Marzano, 2004). A brief examination of a typical classroom dictionary can easily show why. When developing a classroom dictionary, lexicographers strive to conserve space in order to include as many entries as possible. Therefore, definitions are customarily crafted to be precise and concise, ironically omitting the very components that often are most critical to grasping the meaning of a new word: an accessible explanation using familiar language and an age-appropriate example that is relevant to children's own experiences.

To complicate matters further, the rudimentary definitions are written in a miniscule font and often include another form of the target word or obscure synonyms. To illustrate, a struggling reader in search of the meaning of the term categorize in the *Random House Webster's Dictionary* (2001) will encounter this elliptical entry: "to arrange in categories; classify." A polysemous word (i.e. a word with multiple meanings), such as wave, offers additional challenges because a learner must navigate a litany of diverse definitions to find the meaning that is most appropriate to a specific context. The default student response is simply to copy the first or shortest definition without considering its appropriateness.

Directing Students to Derive Meaning from Context

Reading and language acquisition scholars seem to agree that, except for the first few thousand words in common oral usage, most vocabulary learning occurs through extensive reading, with the reader guessing at the meaning of unknown words. Yet, while essential for long-term vocabulary growth, incidental learning from context is at best an inefficient and unpredictable process. Research indicates the odds of deriving the intended meaning of an unknown word from written context is, unfortunately, extremely low, varying from 5 to 15 percent for both native speakers and English learners (Nagy *et al.*, 1985; Beck *et al.*, 2002). Devoid of accompanying instruction, students need to encounter the same word multiple times before they can ascertain and remember its meaning (Stahl and Fairbanks, 1987). In fact, the likelihood of learning a word at a first encounter is almost nil for young readers tackling difficult texts (Kuhn and Stahl, 1998) and English-language learners, who lack a full command of the basic English vocabulary and grammar to be able to exploit linguistic clues to word meaning (Paribakht and Wesche, 1997). Teaching students the word-level skills to exploit context successfully is vital to long-term vocabulary acquisition; however, contextual analysis should never be utilized as the primary or exclusive instructional strategy for supporting students' comprehension.

Relying Primarily Upon Extemporaneous "Teachable Moments"

Often, vocabulary instruction in the classroom is unplanned, driven primarily by student questions and teacher intuitions. However, efficient and effective vocabulary instruction demands informed, intentional planning (Stahl, 1999). To prepare students responsibly for a challenging reading selection, a teacher must first critically analyze the text to determine which words are most central to comprehension and, thus, warrant more instructional time, then consider how to teach these terms in a productive manner, conveying both their meaning and import.

There are a number of reasons to avoid relying on an unplanned, organic approach to vocabulary instruction. Ironically, the students most apt to interrupt the instructional flow to ask a clarification question tend to be the students who are more academically prepared, that is the ones who need the least help. If we largely cater to their immediate lexical needs, we are likely to neglect more imperative vocabulary for less proficient language users. Moreover, carefully worded explanations and illustrative examples are difficult to conceive "on the fly" while working through a reading in class. Conjuring up meaningful word introductions and relevant examples requires more time, creative capital, and instructional stamina than is typically available in class. Yet, haphazard, weak drafts of definitions often amount to little more than what Juel and Deffes (2004) referred to as "context-based mentioning," which can derail the reading process and convey a mixed message about the actual significance of vocabulary development. Teachable moments can indeed enliven and personalize classroom interactions and deepen student understandings. However, we cannot excuse a lack of conscientious vocabulary preparation within lesson planning in the name of creativity and student-centered learning. We should devote our intellectual and creative capital to thoughtful lexical preparation and effective instruction, then tap into our reserves to respond productively to the inevitable challenges and questions that arise during the course of a lesson.

What Does Work

A Comprehensive Vocabulary Development Program Increasing Reading Volume: Necessary but Insufficient

Traditionally, most language experts viewed vocabulary as something more "caught than taught," arguing there are simply too many words to teach feasibly and that incidental word learning via wide reading is responsible for most vocabulary acquisition (Nagy and Herman, 1985). Reading volume is undoubtedly very important in terms of long-term vocabulary development (Cunningham and Stanovich, 1998); however, as previously noted, even with the most adept readers, incidental word learning is a protracted, inefficient, and unpredictable process, providing no way to anticipate which words will be learned and when, nor to what degree. Developing readers cannot be expected to simply "pick up" substantial vocabulary knowledge exclusively through reading exposure without guidance. Specifically, teachers must design tasks that will increase the effectiveness of vocabulary learning through reading practice.

Extensive Reading of Informational Text

Research suggests that one contributing factor to the language divide may be children's lack of experience with significant amounts of non-fiction text. Duke *et al.* (2004) documented the striking paucity of non-fiction expository texts utilized in primary grade classrooms, including teacher read-alouds, classroom libraries, and school libraries. Although Duke *et al.*'s (2004) interviews with children indicated that many preferred informational reading to stories, numerous teachers thought non-fiction texts were less age appropriate for young children. Students need abundant exposure to informational texts in elementary school and beyond, because they are the curricular mainstay of secondary school, higher education, and the workplace. Students who have had a steady diet of narrative texts, both in instructional materials and independent reading, are often ill-equipped for the concept- and data-driven reading passages of science, social studies, and high-stakes testing. The syntactic patterns and lexical density of informational texts generally pose formidable challenges for developing readers (Schleppegrell, 2002) and no amount of narrative reading will prepare them for it adequately.

Rationale for Direct Vocabulary Instruction

Over the past two decades, mounting research has challenged traditional views regarding the role of direct teaching in vocabulary development. Numerous studies have documented the positive impact of direct, explicit vocabulary instruction on both immediate word learning and longer term reading comprehension (Baker *et al.*, 1995; Beck *et al.*, 2002; Biemiller, 2004; Marzano, 2004). For example, Paribakht and Wesche (1997) compared incidental vocabulary attainment among students who learned vocabulary through either independent reading or targeted instruction. Their data showed that both approaches led to considerable gains over a 3-month period. However, students learned more words through targeted instruction and learning exclusively through independent reading often led to only a superficial understanding of many vocabulary words. Thus, the fundamental question of whether vocabulary is best acquired indirectly via reading or directly via explicit teacher instruction is in itself a false dichotomy. Students need a comprehensive vocabulary program that incorporates both direct and indirect approaches to lexical development.

A Model for Comprehensive Vocabulary Development

Lexical scholars tend to focus their research on very specific dimensions of vocabulary growth, running the gamut from voluntary pleasure reading to explicit morphemic analysis. We agree wholeheartedly with Graves' (2000) vision that a balanced or comprehensive model of vocabulary development must include four essential elements.

1. Wide reading: vocabulary grows as a consequence of independent reading and increasing reading volume (Nagy *et al.*, 1985; Cunningham and Stanovich, 1998).
2. Direct teaching of individual words: students learn new words via various teacher-directed instructional strategies (Stahl and Fairbanks, 1987; Beck *et al.*, 2002).
3. Teaching word learning strategies: students independently learn new word meanings when they learn to use word learning strategies, such as exploiting context and analyzing prefixes (Edwards *et al.*, 2004; Graves, 2000).
4. Fostering word consciousness: vocabulary develops when students engage in various activities to increase language play, word choice in writing, and sensitivity to word parts (Nagy and Scott, 2000; Blachowicz and Fisher, 2006).

Research clearly indicates that, while each component supports lexical growth, a schoolwide vocabulary development program integrating all four components holds greater potential for narrowing the language divide. For the purposes of this paper, however, we focus on the second element, directly teaching new words, coupled with strategies to ensure that students apply their newly acquired vocabulary in academic speaking and writing contexts.

Robust Vocabulary Instruction: A Powerful Teaching Routine

A distillation of vocabulary research, together with our 50+ years of combined classroom experience, provides a clear foundation for an effective and efficient vocabulary instructional routine. Something as rudimentary and essential to teachers as how to teach an important new word effectively is rarely mentioned in both language arts and content area curricula. Surprisingly, teacher's editions of core curricula routinely direct teachers to address central lesson vocabulary with little more than the brief exhortation to preview, cover, review, or introduce key terms. Meanwhile, they neglect to provide any explicit direction in how to teach word meanings effectively and efficiently.

The following steps can most certainly be elaborated and adapted, depending upon the relative importance of the words in question and students' background knowledge. However, in our experience, students greatly benefit from a consistent and recognizable approach that incorporates the following steps.

Instructional Steps for Teaching a New Term

- pronounce
- explain
- provide examples
- deepen understanding and coach use
- assess.

Instructional Steps

PRONOUNCE

Classroom observations indicate that, far too frequently, the teacher is the only person who pronounces and uses the academic language of the disciplines. Thus, the first step in teaching a new term is guiding students in correctly pronouncing the word. This will support learners in decoding the word confidently, while also supporting both auditory and muscle memory (Shaywitz, 2003). Engage all students in saying the word together two or three times. If it is a long and/or unusual term, it is often helpful to emphasize each syllable. For example:

> One of our lesson terms is accurate. It is an adjective or describing word. Please say the word with me everyone: "Accurate." Good, let us pronounce it by syllables: "Ac" "cu" "rate." Say it again please: "Accurate." Excellent!

EXPLAIN

Understanding the meaning of a new term requires a clear explanation of the meaning, using language familiar to the students (Stahl, 1999; Beck *et al.*, 2002). If possible, provide a synonym or known phrase to solidify the connection between the new vocabulary term and the student's prior knowledge. Simply presenting unintelligible dictionary or textual definitions is of little value until students can grasp the gist of what a word means, within the context of the language that is already present in their lexicon.

> The word "accurate" means true, correct, or precise. I might say the report in the newspaper about our successful canned food drive was completely true; it was absolutely _____ (students chorally say "accurate").

PROVIDE EXAMPLES

Students will usually need at least two or three examples of a new term to firmly grasp the meaning. Moreover, these examples should be drawn from a variety of contexts, not only the one used in the reading or lesson (Baker *et al.*, 1995; Beck *et al.*, 2002). Multiple examples serve to build students' semantic network, allowing them to incorporate the term into their lexicon beyond mere surface understanding. It is helpful to phrase the examples such that the students repeat the target word in completing the example. This allows students to become more comfortable using the word orally, a key step in building expressive vocabulary.

> Test scores alone do not always provide a true picture of the quality of a school. Test scores present an image that is not always _____ (students say "accurate").

> When I check my bank account each month, I want to be sure the numbers are correct or _____ .

DEEPEN UNDERSTANDING AND COACH USE

Research in cognitive psychology consistently indicates that learners understand and remember information better when they elaborate on it themselves (Marzano *et al.*, 2001). Thus, students' understanding of new vocabulary terms is strengthened when they are given opportunities to deepen understanding of word meanings by generating their own additional examples, non-examples, visual representations, and so forth. For words important enough to warrant direct teaching it is imperative to structure opportunities for students to use the terms in appropriate academic contexts.

> Imagine you are a reporter writing an article about our school. Come up with one accurate and one inaccurate statement about the school using our new term in a complete sentence. Copy this sentence starter to get you started.

> Of the many things said about Adams High School, one accurate statement is_____ .

> Visualize a tabloid newspaper headline saying, 'Elvis Lives!'

ASSESS

Researchers such as Kame'enui *et al.* (2004) and Marzano (2004) have documented the importance of incorporating regular informal vocabulary assessment into the instructional process, especially with academically diverse learners. Assessment of vocabulary involves both formative, quick informal checking for understanding during the lesson and summative evaluation as students subsequently take a formal quiz or test.

In the assessment of important terms, those that are either essential to comprehension or critical for general academic competence, it is advisable to go beyond simple memorization or matching tasks and require students to demonstrate some deeper level of thinking and understanding. Effective checks on understanding tend to fall into two basic categories: discrimination tasks, such as answering focused questions, and generative tasks, such as developing additional examples.

Discrimination: focused questions:
- Is it accurate to say our school is the largest in town?
- Does the book *Holes* give an accurate view of juvenile justice?

Generative tasks:
- Completion activity:

    Complete the following sentences so that the second part further explains the first part and clearly demonstrates your understanding of the underlined words.

    I could tell the newspaper article about our new gym was not *accurate*; _____ _____ _____ .

- Yes–No–Why activity:

    Decide whether the following sentences make sense, paying attention to the underlined words in each sentence. If the sentence makes sense, write YES in the space to the left, then explain why it is logical. If the sentence does not make sense, write NO and explain why.

    School report cards always provide an *accurate* and *reliable* description of a student's work. _____ _____ _____ .

Carrying Learning Further

The basic instructional process outlined above is offered as a flexible foundational strategy, not an endpoint. Teachers can spend more or less time in each instructional phase based upon the importance of the term and the language level of their students. Since it takes multiple encounters with a word for a student to actually learn it, teachers need to provide instruction that requires students to interact with essential terms in a variety of ways within a condensed period of time. It is important to engage students in activities that will bolster their expressive vocabulary (i.e. speaking and writing) as well as their receptive vocabulary (i.e. listening and reading). There are limitless strategies to support students in developing and flexing their lexical muscles. Here are a few of the most effective ones:

Vocabulary Note-taking Guides

If vocabulary words are central to lesson comprehension and required for subsequent independent reading, writing, or listening tasks, it is imperative to help students keep track of novel words through a note-taking scaffold (Marzano *et al.*, 2001). A note-taking scaffold has multiple advantages in that it provides (1) an advance organizer of the most essential lesson terms, (2) an accountability for active student engagement during the lesson, and (3) a reference for later rehearsal and study.

SAMPLE VOCABULARY NOTE-TAKING GUIDE

Word	Synonym/Definition	Example/Image/Showing Sentence
accurate, adj.	true, _____, exact, precise	Rumors are often not _____ information. Image of tabloid headline, "Elvis is alive!!"
reliable, adj.	dependable, someone you can count on	Our newspaper is always delivered by 6:00 a.m.; our carrier Luis is very _____ . Image of a newspaper on the front porch.

When working with struggling readers, second-language learners, and other diverse students, it is advisable to fill out the guide in advance partially, leaving blank certain key words that students are directed to fill in during the course of instruction. In this way students can focus their attention on comprehending the explanation and examples, instead of getting bogged down in the writing process and missing vital content. Gradually require students to assume more responsibility for filling in the guide, until they can independently take notes on a blank vocabulary note-taking guide.

Vocabulary Study Strategies

Students benefit from learning efficient and effective strategies for reviewing, practicing, and elaborating newly acquired vocabulary terms after teacher-directed instruction (Kame'enui *et al.*, 2004; Marzano, 2004). Vocabulary study should be limited to lesson-specific terms that are essential to comprehending the big ideas central to the subject matter and high-incidence academic terms that are needed to discuss and write about the topic.

There are three productive vocabulary study strategies.

1. Read, cover, recite, check (RCRC) (Archer and Gleason, 2002): a verbal rehearsal strategy in which students learn to read the word to themselves, cover it up with their hand, recite the definition and related examples to themselves, and then check by reviewing the recorded information from the note-taking guide or other written record.
2. Vocabulary study cards, wherein students create 3-inch × 5-inch cards containing useful information related to the term, such as definition, synonyms, examples and non-examples, associated images, sentences, and the like. Students can study their cards individually (using rehearsal strategies like RCRC), with a partner, and in class-wide vocabulary games like Jeopardy.
3. Vocabulary notebooks, in which students write down terms pre-taught by the teacher as well as self-selected terms that students cull from the reading. It is helpful to have an explicit organizational scheme for what information is recorded in the notebook, such as synonyms, images, sentences, part of speech, etc.

Accountable Contexts for Speaking and Writing

All too often, the teacher is the only individual in the classroom who actually uses academic language, while students are allowed to listen passively or use casual, daily vernacular. If one of our instructional priorities is significantly narrowing the lexical divide, we must structure daily classroom contexts so that all students are accountable for using newly introduced terminology in their speaking and writing. Students with impoverished academic vocabulary and little self-confidence will need more than encouraging words and motivating topics to develop rich expressive vocabulary for scholastic success (Scarcella, 1996; Fillmore and Snow, 2000; Gersten and Baker, 2000; Dutro and Moran, 2003). Students benefit greatly from brief, daily classroom opportunities to use academic language in speaking and writing. One efficient way to get students to apply academic language is to provide opportunities for "prepared participation," which affords them time to collect their thoughts and complete a written response starter. For example, in discussing the topic of bullying prior to a reading on the subject, a teacher could set the stage by first asking students to compile an individual list of examples of bullying they had witnessed or heard of. After this initial idea generation, students could be given a few sentence starters like the following (including key terms from the relevant vocabulary list) and directed to write two sentences in their notebook in preparation for the discussion.

One form of verbal/non-verbal bullying I have witnessed in our
school is . . .

I am aware of several forms of verbal/non-verbal bullying at our
school, but the most serious is . . .

A prevalent form of bullying at our school is . . .

Students could be prompted to rehearse their favorite example sentence
with a partner in preparation for a subsequent class discussion. The teacher
could then lead a discussion of these examples within a structured idea
wave, allowing multiple students to read one prepared sentence aloud while
synthesizing and elaborating as appropriate.

Teaching Words that Matter Most

Intensive vocabulary instruction is absolutely necessary to produce in-depth
word knowledge. However, only a fraction of the potentially unfamiliar
words in a standards-based, cognitively demanding lesson can be taught,
particularly within a diverse, mixed-ability classroom. Thus, the first challenge is to determine which words warrant direct and detailed teaching.
Without careful analysis of the lexical demands of a text, a teacher can
squander vital instructional time on words that may be unfamiliar but have
little bearing on comprehension of the focal concepts.

Intensive instruction is most worthwhile either when words are related
to the central lesson concepts or when words have general utility in
academic contexts. Although we want to engender curiosity and playful-
ness with language learning, it is easy to engage in "lexical accessorizing"
throughout a lesson, spending an inordinate amount of time explicating
words peripheral to the central themes and issues, yet intriguing to the
teacher or a small cadre of precocious students.

Relying on publishers to designate the words that warrant instruction
can be derailing and unproductive. Textbook publishers often highlight
words simply because they are rarely used or idiomatic. Language arts
materials have the greatest tendency to focus heavily on unusual or
provocative words for the more sophisticated reader, while neglecting
central lesson terms and high-utility academic words that are vital for less-
proficient readers. The other core subject areas characteristically provide a
fairly reliable list of lesson-specific terms tied to content standards, while
neglecting to mention high-use academic terms students will encounter
across the disciplines. For example, in a sixth-grade U.S. history chapter
addressing the American Revolution, terms such as patriot, loyalist, and
Stamp Act will predictably be highlighted. However, the plethora of

vocabulary necessary for students to understand and discuss the cause/effect relationships of this historical period will not be clarified (e.g. impact, subsequent, factors, and consequences). Because of the sketchy and rather arbitrary nature of key terms selected by publishers, it is incumbent upon teachers to have a viable framework for choosing words that require planned explicit teaching.

Guidelines for Choosing Words to Teach

1. Choose "big idea" words that name or relate to the central concepts addressed in the passage (e.g. democracy, independence, fossil fuels, and ecology).
2. Choose high-use, widely applicable "academic toolkit" words that students are likely to encounter in diverse materials across subject areas and grade levels (e.g. aspect, compare, similar, and subsequently).
3. Choose high-use "disciplinary toolkit" words that are relevant to your subject area and that you consider vital for students to master at this age and proficiency level (e.g. metaphor, policy, economic, application, and species).
4. Choose "polysemous" (multiple meaning) words that have a new academic meaning in reading in addition to a more general, familiar meaning (e.g. wave as in "wave of immigrants" versus a greeting or ocean wave).
5. Especially when dealing with narrative texts, identify additional academic words (not included in the reading selection) that students will need to know in order to engage in academic discourse about the central characters, issues, and themes.

Concluding Thoughts

Word poverty and its attendant woes are beginning to merit much-deserved attention. Schools need to commit themselves to implementing rigorous and informed vocabulary and language development programs so that they can aggressively address the challenges inherent in narrowing the endemic language divide. Teachers across the grade levels and subject areas have to work collaboratively to shoulder the responsibility of equipping students with the lexical skills to navigate today's high-stakes, standards-based educational environment successfully. We must keep in mind, however, that teaching vocabulary robustly is not an end in itself but only a means to an end. The critical outcome is how well we equip students to thrive in academic contexts.

Appendix: Follow-up Application Activities—Self-study Applications

Choosing Important Words to Teach

1. Clarify the meaning of "academic toolkit" words.

2. Why is it essential for students to know and use these terms?

Task: choose any textbook chapter, informational article, or other appropriate reading from your curriculum and identify five "academic toolkit" terms that are either used in the reading itself or in the questions suggested in the teacher's edition (e.g. end of the chapter). Share the terms you've selected with a colleague including the rationale, how do you know this is an "academic toolkit" word?

3. What is a "big idea" discipline specific word?

Task: examine the same chapter/article used in the first activity and identify five essential "big idea" discipline specific terms that are essential for students to understand in order to comprehend the reading. Share the terms you have selected with a colleague and justify why they qualify as an essential word to pre-teach.

Explicit Teaching Important Words

1. Clarify the five key steps in effectively teaching a new term.

Task: prepare a vocabulary lesson plan for the ten terms identified above. Be sure to include a note-taking guide for each term. Practice teach two to three words with a colleague and give one another feedback. Then teach the ten terms to your students using the process outlined in the chapter.

Structured Use of New Terms in Academic Contexts: "Academic Talk"

1. Why is it so important to structure student use of recently taught terms and engage in "academic talk"?

Task: create two appropriate "sentence starters" using two or more of the terms identified in the previous activities. Plan a discussion sequence in which *all* students would be required to use their "academic talk" including the sentence with the target vocabulary (e.g. writing the sentences, partner rehearsal, whole class discussion, etc.). Utilize these strategies in structuring an academic discussion in your classroom. Reflect on the results. Did every student participate? Was everyone using the target vocabulary terms? What would you do differently next time? Why?

Assessment

1. Why is it important to go beyond simple matching or multiple choice assessments for important terms?
2. What do we mean by "generative tasks" for assessment? Provide one example.

Task: create three generative assessments (e.g. "yes–no–why?") for at least four of the terms from the above activities. Utilize these assessments with your students and evaluate the results.

Vocabulary Study

1. Identify at least three specific strategies for vocabulary study.

Task: create four sample "vocabulary study cards" using terms from the above activities. Guide your students in creating their own vocabulary study cards and teach them the verbal rehearsal strategy RCRC. Informally assess their retention of the terms studied within 2–3 days. What was their level of retention? What would you do differently to improve your students' study strategies?

Appropriate Dictionaries

Many traditional classroom dictionaries are not helpful to struggling readers because they use more sophisticated language in defining the term (e.g. "inherently means intrinsically") or other forms of the word in question (e.g. "gratitude is the act of being grateful"): in either case it leaves the student confused and lacking basic understanding of the term. However, there are so-called "learner dictionaries" crafted for striving readers and English learners that are far superior to traditional classroom dictionaries.

Task: Visit www.ldoceonline.com/ and access the free online *Longman Dictionary of Contemporary English*. Look up three of the "academic toolkit" terms from the first activity and describe their appropriateness for your students (i.e. would your student be likely to understand the definition and example provided). Do the same thing with three more terms with the Heinle & Heinle online *Newbury House Dictionary of American English* (http://nhd.heinle.com/home.aspx).

Web-based Vocabulary Resources

The Internet contains a treasure trove of lexical resources and related tools if one knows where to look! Below are a handful of the sites that we have found to be most useful to educators.

Pacific Regional Educational Lab

www.prel.org/programs/rel/vocabularyforum.asp

The Pacific Region Education Lab recently hosted the Focus on Vocabulary Forum with leading researchers and has released an excellent booklet summarizing their findings, along with copies of the handouts and PowerPoint slide presentations.

Lexile Power Vocabulary

www.lexile.com/DesktopDefault.aspx?view=ed&tabindex=2&tabid=16&tab pageid=183

The Lexile Power Vocabulary is an interesting electronic resource for vocabulary instruction posted by the folks at Lexile.com. This tool is linked to specific titles that are commonly found on core literature lists, basal anthologies, etc. It also provides the identification of key vocabulary and tools for teaching and assessment. Have a look!

Reading Online—International Reading Association

www.readingonline.org/articles/art_index.asp?HREF=/articles/curtis/index.html

One of the most interesting and practical research studies to focus on vocabulary instruction with adolescents is posted at the International Reading Association's website. This article describes a 16-week intervention by Mary Longo and Ann Marie Curtis in which the comprehension of middle and high school students reading below grade level was improved significantly by instruction that developed their vocabularies through listening, speaking, reading, and writing. Guiding principles for the intervention are discussed and sample activities are provided.

American Federation of Teachers: American Educator

www.aft.org/pubs-reports/american_educator/spring2003/chall.html

A recent issue of American Federation of Teachers' *American Educator* has a wonderful article on The Fourth Grade Slump, which features vocabulary knowledge and related instructional challenges/solutions as the core focus. A *must* read!

The Academic Word List

http://language.massey.ac.nz/staff/awl/awlinfo.shtml

The Academic Word List is an interesting site hosted by New Zealand linguist Dr. Averil Coxhead. The central idea here is to identify the critical academic vocabulary used across disciplines (e.g. compare, similar, and vary) that is essential for students to understand in academic reading and writing.

Text Project

www.textproject.org/

Text Project is sponsored by Dr. Elfrieda (Freddy) Hiebert and colleagues and is loaded with wonderful downloadables of papers, chapters, PowerPoint shows, etc., plus details on the new Quick Reads program based on Dr. Hiebert's research.

The Reading Corner

www.scoe.org/reading

These are the webpages maintained by one of the authors (Kevin Feldman), and contain many useful resources, web links, downloadable files, etc.

References

Archer, A. & Gleason, M. (2002). *Skills for school success.* North Billerica, MA: Curriculum Associates.

Baker, S. K., Simmons, D. C., & Kame'enui, E. J. (1995). *Vocabulary acquisition: Synthesis of the research* (technical report No. 13). Eugene: University of Oregon, National Center to Improve the Tools of Educators.

Baumann, J. F. & Kame'enui, E. J. (Eds.) (2004). *Vocabulary instruction: From research to practice.* New York: Guilford Press.

Beck, I. L. & McKeown, M. G. (1987). Getting the most from basal reading selections. *The Elementary School Journal, 87* (3), 343–356.

Beck, I. L., McKeown, M. G., & Kucan, L. (2002). *Bringing words to life: Robust vocabulary instruction.* New York: Guilford Press.

Biemiller, A. (2004) Teaching vocabulary in the primary grades: vocabulary instruction needed. In J. F. Baumann & E. J. Kame'enui (Eds.), *Vocabulary instruction: From research to practice* (pp. 159–176). New York: Guilford Press.

Blachowicz, C. L. Z. & Fisher, P. (2006). *Teaching vocabulary in all classrooms* (2nd ed.). Columbus, OH: Prentice-Hall.

Carlo, M. S., August, D., McLaughlin, B., Snow, C. E., Dressler, C. *et al.* (2004). Closing the gap: Addressing the vocabulary needs of English language learners in bilingual and mainstream classroom. *Reading Research Quarterly, 39*, 188–215.

Chall, J. S. (2000). *The academic achievement challenge: What really works in the classroom?* New York: Guilford Press.

Chall, J. S., Jacobs, V. A., & Baldwin, L. E. (1990). *The reading crisis: Why poor children fall behind.* Cambridge: Harvard University Press.

Cunningham, A. E. & Stanovich, K. E. (1998). What reading does for the mind. *American Educator, 22* (1–2), 8–15.

Curtis, M. E. & Longo, A. M. (1999). *When adolescents can't read: Methods and materials that work.* Cambridge: Brookline.

Duke, N. (2004). The case for informational text. *Educational Leadership, 61* (6), 40–45.

Durkin, D. (1979). What classroom observations reveal about reading comprehension instruction. *Reading Research Quarterly, 14,* 481–538.

Dutro, S. & Moran, C. (2003). Rethinking English language instruction: An architectural approach. In G. Garcia (Ed.), *English learners: Reaching the highest level of English literacy* (pp. 227–258). Newark, DE: International Reading Association.

Edwards, E. C., Font, G., Baumann, J. F., & Boland, E. (2004). Unlocking word meanings. In J. F. Baumann & E. J. Kame'enui (Eds.), *Vocabulary instruction: From research to practice* (pp. 159–176). New York: Guilford Press.

Fillmore, L. W. & Snow, C. E. (2000). What teachers need to know about language. Special report from ERIC Clearinghouse on language and linguistics (Online). Available: www.cal.org/ericcll/teachers/teachers.pdf

Gersten, R. & Baker, S. (2000). Effective instruction for English-language learners: What we know about effective instructional practices for English-language learners. *Exceptional Children, 66* (4), 454–470.

Graves, M. F. (2000). A vocabulary program to compliment and bolster a middle grade comprehension program. In B. M. Taylor, M. F. Graves, & P. Van den Broek (Eds.), *Reading for meaning: Fostering comprehension in the middle grades* (pp. 116–135). Newark, DE: International Reading Association.

Hart, B. & Risley, T. R. (1995). *Meaningful differences in the everyday experience of young American children.* Baltimore: Paul H. Brookes.

Hirsch, E. D. (2003). Reading comprehension requires knowledge of words and the world: Scientific insights into the fourth-grade slump and the nation's stagnant comprehension scores. *American Educator, Spring,* 10–20.

Juel, C. & Deffes, R. (2004). Making words stick. *Educational Leadership, 63* (6), 30–34.

Kuhn, M. R. & Stahl, S. A. (1998). Teaching children to learn word meanings from context: A synthesis and some questions. *Journal of Literacy Research, 30,* 19–38.

McIntosh, R. & Vaughn, S. (1994). Observations of students with learning disabilities in general education classrooms. *Exceptional Children, 60* (3), 249–262.

McKeown, M. G. (1985). The acquisition of word meaning from context by children of high and low-ability. *Reading Research Quarterly, 20,* 482–496.

Marzano, R. J. (2004). The developing vision of vocabulary instruction. In J. F. Baumann & E. J. Kame'enui (Eds.), *Vocabulary instruction: From research to practice* (pp. 159–176). New York: Guilford Press.

Marzano, R. J., Pickering, D. J., & Pollock, J. E. (2001). *Classroom instruction that works: Research based strategies for increasing student achievement.* Alexandria, VA: Association for Supervision and Curriculum Development.

Moats, L. (2001). Overcoming the language gap. *American Educator, Summer,* 5–9.

Nagy, W. E., Herman, P. A., & Anderson, R. C. (1985). Learning words from context. *Reading Research Quarterly, 20,* 233–253.

Nagy, W. E. & Scott, J. A. (2000). Vocabulary processes. In M. L. Kamil, P. B. Mosenthal, D. Pearson, & R. Barr (Eds.), *Handbook of reading research* (Vol. 3) (pp. 269–284). Mahwah, NJ: Erlbaum.

National Assessment of Educational Progress. (2004). *Group results for sex, region, and size of community.* Washington, DC: U.S. Government Printing Office.

National Reading Panel. (2000). *Teaching children to read: An evidence-based assessment of the scientific literature on reading and its implications for reading instruction.* Bethesda, MD: National Institute of Child Health and Human Development.

Paribakht, T. S. & Wesche, M. (1997). Vocabulary enhancement activities and reading for meaning in second language vocabulary acquisition. In J. Coady, T. Huckin, M. H. Long, & J. C. Richards (Eds.), *Second language vocabulary acquisition: A rationale for pedagogy* (pp. 174–199). New York: Cambridge University Press.

Saville-Troike, M. (1984). What really matters in second language learning for academic achievement? *TESOL Quarterly, 18* (2), 199–220.

Scarcella, R. C. (1996). Secondary education and second language research: ESL students in the 1990s. *The CATESOL Journal, 9*, 129–152.

Schatz, E. K. & Baldwin, R. S. (1986). Context clues are unreliable predictors of word meanings. *Reading Research Quarterly, 21*, 439–453.

Schleppegrell, M. (2002). Linguistic features of the language of schooling. *Linguistics and Education, 12*, 431–459.

Schmitt, N. & Carter, R. (2000). The lexical advantages of narrow reading for second language learners. *TESOL Journal, 9*, 4–9.

Scott, J. A. & Nagy, W. E. (1997). Understanding the definitions of unfamiliar words. *Reading Research Quarterly, 32*, 184–200.

Shaywitz, S. (2003). *Overcoming dyslexia: A new and complete science-based program for reading problems at any level.* New York: Knopf.

Stahl, S. A. (1999). *Vocabulary Development.* Cambridge: Brookline.

Stahl, S. A. & Fairbanks, M. M. (1987). The effects of vocabulary instruction: A model-based meta-analysis. *Review of Educational Research, 56*, 72–110.

CHAPTER 2

Evidence-based Strategies for Vocabulary Instruction/Intervention

JUDY K. MONTGOMERY

Teacher: "It's your turn to read, Gregg. Start here on this page."

Gregg (a 12-year-old struggling reader): "I know a lot of these words."

Teacher: "Good, then this will be easy to read."

Gregg: "Yikes, they put some new words in here."

Teacher: "You can read those words, too, Gregg. Start reading here."

Gregg (still avoiding the reading event): "I already know 100 words from that big list you gave me."

Teacher: "Wonderful. I am proud of you for knowing 100 words. Now, let's start reading here."

Gregg (looking at the teacher with genuine concern in his face): "Hey, Mrs. M. . . . I was just wondering how many more words are there to learn?"

Vocabulary knowledge is among the best predictors of successfully learning to read (National Institute of Child Health and Human Development, NIH, DHHS, 2000). It is one of the most visible aspects of language acquisition in children. As Richgels (2004) noted "The number of words in a child's vocabulary is an indicator of his or her linguistic health and a factor in his or her ability to use language in varied contexts and for multiple purposes" (p. 473). Acquiring the necessary vocabulary begins in the first year of life.

Typically developing young children need to hear at least 33 million words by age 3 years (Hart and Risley, 2003). Once formal education begins, children acquire five new words a day (Nagy and Anderson, 1984). Our schools place a high priority on providing effective vocabulary instruction in all grades. Command of a large vocabulary frequently sets high-achieving students apart from less successful ones. Word knowledge is closely related to overall language development, reading proficiency, and academic achievement. From their earliest years, children know the wonder and power of words. They are entertained by the sound and meaning of words and they never appear to tire of the game of "what's that?" (McGregor, 2005). Gregg, the student in the vignette above, would be chagrined to discover that the answer to his query about the number of words in English is approximately 450,000 (Stahl, 1999). With attentive adult support, there is a never-ending supply of new words for students to learn.

However, students who experience disabilities learn with great effort or those who acquire English as their second or third language often find vocabulary acquisition less joyful. Indeed, a limited vocabulary is the hallmark of language and learning disorders. Identifying language or learning disorders early in their educational career is crucial in order for students to receive the specific instruction or interventions they need. Teaching vocabulary skills to culturally and linguistically diverse children in preschool and the early grades is crucial to their success (Champion and Hyter, 2003; Roseberry-McKibbon, 2007). Students with learning disabilities (Westby, 1999) and students with complex communication disabilities (Lowe, 2003), as well as typical elementary and secondary students (Beck et al., 2002; McCardle and Chhabra, 2004) all benefit from extended conversations and a rich vocabulary environment. Teachers need to know —and use—the most effective ways to instruct all of these student populations. Adolescents may pose a special challenge. Speech–Language pathologists, classroom teachers, other education specialists, and parents regularly address vocabulary goals on the individual education plans they write for these students. They need vocabulary intervention strategies that produce positive outcomes.

This leads us to ponder how should we go about teaching new vocabulary to adolescents? Five queries about teaching vocabulary to students from age 11 to 17 years are posed in this chapter.

1. How is vocabulary learned at this age?
2. What words should we use for general and special education students?
3. How can we work collaboratively to supplement the general education curriculum?

4. How can we enrich the semantic environment for both high-achieving and low-achieving students?

5. How can we teach or intervene with students in an explicit, systematic, and intensive way? In short, *what works?*

Each of these queries will serve as a topic in this chapter. The topic will include a description, some key evidence-based statements to guide educators, a discussion of the impact of those statements, and an example of an instructional or intervention strategy for secondary grade levels in the form of a lesson. Each entry is a short statement of how the research informs the practice described in the activity.

Evidence-based Practice

Two key federal education laws in this century require educators and specialists to use "scientifically based reading research" (U.S. Dept. of Education, 2002) or "evidence-based interventions to the extent possible" (U.S. Dept. of Education, 2004). The evidence-based statements used in this chapter will serve as a freeway exit to quickly find the most relevant information within the vast amount of empirical research that instructors and interventionists have published about adolescents.

Evidence-based practice is not only stipulated in law; it is the most ethical way to teach all children. Educators need to know the defining research that directs their choice of instruction. Fortunately, vocabulary is one of the "most clearly articulated lines of research in literacy education" connecting word knowledge with reading comprehension (Blachowicz and Fisher, 2004, p. 66). Though some educators may frown upon the amount of attention "research" is getting in schools, the alternative is teaching by happenstance, emotion, or perhaps by watching what the teacher in the next room is doing. This is not acceptable. Yorkston (2006) maintained a sense of humor when she described evidence-based practice as the right balance between "nothing is good enough" and "anything goes" (p. 7).

Evidence-based practice has been aptly described as "the integration of best and current research evidence with clinical/educational expertise and relevant stakeholder perspectives, in order to facilitate decisions about assessment and intervention that are deemed effective and efficient for a given stakeholder" (Schlosser and Raghavendra, 2003, p. 259). In addition, Justice and Fey (2004) suggested that placing evidence-based practice in applied settings, such as schools, represents an important undertaking in the twenty-first century. There appears to be a need to strengthen this connection as shown when one investigator found that 82 percent of early childhood professionals interviewed reported they did not record learner performances, nor seek that data to make their intervention decisions (Reichle, 2006). Therefore, it appears that some practitioners need to have greater access to evidence-based practice for the key areas they teach. Vocabulary is one of those key areas. Evidence-based practice reviews and chapters like this one may help "to identify the clinical bridges that need to be built—bridges that will get us to our clinical destination in an efficient manner" (Yorkston, 2006, p. 6).

How is Vocabulary Learned?

Vocabulary is learned both indirectly and directly. Students learn indirectly in three primary ways: by having frequent rich and varied conversations with adults, by listening to books read to them, and by reading themselves. The first two methods build oral vocabulary enabling the third method—reading—to develop. Students must learn *all* vocabulary words solely by listening—until they can read.

Students who do not have frequent stimulating adult conversations, are not read to regularly, and do not read well themselves must be taught vocabulary directly. Research shows that children's vocabulary can be built by explicitly teaching types of words, categories of words, and even specific words (Dollaghan, 1998; Roth and Troia, 2006). Explicit instruction may be provided in schools or at home. Explicit instruction is characterized by the use of word games, word learning strategies, and structured spoken and written language activities. These activities need to be interesting and even playful or students will not engage and, therefore, will not learn. Since listening and speaking vocabularies enhance reading and writing vocabularies, the benefits of particular practice activities cross over from one mode to another. Seeing words that they have heard helps students recall letter patterns, giving them more than one way to remember words (Montgomery, 2007). Adolescents who cannot—or do not—read are at a distinct disadvantage in vocabulary development. Once students can read words on a page accurately and fluently they will be able to construct meaning at many levels (Lyon, 1998). Adolescents will increase their vocabulary if they read and they will improve their reading if they recognize more words. That is how vocabulary grows. Reading matters.

Once students are reading independently, decoding some words, but recognizing most words automatically, it is important to teach and use words specifically that will allow them to discuss, summarize, and respond to reading. Students acquire many of these new words first in their spoken language. It is important to discuss new words. An increase in their spoken vocabulary, in turn, makes it easier for them to comprehend text.

Direct word learning strategies are also highly effective after students become readers. When new words are encountered in reading, students should be strongly encouraged to do five things: try to pronounce the word, think of other words that are similar, look for familiar affixes, base words, roots, etc., look for context clues, and use a dictionary (Beck *et al.*, 2002). Kinsella (2004), and others cautioned that dictionary definitions are of questionable value to struggling readers. "Student-friendly" definitions using spoken vocabulary words instead of reading vocabulary words are preferable (Beck *et al.*, 2002).

Evidence-based Statements on How Students Learn Vocabulary

1. Reading aloud to students is most effective when accompanied by discussion before, during, and after reading (Cunningham and Stanovich, 1998; Honig *et al.*, 2000).
2. Context clues work best for recognizing written words that are already in a novice reader's oral vocabulary (Richgels, 2004).
3. Students who are given direct instruction in word meanings are better able to discern meanings of untaught words (Beck *et al.*, 1982).

Each of these statements underscores the importance of the link between oral and written vocabulary for emergent readers and the importance of reading to increase the number of known words continually. Children's literature plays a very important role for young or developmentally young students. Books, stories, and poetry should be read daily as an indirect method to increase word comprehension and then continued through the school years. When characters are richly described and story plots are compelling, children easily absorb new vocabulary words. Authors of good children's literature are unofficially permitted to "talk over children's heads"—using polysyllabic words and advanced syntactic structures—without jeopardizing the interest or loyalty of young minds. This is as true for sixth graders (Stahl *et al.*, 1991) as it is for preschoolers (Justice *et al.*, 2005).

Older students learn the meanings of new words from hearing them in stories in the same way they would have from reading those words. For younger children, listening vocabulary grows faster when they hear words they cannot yet read or write. Some of these words also become part of their speaking or "thinking" vocabularies, showing up in pretend play, children's conversations, and surprise announcements like "this dish of broccoli is enormous!" Adolescents are unlikely to explore words with this same sense of abandon. They might recognize some words they could try to use in a situation, but they are not going to risk looking or feeling foolish.

There is much less experimentation or spontaneity at this age level. Activities must be chosen with this in mind. Here is a sample vocabulary-expanding activity for general education and special education students at the secondary level. It requires you to select a compelling story and read it aloud. This approach seems simple on the surface, but it is powerful. Being read to is always enjoyable for all students, including adolescents, and it engages them effortlessly. Adolescents who are poor or unmotivated readers get few opportunities to hear and discuss good literature that is less than novel length.

An example of a strategy to enhance the learning of vocabulary through the use of literature is shown in Lesson 1.

Lesson 1

Literal to Inferential Questioning From a Read-aloud Story

Read a carefully selected short story or book for 5–8 minutes. A website for book selections is at the end of the chapter. If you do not finish the book, do so another time. Begin a discussion of the book with literal questions and then shift to more inferential ones. Intentionally, use and reuse the vocabulary in the book as you ask the questions and discuss the answers.

If you chose to read *The Wall* by Bunting (1992) it would take about 7 minutes. It is about the Vietnam Memorial in Washington DC, through the eyes and experiences of a young boy who knows little about the war and his father's great loss. They are looking for the little boy's grandfather's name on the wall—he lost his life in Vietnam in 1967. The answers to the questions become quite significant. History, politics, and strong emotions are at stake.

The author brings in interesting words that may not be in some adolescents' vocabulary and should be discussed, defined, and used by the teacher: march, medals, squashed, weighted, mutters, stares, bunch, rather, uniforms, laid, honor, bent, blurs. They are not particularly complex or polysyllabic words, but they have specific meanings that reveal the strong emotions in the story.

Here are sample questions for *The Wall* which demonstrate how the questions transition from literal to inferential levels.

1. Who are the characters?
2. When did the story happen?
3. Where did it take place?

4. What was the problem in the story?
5. How was the problem solved?
6. Did you like how the story ended?
7. What would you have changed? Why?
8. What lesson or moral was taught?
9. Did the man intend to influence the boy's feelings? What makes you think that?
10. Does the lesson have any connection with your life? In what way?
11. What other stories could this author write to teach this lesson?
12. Why do you think the author wrote this story?

What Words Should We Use for General and Special Education Students?

At the secondary level, it is important to use materials that reflect the curriculum being taught in the classes, as well as the "unstated" vocabulary or what Beck *et al.* (2002) called "tier two vocabulary." Adolescents who know many "tier two words" make good academic progress. Tier one words are basic words such as sight words, words found in early readers, and the 5000–7000 words we use for everyday conversation. Tier two, on the other hand, consists of high-frequency words for more mature users. Words in this tier are likely to be used in many academic courses and have multiple meanings. They are often not taught since they appear "common," but in fact, they are not well understood by many students. Tier three words are usually connected to specific domains or subject areas and are used with less frequency. Students need to learn all three tiers of words, in an ascending order.

Secondary students who can converse and read likely have acquired most tier one words. If they have not, they need to be directly taught first. Subject area teachers are most likely to teach tier three words, which is appropriate. However, that often leaves tier two words—those more mature words that are commonly used in all areas—overlooked. Table 2.1 shows examples of words at all three tiers. Adolescents who do not know tier two words because they have not been explicitly taught are at a disadvantage. Presenting tier two words in varied ways with lots of active engagement will support academic success at the secondary level. Beck *et al.* (2002) recommend explicitly teaching tier two words. There are approximately 7000 words in this tier, so obviously not all of them can—or should—be taught. Teaching 700 new words a year for 10 years is not an appropriate goal; however, judiciously selecting three tier two words each week for instruction is valuable.

TABLE 2.1 Examples of words in each tier

Tier One Words	Tier Two Words	Tier Three Words
Kite, bag, jump, because, race, mild, and singing	Docile, expression, fragrant, expensive, density, vintage, and conflagration	Lathe, chasm, democracy, cardiovascular, sulfur, and photosynthesis

Evidence-based Statements Related to Teaching Words and Word Usage

1. Semantic mapping and categorizing has been found to improve both students' recall of targeted words and their comprehension (Honig et al., 2000).
2. Students benefit when they are given not only definitions but also examples of word usage in a wide variety of contexts (National Institute of Child Health and Human Development, NIH, DHHS, 2000).
3. Educators are able to teach only eight to ten new words per week thoroughly, so words need to be chosen carefully (McCardle & Chhabra, 2004).

An activity to directly teach tier two words that are critical for mathematics is shown in Lesson 2. Different core subject areas can be selected from the resource listed in Lesson 2.

Lesson 2

Positive "Overusing" of Tier Two Words

Word lists that constitute the "materials" of teaching vocabulary may be found in *The Reading Teacher's Book of Lists* (Fry *et al.*, 1993). Take three words from the list each week and write student-friendly definitions, use them in word games, make flash cards with the definition on the back, and overuse the words in your daily conversation to get students to notice them.

For instance you can say to your group or class, "The weather today includes a combination of wind and rain. That combination makes me stay indoors. Now a combination of wind and sun would make me want to go sailing. If I did go sailing, I would use my new combination lock on my sea bag. But since I am staying indoors today and only dreaming of sailing, I will plan on a combination of hot soup and a sandwich for lunch." Invariably, students look quite puzzled and ask why do you keep saying that word? "What word?" I say. "You know—that word." "What word?"

I say. "Combination," one of them says. "Oh yes, that word—combination. I like that word," I say.

List of tier two words in intermediate mathematics:

combination, deviation, exact, include, increase, notation, origin, proportion, reverse, successive, terminate, and variable

(Fry *et al.*, 1993, pp. 50–51)

How Can We Work Collaboratively to Supplement the General Education Curriculum?

The general education curriculum has more indirect vocabulary opportunities and less direct ones. With the possible exception of spelling words and unit words, classrooms in grades six through to twelve have few direct word-learning lessons. Teachers focus more on the facts and operations that adolescents need to know than the words they need to know to speak, read, or write about those complex ideas. This is sufficient for many general education students who are learning new words on their own. For others with learning challenges, a small vocabulary is a barrier to this advanced learning. Special educators can supplement the general education curriculum by co-teaching in classes in which their target students are enrolled. Collaborative planning and co-teaching occurs when teachers like and respect each other's teaching styles. These styles do not need to be the same, but they do need to blend well in one classroom. Sometimes it is best to plan together but carry out the instruction in different places. This can be effective as well. Adolescents benefit from the give and take of two instructors in the room. They learn from the conversations we hold, the way we support each other's ideas, and the way we work out differences. For some students, this is the first time they have observed adults using language to solve a problem. It can be highly instructive for them.

Teachers may be more focused on standards and presentation of the content for the entire class, while the special educator is influenced by the individual learning style and needs of a student with a disability. The teacher looks for evidence that a curricular activity will be applicable for all students, while the special educator seeks evidence that this approach will benefit this adolescent.

Combining standards and evidence-based practices takes effort and there are a limited number of teaching resources or tools available for education teams to use together (Montgomery, 2007). Besides teachers teaching together, adolescents need to be working together on projects that meet both group and individual needs. The concept cube described below is one such activity that allows students to all construct the same learning tool, but then master it—and the other cubes in the room—at their own pace. New vocabulary information will progress through the three levels of word knowledge (Armbruster and Osborn, 2001). The three levels are: unknown (I do not know this word), acquainted (I have seen or heard this word, but it is not mine yet), and established (I know this word, what it means, and how and when to use it). Reaching the final stage may take a considerable length of time with direct and repeated practice, facilitated in the collaborative environment.

Evidence-based Statements Related to Collaborative Work

1. Challenging students to create original sentences with target words increases personal interest and word learning (Beck *et al.*, 2002).
2. Arranging thoughts, concepts, and, eventually, words into categories facilitates meaning, memory, and retrieval (Roth and Troia, 2005).
3. Progress through three levels of word knowledge—unknown, acquainted, established—can be facilitated with direct and repeated practice (Armbruster and Osborn, 2001).

Using these evidence statements, an activity for collaborative work is shown in Lesson 3.

Lesson 3

Concept Cube

Students are given a six-square pattern on tagboard or stiff paper that can be folded and taped into a three-dimensional cube, which will be four inches on each side. (Cube pattern is on the website listed at the end of this chapter.) Before they fold it up, they must write clearly in each square and follow these directions. Each student is given one challenging vocabulary word from a recent reading, core subject unit, or grade level list. Broader, more complex words work best for this task. (See the discussion of tier two words in this chapter for ideas.)

1. Write the assigned vocabulary word in one square.
2. Write a synonym (word or phrase) in another square.
3. Write an antonym (word or phrase) in another square.
4. Write a category or categories it could belong to.
5. Write the essential characteristics of the concept of this word.
6. Give one example.

Then fold along the lines and tape it into the shape of a cube. Roll the cube and read what comes up on the "top" of it. The student must tell the relationship of that word or phrase to the original word.

For example, if the word was "bellicose" and the student rolled the cube and it came up "soft spoken" the student would say "It is the opposite." If it came up "types of verbal expression" the student would say "It is the category." Teachers scaffold student learning as needed. After students know their own cube without any errors, they exchange with someone in the room and learn another word. Cubes can be turned from face to face, rather than rolled if you do not wish to have as much activity in your room.

How Can We Enrich the Semantic Environment for Both High-achieving and Low-achieving Adolescents?

An ultimate goal of vocabulary intervention is not to continually teach new words, but rather to teach students to learn words on their own. Vocabulary instruction should focus on three types of words: important words (key words to help readers make sense of the text), useful words (words they will encounter often), and difficult words (words with multiple meanings, figurative language, idiomatic words, etc.). Both high-achieving and low-achieving students need an enriched semantic environment so they will come in frequent contact with unusual and interesting words. High-achieving students have greater word curiosity than struggling adolescents. This is primarily because the learning process for less-skilled students is more energy- and time-intensive. It takes a vast amount of focus, attention, and literally all of their cognitive reserves to figure out new words they encounter. They do not seek out those energy-draining experiences as exuberantly as quicker learners often do. Nevertheless, both types of learners need assistance with at least one of the three types of words listed above—difficult words. There are several ways to enrich their semantic environment.

Teaching students multiple meanings (I eat cake, the mud will cake on my shoe; I wear a winter coat, this is a coat of arms, it needs a coat of paint, the animal's coat was matted) builds on known words to extend their vocabulary. It is an effective and efficient instructional activity (McCardle & Chhabra, 2004).

Idioms are used throughout everyday conversation, in casual reading materials, and in more sophisticated novels and literary works. Idioms are a formidable challenge for English learners. They carry a tremendous amount of meaning in a few short words. Idioms are used to explain highly familiar sets of experiences, attitudes, and feelings in a type of verbal shorthand. Although idioms may be taught from their literal form (the historical part) to their figurative form, it is not necessary. We all use idioms accurately and we learn new ones from oral conversation, without knowing the original story behind the words. While high achievers may benefit from learning how the lifestyle and mannerisms of the European Middle Ages spawned so many idioms we use today, lower achievers may not. You can differentiate your teaching to engage both groups meaningfully. Several particularly good idiom books for adolescents are listed at the end of the chapter.

Evidence-based Statements Related to an Enriched Semantic Environment

1. Multiple-meaning words and compound words encourage students to cross-check meaning with the context of the sentence and increase the likelihood of remembering the word (Bannon *et al.*, 1990; McCardle and Chhabra, 2004).
2. Students do not learn vocabulary words based on their age or their grade. They learn words based on their experiences (Beck *et al.*, 2002).
3. Lengthy and robust instruction involving active learning, prior knowledge, and frequent encounters is more powerful (Graves, 2006).

An activity to enrich the semantic environment is included in Lesson 4.

Lesson 4

Learning Idioms by Themes

One hundred and ninety-eight English idioms can be taught in ten major thematic units for interest, organization, and easy recall (Conger, 2006). These are very useful for English learners. The ten categories are school, clothes, food, color, animals, head and face, arms and legs, sports, money, and numbers. The clothes and numbers idioms are listed below. Adolescents go through a series of activities with each idiom in order to have lengthy and robust instruction with repeated encounters with the same idiom within the theme. These include cartoons and images, vignettes, short dialogues, mini-quizzes, writing original sentences, and scaffolded discussion. The reference is in the list at the end of this chapter. The activity series is not listed here, only a sample of three category entries. Teachers should introduce two per week from the same category, do the series of activities, and then review all idioms introduced at the end of each month. There are mini-quizzes provided to monitor progress and check retention periodically. Students view it as a challenge and find the vocabulary instantly useful in speaking, reading, and writing.

CLOTHES

- at the drop of a hat
- walk in her shoes
- talking through his hat
- take my hat off to you
- fly by the seat of my pants
- feather in my cap
- off the cuff
- stuffed shirt
- wolf in sheep's clothing
- fill her shoes
- keep it under your hat
- eat your hat
- ants in his pants
- roll up your sleeves
- something up his sleeve
- old hat
- pull one out of his hat
- bursting at the seams.

NUMBERS

- on cloud nine
- take five
- two left feet
- back to square one
- forty winks
- two shakes of a lamb's tail
- dress to the nines
- the whole nine yards
- the eleventh hour
- fifth wheel
- behind the eight ball
- two heads are better than one.

How Can We Teach or Intervene with Students in an Explicit, Systematic, and Intensive Way?

This is the fifth and final question posed in this chapter because it pulls together the other four questions and discussions and asks teachers and specialists to instruct vocabulary with a plan in mind. The plan is not merely to expose students to "new" words, but rather to use the evidence-based practices that we know are successful: select words with care, present lessons in a meaningful way, and monitor students' progress as they acquire new words. As noted earlier, students learn some vocabulary indirectly. They do so with robust discussion with adults, being read to, and reading on their own. When students do not engage in those activities routinely and with purpose, they have a meager oral vocabulary on which to build their reading vocabulary and comprehension. Thus, they need direct vocabulary instruction earlier. Direct translates to explicit. Explicit teaching requires us to select the words using the methods described in this chapter and others in this book and teach them in the most engaging and motivating ways we know.

Systematic refers to the sequence, order, and precision of teaching those words. Each lesson has demonstrated how fewer words are presented, elaborated upon, and practiced in numerous ways. Teachers and specialists should always know precisely what words they are teaching in effective vocabulary work and be pleasantly surprised when other words are acquired simultaneously. Vocabulary words are learned when the student has a need for them in oral or written language. Systematic teaching includes our creating a need for students to use their expanding vocabulary.

Intensity refers to time and frequency. Shorter lessons repeated more frequently seem to stabilize new word learning (Graves, 2006). Collaborative teaching provides multiple opportunities for students to have short, intensive strategy sessions in which formally taught vocabulary can be applied and molded until the student "owns it." Specific words can be introduced in the classroom in one round of exercises, reinforced by the speech language pathologist later in the week, and then practiced in a small group or independently utilizing a highly explicit, systematic, and intensive weekly routine (Montgomery, 2007). Although we know that students may learn after one exposure, fast mapping, this is only at the receptive level and it takes considerably more exposures for students to establish that word at the expressive level in speaking, reading, or writing (Wagovich and Newhoff, 2004). Intensive instruction and intervention provides those multiple exposures.

Evidence-based Statements Related to Explicit Intervention

1. Students need to encounter a word about twelve times before they know it well enough to improve their comprehension (McKeown *et al.*, 1985).
2. Engage students in active and deep processing of new words (Graves, 2006).

3. Twenty common prefixes account for 97 percent of the prefixed words in printed school English (White *et al.*, 1989).

A sample activity for providing instruction and/or intervention in an explicit, systematic and intensive way is shown in Lesson 5.

Lesson 5

Fix the Prefix

Prefix instruction in grades six through to ten can yield significant instructional pay-off for the teaching time involved. This is because prefixes tend to be consistent in spelling and meaning and just nine prefixes account for three-quarters of words with prefixes. (White *et al.*, 1989). See Figure 2.1 for a list of the twenty "top prefixes" and the shaded area shows the top nine, which account for 75 percent of the prefixed words in English.

Concentrate on the top three prefixes, then the top six, then the top nine. Write or type the prefixes in large letters on 3-inch × 5-inch cards. Have five to eight students in a group with the prefix cards face up on the desk in the middle.

Read a word and its definition. "The word is proper. Proper means that everything is done correctly or in the right way. What is the opposite of proper?" Students are quickly to take the prefix card that they think will create the opposite. One should select "im" and say the new word. "Improper." Say "What does improper mean?" Scaffold the student answer until you get a response similar to "improper means that things are not done correctly or in the right way." If the student selects an incorrect prefix, indicate that it is not that one and someone else in the group takes a turn. Have each student say the correct prefixed word. Later have them write the words—both with and without the prefixes, based on your spoken definitions. Repeat until each word has been practiced about twelve times. Guided practice and independent student worksheets are provided in the resource listed in the references (Montgomery, 2007).

Summary

This chapter asked and attempted to answer five questions about how vocabulary can be enhanced for adolescents, with and without identified learning difficulties. Five queries about teaching vocabulary to students from age 11 to 17 years were posed.

1. How is vocabulary learned at this age?
2. What materials should we use for general and special education students?

Prefixes		Number of words with the prefix	
un	(not)	782	
re	(again)	401	
in, im, ir, il	(all mean "not")	313	
dis	(opposite)	216	
en, em	(make)	132	
non	(not)	126	
in, im	(all mean "into")	105	
over	(too much)	98	(75% of words)
mis		83	
sub		80	
pre		79	
inter		77	
fore		76	
de		71	
trans		47	
super		43	
semi		39	
anti		33	
mid		33	
under		25	
Total		2,859 Words	

Figure 2.1 Twenty most frequent prefixes in English
Source: Adapted from Graves (2006) and White *et al.* (2006)

3. How can we work collaboratively to supplement the general education curriculum?
4. How can we enrich the semantic environment for both high-achieving and low-achieving students?
5. How can we teach or intervene with students in an explicit, systematic, and intensive way?

The discussion of each query involved a discussion of the topic, evidence-based statements from the literature as guidelines for the reader, and closed with a lesson in which the research informed the practice in our schools. Lessons were selected that could either be presented solely from the instructions in the chapter or the source was given so teachers and specialists could access the complete lesson and materials needed. So what works? When educators know their students well, understand how vocabulary develops, plan and execute explicit, systematic, intensive lessons, monitor progress, and have high expectations, vocabulary intervention works.

Questions and Action Research Assignments

1. Describe how vocabulary size is one of the best predictors of language development. List methods in which vocabulary size may be measured at various age levels.
2. What does evidence-based practice mean for teachers and education specialists? How can it be used to plan instruction for general education students and intervention for special education students? Explain the legal basis for evidence-based practice. Do you think it improves our educational environment? Why or why not?
3. Select one of the five queries in this chapter and design and create a PowerPoint presentation to teach the important points to a group of paraprofessionals who work with struggling students in a seventh or eighth grade class. Include examples of the evidence statements that are appropriate for this grade level. Teach the lesson that is included in this chapter and add one more lesson of your own.
4. Look up the Fry *et al.* (1993) reference, select a group of tier two vocabulary words for a core subject area, and develop a short lesson to teach these words to a group of adolescents with identified learning disabilities. Include a method to monitor progress.
5. Proverbs, like idioms, are examples of figurative language. Investigate proverbs and compare and contrast them with idioms described in this chapter. Make a list of ten proverbs that might have significance for secondary level students' lives today. Three of your ten proverbs should be from a language and culture different than the dominant culture of U.S. schools.

Vocabulary Websites

Concept Cube

www.mury.k12.ut.us/MHS/apus/handouts/concept-cubeassignment.html

Pattern for the Concept Cube lesson.

Digital Kids Club

www.adobe.com/education/digkids/lessons/idiom.html

Very creative lessons to teach idioms with Adobe PhotoShop Elements.

Read Write Think

www.readwritethink.org/lessons/lesson_view.asp?id=254

Lessons to teach idioms.

Teachnology

www.teach-nology.com/teachers/lesson_plans/language_arts/vocab/

Vocabulary lessons that incorporate technology at the middle and high school level—most are directly related to core subject vocabulary.

Trelease on Reading

www.trelease-on-reading.com

Books lists for read-aloud to middle school and high school students.

Web English Teacher

www.webenglishteacher.com/idioms.html

A wide range of lessons that may be easily adapted for English learners and students with disabilities.

References

Armbruster, B. B. & Osborn, J. (2001). *Put reading first.* Jessup, MD: National Institute for Literacy.

Bannon, E., Fisher, P. J., Pozzi, L. & Wessel, D. (1990). Effective definitions for word learning. *Journal of Reading, 34,* 301–302.

Beck, I. L. & McKeown, M. G. (2002). *Bringing words to life: Robust vocabulary instruction.* New York: Guilford Press.

Beck, I. L., Perfetti, C. A., & McKeown, M. G. (1982). Effects of long term vocabulary instruction on lexical access and reading comprehension. *Journal of Educational Psychology, 74* (4), 506–521.

Blachowicz, C. & Fisher, P. (2004). Vocabulary lessons. *Educational Leadership, 61* (6), 66–69.

Bunting, E. (1992). *The Wall.* New York, NY: Clarion Books.

Champion, T. B., Hyter, Y. D., McCabe, A., & Bland-Stewart, L. M. (2003). A matter of vocabulary. *Communication Disorders Quarterly, 24* (3), 121–127.

Conger, M. (2006). *Read between the lines!* Greenville, SC: Super Duper Publications.

Cunningham, A. E. & Stanovich, K. E. (1998). What reading does for the mind. *American Educator, 22,* 8–15.

Dollaghan, C. (1998). Spoken word recognition in children with and without specific language impairment. *Applied Psycholinguistics, 19,* 193–207.

Fry, E. B., Kress, J. E., & Fountoukidis, D. L. (1993). *The reading teacher's book of lists.* (3rd ed.) Englewood Cliffs, NJ: Prentice Hall.

Graves, M. F. (2006). *The vocabulary book.* New York: Teachers College Press.

Hart, B. & Risley, T. (2003). The early catastrophe: The 30 million-word gap. *American Educator, 27* (1), 4–9.

Honig, B., Diamond, L., & Gutlohn, L. (2000). *Teaching reading sourcebook for kindergarten through 8th grade.* Novato, CA: Arena Press.

Justice, L. M. & Fey, M. E. (2004). Evidence-based practice in schools: Integrating craft and theory with science and data. *The ASHA Leader, 9*, 4–5, 32.

Justice, L. M., Meier, J., & Walpole, S. (2005). Learning new words from storybooks: Findings from an intervention with at-risk kindergartners. *Language, Speech, and Hearing Services in Schools, 36*, 17–32.

Kinsella, K. (2004, March 13). *Vocabulary presentation vs. vocabulary decoration across the subject areas.* Keynote address presented at the Orange County Reading Association, Orange, CA.

Lowe, M. A. (2003). Selecting reading and writing vocabulary for the AAC user. *Perspectives: Augmentative and Alternative Communication, 12* (2), 3–7.

Lyon, G. R. (1998). *Reading development, reading disorders, and reading instruction: Research-based findings.* Washington, DC: Formal Report and Senate Testimony provided to the Committee on Labor and Human Resources, The United States Senate.

McCardle, P. & Chhabra, V. (2004*). The voice of evidence in reading research.* Baltimore: Brookes.

McGregor, K. K. (2005). Children's word learning: An introduction. *Perspectives in Language Learning and Education, 12* (3), 3–4.

McKeown, M. G., Beck. I. L., Omanson, R. C. & Pople, M. T. (1985). Some effects of the nature and frequency of vocabulary instruction on the knowledge and use of words. *Reading Research Quarterly, 20*, 522–535.

Montgomery, J. K. (2007). *The bridge to vocabulary.* Bloomington, MN: Pearson/AGS.

Nagy, W. E. & Anderson, R. C. (1984). How many words are there in printed school English? *Reading Research Quarterly, 19*, 304–330.

National Institute of Child Health and Human Development, NIH, DHHS. (2000). *Report of the National Reading Panel: Teaching children to read: Reports of the subgroups (00–4754).* Washington, DC: U.S. Government Printing Office.

Reichle, J. (2006). Implementing evidence-based instruction: Talking the talk and walking the walk. *Perspectives on Augmentative and Alternative Communication, 16* (3), 11–15.

Richgels, D. J. (2004). Paying attention to language. *Reading Research Quarterly, 39* (4), 470–477.

Roseberry-McKibbon, C. (2007). *Language disorders in children.* Boston: Pearson Allyn-Bacon.

Roth, F. P. & Troia, G. A. (2005). *Vocabulary instruction for children and adolescents with oral language and literacy deficits.* Presentation at 2005 Council for Exceptional Children Annual Convention, Baltimore, MD.

Roth, F. P. & Troia, G. A. (2006). Collaborative efforts to promote emergent literacy and efficient word recognition skills. *Topics in Language Disorders, 26* (1), 24–41.

Schlosser, R. W. & Raghavendra, P. (2003). Towards an evidence-based practice in augmentative and alternative communication. In R. W. Schlosser (Ed.), *The efficiency of augmentative and alternative communication: Towards evidence-based practice* (pp. 259–297). New York: Academic Press.

Stahl, S. A. (1999). *Vocabulary development.* Cambridge, MA: Brookline Books.

Stahl, S. A., Richek, M. G., & Vandevier, R. (1991). Learning word meanings through listening: A sixth grade replication. In J. Zutell & S. McCormick (Eds.), *Learning factors/teacher factors: Issues in literacy research. Fortieth yearbook of the National Reading Conference* (pp. 185–192). Chicago: National Reading Conference.

U.S. Department of Education. (2002). No Child Left Behind Act of 2001: Reauthorization of the Elementary and Secondary Education Act (Online). Available: www.ed.gov/offices/OESE/esea/index.html.

U.S. Department of Education. (2004). Reauthorization of the Individuals with Disabilities Education Act (IDEA) PL 108–446 (Online). Available: www.cde.ca.gov/sp/se/lrideareathztnasp

Wagovich, S. A. & Newhoff, M. (2004). The single exposure: Partial word knowledge growth through reading. *American Journal of Speech-Language Pathology, 13* (4), 316–328.

Westby, C. (1999). Beyond decoding: Critical and dynamic literacy for students with dyslexia, language learning disabilities (LLD) or attention deficit–hyperactivity disorder (ADHD). In K. G. Butler and E. R. Sillliman (Eds.), *Speaking, reading and writing in children with language learning disabilities: New paradigms in research and practice* (pp. 73–107). Mahwah, NJ: Lawrence Erlbaum.

White, T. G., Sowell, J., & Yanagihara, A. (1989). Teaching elementary students to use word-part clues. *The Reading Teacher, 42*, 302–308.

Yorkston, K. M. (2006). Evidence-based practice: A roadmap to intervention. *Perspectives in Augmentative and Alternative Communication, 16* (3), 6–8.

CHAPTER 3

Teaching Academic Vocabulary to Adolescents to Improve Comprehension[1]

MARY E. CURTIS AND ANN MARIE LONGO

Introduction

The importance of vocabulary to reading achievement—and more specifically to reading comprehension—has long been established (Thorndike, 1917; Davis, 1944). Knowledge of word meanings and the ability to access that knowledge efficiently are recognized as important factors in reading and listening comprehension, especially as students progress to middle school and beyond (Chall, 1983, 1996; Marzano, 2004).

Although growth in vocabulary knowledge occurs rapidly and almost effortlessly for some children, the rate at which word meanings are acquired can vary greatly. Many children with reading problems have poor vocabularies and the gap between the vocabulary they need and the one they have widens over time (Biemiller, 1999).

In this chapter we describe an intervention we developed to meet the needs of adolescents who lack the vocabulary knowledge they need to comprehend materials written at their grade level.

The vocabulary intervention is one of a set of four 16-week courses that make up a remedial reading curriculum known as *Reading Is FAME* designed for the students and teachers at Girls and Boys Town in Boys Town, Nebraska (Curtis and Longo, 1997).

The theoretical framework for the *FAME* curriculum is Chall's (1983, 1996) stages of reading development. The first course—for students reading below the fourth grade level—teaches the relationships among the most common letter combinations and sounds. The goal of the second course—intended for students reading between the fourth and sixth grade levels—is to promote fluency in recognizing words and their meanings. The third course (and the one we focus on in this chapter) seeks to build up the vocabulary knowledge of students reading between the sixth and eighth grade levels. In the fourth course—designed for students reading at the eighth grade level and beyond—the emphasis is on improving the integration of text information via both reading and writing (Curtis and Longo, 1999).

Students get placed in a particular course in the sequence based on an initial assessment of their reading achievement using the Diagnostic Assessments of Reading (Roswell *et al.*, 2005). Oliver is typical of the students who get placed in the vocabulary course after testing. As a ninth grader, Oliver was able to read aloud material at the high school level with ease. But he was not able to understand what he read. Some of Oliver's teachers wondered whether he had attentional problems. Others believed that he just lacked motivation. But when he took the Word Meaning subtest on the Diagnostic Assessments of Reading, we discovered that he knew the meanings of very few words above the fourth grade level. Because of his vocabulary difficulties, Oliver's comprehension suffered. And because his comprehension suffered, he was unable to use context as a way to acquire new word meanings.

For Oliver—and for the multitude of adolescents like him—direct vocabulary instruction can be one of the most efficient and effective routes for improving comprehension.

Overview to the Vocabulary Intervention

The vocabulary intervention is based on what previous research had told us about effective vocabulary instruction. So, in this sense, our intention from the outset was derivative and readers will recognize at least some of the instructional activities we use as familiar ones.

In another sense, however, two features make our approach different from typical classroom vocabulary instruction. First, even though the goal is to improve students' reading comprehension, all of the instructional time in the intervention is focused on developing students' vocabularies. Second, teachers use a word list as the base for their instruction, introducing each word first in isolation before presenting it in context. The reasoning behind these decisions is described below.

Focusing on Vocabulary Learning

In our experience, much of the failure of remedial reading instruction results from doing too much rather than too little. We wanted to make sure that our intervention focused on the knowledge and skills most needed by our students to advance their understanding.

Weak vocabularies can cause students' comprehension to suffer and difficulties in comprehension can cause their vocabularies to remain weak (Chall, 1983, 1996; Curtis, 2006). But—in order to influence their comprehension—students need at least ten to fifteen encounters with each word's meaning (Beck *et al.*, 1987). So we decided to devote all of the instructional time available—45 minutes a day, 5 days a week for 16 weeks—to direct teaching of vocabulary and its application in context.

Moving from Isolation to Context

We knew that, to be effective, vocabulary learning must occur in context (Sternberg, 1987). However, we wanted to design an intervention where students would be the ones to create the contexts in which they learned word meanings.

In more traditional vocabulary instruction, the lesson usually begins with a story or article that students are reading (the context) and words are selected for further discussion (in isolation). In our course, teachers and students always begin with a discussion of a set of words and their meanings (in isolation), following which students complete activities requiring them to apply knowledge about the word meanings they are learning (the context).

The emphasis is always on getting students to make inferences about contexts in which word meanings will fit (rather than asking them to make inferences about word meanings from contexts they are given).

Selecting Words for Instruction

Knowledge of word meanings is rarely (if ever) an all or none matter, especially for adolescents who have experienced difficulties in learning to read. Because of gaps in background knowledge, they tend to recall very little from typical instructional experiences designed to acquaint them with grade appropriate word meanings. And in cases when they are already familiar with a word's meaning, their knowledge is frequently based on their aural experiences with the word (rather than any encounters they might have had with the word in print).

A framework we have found useful in our thinking about this is Dale's (1965) "stages of word knowledge." According to Dale (1965), four stages of comprehension are involved in word knowledge: words whose meanings are known (stage four), words whose meanings are recognized in some contexts but not others (stage three), words that have been seen or heard, but whose meanings are not known (stage two), and, finally, words that have never been heard or seen before (stage one).

A typical unit in our vocabulary intervention consists of ten words, about half of which students are likely to have some familiarity with (stage three) and about half of which are likely to be new (stages one to two). For example, one unit includes the following words: persistent (refusing to give up or let go), astound (to fill with surprise or sudden wonder), confine (to keep or hold in), elusive (hard to describe or understand), remote (far off in place or time), spectacular (making a very unusual or impressive sight or display), extinguish (to put out; do away with), longevity (a long duration of life), taunt (to insult or ridicule; mock), vital (having to do with or necessary for life).

In the case of some of the stage one and two words, we expect that students will start out with some relevant conceptual knowledge (e.g. *taunt*), while for others, we know they might not (e.g. *elusive*). For stage three words, students' prior knowledge will be connected to particular situations (e.g. fire *extinguish*er or *remote* control) and might be intertwined with similar words (e.g. insistent versus *persistent*).

In choosing words for instruction, we apply an additional criterion. Since our students are adolescents comprehending about 2–3 years behind their grade level in school, we look for words found in reading materials across the content areas at the sixth to eighth grade levels, ones likely to disrupt comprehension if their meanings are not known. Words like these have been referred to as "high-utility academic vocabulary" (Laufer and Nation, 1999) or "tier two words" (Beck *et al.*, 2002).

As the name implies, high-utility academic words are ones that are used in all of the content areas—words like assume, evaluate, manipulate, simultaneous, and so on. (See Corson (1997) for a list of some of the most frequently and widely used academic words.) Because these words are abstract words that are common in a variety of school subjects, direct and systematic vocabulary instruction that focuses on them can have a powerful impact on comprehension. This is especially true for English-language learners, where deep and extensive exposure to vocabulary seems to produce the best results (Gersten and Jiménez, 1994).

One condition that we do not use for word selection is semantic category. Research shows that grouping words thematically is not necessary if vocabulary instruction is varied and rich (see Stahl (1999) for a summary of this work). Since we want our students to create their own connections among words, we feel that they might be hindered in that process if we use words where relationships are already built in.

Five principles guide the teachers' and students' movement through each week of the intervention:

- introduce and activate word meanings
- present words in a variety of contexts

- provide multiple opportunities to learn and expand on meanings
- promote active and generative processing
- provide ongoing assessment and communication of progress.

We explain each of these principles in further detail in what follows, and provide illustrations of each from one of the units in the curriculum.

Introduce and Activate Word Meanings

The initial goal for every vocabulary unit is the same: to promote word knowledge and skills with explicit instruction. Each word and its meaning are introduced, followed by a discussion of the contexts in which the word and meaning can be applied. So, for example, in the case of *persistent*, the teacher might say:

> A persistent person is someone who hangs in there despite difficulties. We often hear or read about people like this . . . people who overcame a bunch of obstacles to succeed. Like an athlete who was persistent even though he or she had injuries—they refused to give up. Can anyone think of someone they know or have heard about who was persistent, who refused to give up?
>
> We had at least one word in an earlier unit that is related to persistence—can anybody think of one? The one I thought of was *endurance.* What connections do you see between endurance and persistence?
>
> Could persistence ever be a negative thing—can anybody think of a situation when someone's refusal to give up or let go might be harmful?

Notice that—as emphasized earlier—the teacher always directs the focus during the introduction of the word on helping students to come up with contexts in which the word meaning can be applied (versus asking students to infer something about the meaning of the word from contexts the teacher supplied).

Once the words and meanings for the week are introduced and discussed, students begin to make further connections between the new information and their prior knowledge. This is accomplished by working in small groups or individually on an exercise referred to as the completion activity. Some examples are:

> I was very persistent when . . .
>
> Things that can be confined are . . .

Concepts elusive to many people include . . .

People often extinguish . . .

Discussion of answers to the completion activity provides students with an opportunity to listen to and learn from each other. It also gives teachers a chance to clarify word meanings further. The completion activity also sets the expectation—from the outset—that vocabulary learning is much less about coming up with a single "correct" answer than it is about making connections to what you already know.

Present Words in a Variety of Contexts

Since we begin with a set of isolated words, we know that we need to provide students with opportunities to use them in a variety of contexts and to receive feedback about their success in doing so. One of the ways in which we accomplish this is via cloze or fill-in-the-blank sentences such as the following:

Even though the fire was out of control, the firemen _____ and were able to contain it.

and

The dog was _____ to the backyard so he would not chase the neighbor's cat.

Students are instructed to use each word only once in this activity, presenting many of them with great difficulty initially. This is especially true when more than one word can fit into a sentence frame. Through teacher modeling and small group discussion, however, students quickly figure out the best ways to fill in the blanks. The cloze format also provides teachers and students with an opportunity to discuss inflectional endings (e.g. -ed, -er, and -s) and the relationship between root words (e.g. persist) and derived words (e.g. persistent, persisted).

In addition to the sentence cloze task, each unit also includes a paragraph cloze activity such as the following:

____ winds refused to let up and continuously whipped the flames higher and higher. The burning building became an illuminated monster with hundreds of red tongues lashing out at the black sky.
    Gravity defying streams of water sought out the flames that refused to be _____ or _____ . Again and again fiery fingers

teased and _____ the firefighters below. It was _____ that the source that sustained the monster's fury be located. For several hours, however, the source proved to be _____, and the room it was located in was too _____ for the firefighters to find.

The battle was captivating. Human beings protecting their environment pitted against an all consuming force that hissed and spewed jetting sparks in a desperate attempt to prolong its _____. Onlookers were _____ by the _____ sight.

We find that most teens with reading difficulties view the paragraph cloze as even more of a challenge than the sentence task, accounting for why their efforts to use context to figure out the meanings of unknown words has so little pay-off. In working on the paragraph fill-ins, teachers show students how to complete the activity in stages and model for them the kinds of decisions that skilled readers make as they process text.

For example, to introduce the task, teachers first read through the whole paragraph, showing students how to get an overall sense of the topic. Then, using a "think-aloud" procedure, teachers work through the blanks, drawing attention to the context clues that helped to narrow down possible choices (e.g. "Looking at the first sentence, it seems to me that winds could be either *spectacular* or *persistent*. In this sentence, though, it describes the winds as refusing to let up, so this tips me off that *persistent* would probably be the better choice."). Teachers also show how to skip blanks they cannot answer the first time through, cross out words they have already used, and pencil in possibilities when they are not sure which choice is best.

Over the next few weeks, the whole class works through the exercise together, with the teacher acting as a scribe and monitor (e.g. "Is that the only word that fits?" and "How do we know that's a good choice?"). Students then work in small groups or pairs, following the same process. Finally, students complete the activity on their own and class time is spent discussing and defending choices.

Students also experience their vocabulary words in a variety of contexts via a read and respond activity. As part of each unit, students read several short, informational articles written about topics of general interest. Although occasionally the articles include one or more of the course vocabulary words, this is not a factor we used in their selection. Instead, we pick articles that we feel lend themselves to application of the words, meanings, and concepts that the students are learning. To facilitate application, we write a set of questions to accompany each article that incorporates some of the vocabulary words. So, for example, if the text is about the function of the pyramids and the process of mummification, the questions might be as follows.

1. Reaching a *consensus* on how the pyramids were built has been *elusive*. What is your *hypothesis?*
2. Why do you think the process of mummification was *vital* to the Egyptians' beliefs?

Before reading, teachers choose which question(s) they want students to answer and in which form the answer should occur (i.e. oral or written). Teachers also preview any information students might already know or need to know about the topic of the article (e.g. what do pyramids look like?) and any key terms (e.g. "pharaoh").

Still another way teachers provide students with different contexts in which to think about their vocabulary words is a read-aloud activity. Reading aloud is done frequently with young children; however, older students' vocabularies have been shown to benefit from listening as well (Stahl, 1999). Each of our units contains two stories that can be read aloud by the students and/or teachers. As in the case of the read and respond activity, the question accompanying each story helps to focus students' attention during reading and enhance their understanding of how the story relates to their vocabulary words.

So, for the unit we have been discussing, a story and question used might be:

"Jason and the Golden Fleece, Part 3", in W. F. Russell's (1989) *Classic Myths to Read Aloud*. New York: Three Rivers Press.

As you listen to the third and final portion of the story, answer the following:

What part of this whole saga most *astounded* you?

Provide Multiple Opportunities to Learn and Expand on Meanings

Virtually every discussion of effective vocabulary instruction emphasizes the importance of providing students with multiple, meaningful encounters with word meanings (e.g. Baumann and Kame'enui, 2004; Graves, 2006). Two ways that we find to be especially beneficial in providing these kinds of encounters are yes–no–why activity and analogies.

We modeled the yes–no–why activity after one designed by Beck *et al.* (1982). Questions are constructed by pairing the words in the unit and students are asked to answer each question as well as to provide a reason for their answer. For example, some yes–no–why questions might be as follows.

1. Is something *elusive* also *remote?*
2. Can *confinement* affect *longevity?*
3. Is something *astounding* always *spectacular?*
4. Could something *persistent* ever be *extinguished?*
5. Is *taunting* ever *vital?*

There are no right or wrong answers to the questions and teachers provide a model for students of how to give support for their answers. By encouraging students to make their thinking explicit, additional relationships among the words and concepts are discovered and discussed.

By far the most challenging among the word activities is the analogies task. One reason for this is that the analogies are open-ended ones, with more than one correct answer. Another reason, though, is that many of our students are unfamiliar with the "rules" of analogical reasoning.

Teachers begin with a discussion of the many ways in which words can be related (e.g. synonyms–antonyms, cause–effect, category–example, part–whole, object–use, etc.). Once students are familiar with the different kinds of word relationships, the teacher models the process of identifying the relationships between the first two words in each analogy. Once a relationship was identified, the teacher then leads the class in a discussion of words that would complete the second half of the analogy.

Because we use an open-ended format—encouraging as many "correct" answers as possible—the analogy activity is a powerful tool for increasing vocabulary learning. Some examples include the following.

confine : fences :: constrict : ?

extinguish : firefighter :: tabulate : ?

persistent : achievement :: determination : ?

spectacular : fireworks :: baffling : ?

Promote Active and Generative Processing

Writing is one of the primary ways in which students are encouraged to process word meanings in an active and generative way. Each week, teachers assign at least one topic for students to write about, using at least five of the vocabulary words for the unit, along with any past words they can incorporate.

In the case of our sample unit, one of the writing assignments asks students to describe what you would hear, feel, see, and taste if you were sitting on an ocean beach in the middle of the day. Some of the responses generated by students (with vocabulary words in italics) have included the following.

If I was to go to the beach right now I would be *astounded*. It would be a *spectacular* day. I would see the ocean *shimmer*. It would be *appealing*. When I got there I would move to a *remote* place and not be near anyone. The waves would be crashing *persistently*. I would feel the sun burning on my *sensitive* skin (Rick).

Quietly sitting on the *shimmering* sand of a beach, in a *remote* location, a soft, cool, salty wave *taunts* my fiery extremities with its breath. The *vital* air *extinguishes* the *extensive* heat of the high sun, which *subtly* burns the skin on my arm (Mike).

I would feel *astounded* sitting on the beach wall watching a *spectacular* sunset. I would make sure my beach would be on a *remote* island. If I constantly live on the beach and ate healthy my life would be full of *longevity*. I would live in a *confined* home so no one would *taunt* me. But my dream would be *extinguished* when the alarm clock would go off (John).

It would be a very *spectacular* moment if I could be in the middle of the ocean. The view would be so *astounding* my heart would stop. The waves splashing *persistently* and the wind howling voices into my ears. Howling a song so soft and sweet. Telling me to relax and that it is *vital* for me to relax or my *longevity* will go down. The wind song told me to go to a *remote* place to chill out sometimes or I will go crazy. As the wind kept singing the water would splash a light mist on my face that would *evaporate* instantly. The water soaking into my skin going through my blood stream. Making me feel happy inside. It *extinguished* the fire inside me and I no longer had the *determination* to *taunt* or make fun of anyone. Then the incredible experience would be over and I wouldn't be able to explain this *elusive* experience (Jacob).

Another of the writing assignments for each unit asks students to discuss whether they agree or disagree with a quotation. The quote for the sample unit is "Many of life's failures are people who did not realize how close they were to success when they gave up" (Thomas Edison). Responses from students included the following.

Although this quote seems to make sense, there are many reasons why I disagree with it. Many people might be striving for a goal and they did not want to finish it for some reason. Many people have *spectacular* goals but people just got rid of them like kitchen fires with fire *extinguishers*. Many goals were *diminished* because of boredom. People do not want to do it any more or they *detract* from their goal because of something important like a baby. They might be so *astounded* by the baby they do not want to go back to the goal. Other people might *regret* giving up a goal they have been working on. People have to make decisions that are *vital* to their happiness. They might have to move to a *remote* environment to forget about their goals. Other people might throw their goals away because someone likes to *taunt* them about their dream. Even if you do not achieve your goal it will always be *confined* in your head (Rick).

For someone to become a successful person is a *spectacular* and *elusive* thing because no one can *foresee* his future or know his *destiny*. Working hard to reach something will never turn against you. I disagree with the statement that says life failures were close to success or *triumph*. People know when they are close to success. That is why they *persist* to reach the *vital* goal to *astound* themselves and the world too (Ari).

In responding to students' writing, teachers used an evaluation sheet that consists of two parts. The first part lists criteria that students are instructed to apply to their writing before submitting their assignment. For instance, did they do the following.

1. Write so that readers could relate to it, understand it, feel it?
2. Stick to the topic and make sense?
3. Make great choices about the words they used?
4. Use all their words correctly?
5. Express a complete thought in each sentence?
6. Vary their sentence length and structure?
7. Punctuate correctly?
8. Spell all their words correctly?

The second part contains a four-point holistic scoring guide that teachers use to communicate their assessment of how well students met the criteria. The four points are as follows.

4. Beautifully done. What you said really stuck with me, and you met most criteria.
3. Great job. I like what you had to say. See criteria you should check more carefully next time.
2. Pretty good response. See criteria to check more carefully next time.

1. You can do a better job. See criteria that you need to check more carefully next time.

Although students find it difficult at first to do the writing assignments, most are able to see progress fairly quickly. Linda's writing is typical of the pattern of growth that we have observed:

A person who I think is *unique* is my little sister. Her name is Holly. She has made it through Pendleton to sixth grade. She loves to draw and dance. It is not fair because she is very good at singing. Holly does not like soccer that much but she is still playing. She plays on a rec team. I love my little sister. I know she is going to be pretty when she grows up. My little sister still plays with dolls but she is cute so it is ok. She is one of the youngest in her class and one of the smallest too. I think she has ADD but she is still in Pendleton so I am proud of her (Linda, unit 1).

Yes, I believe that "continuous effort is the key to unlocking our potential." If you are *judicious* with the decisions you make then you may be able to unlock that *potential* faster. It might be very *hectic* to keep on trying and not give up, but it's all for the best. If you are not used to working a lot then you will have to *adapt* which might take awhile. You will need to *resolve* on what you like the most so you can work on it more. You will feel very *triumphant* when you accomplish your *resolution*. People might just start to *envy* you later. The more you *ponder* the more ideas you will get. But do not make this an *obsession* because you do not want it to take over your life. You might even find something *mysterious*. So be *determined* and do not give up (Linda, unit 7).

This summer and through this year things have happened that have made me more aware of my life. Two of my best friends met their *demise* this summer in a car accident around the time I was getting my license. I was so *devastated* by their deaths that it *diminished* my desire to drive anymore. There have been five more *gruesome* accidents this year that make me *sensitive* to driving *conservatively*. Kids need to make sure that they do not *exceed* the speed limit and always wear their seat belts. There can be *traumatic* consequences when you do not obey the driving laws. When I drive I am very careful. I cannot see how my dad is so *tranquil* when I am driving (Linda, unit 12).

On her first writing assignment, when asked to describe a unique person, Linda used simple sentence structure and produced a piece with minimal cohesion. By mid-course, when asked to agree or disagree with a quote, she used more complex sentences and she was able to include several of the vocabulary words. She also used more transition words, which improved the coherence of her text, although her overall organization was still weak. Toward the end of the course, in a reflection, she began to show some comfort in using the vocabulary to make the transition from what Shaughnessy (1977) called "sentences of thought" to "passages of thought."

Writing is an invaluable tool for providing students with opportunities to improve their expressive vocabulary. What teachers find most challenging about it, though, is the minimal emphasis that our instruction places on writing itself. However, when teachers see that even the most reluctant writers can be motivated if focus remains on vocabulary use, they become more comfortable with using writing without providing explicit writing instruction.

Also helping to ease teachers' concerns about the need to work on writing is an activity called Improving Sentences. Sentences containing errors—patterned after the kinds of errors we have observed students make during vocabulary acquisition—are part of each unit. Teachers and students examine each of the sentences that contain incorrect usage of the unit's vocabulary words and then discuss ways in which to revise and improve them. Some examples are as follows.

1. He lives *remote* from everyone else in the family.
2. The *astound* news caused the community disbelief.
3. His toothache *persistent* through the night.
4. *Vital* construction made the building able to withstand the earthquake.
5. The mustang *elusive* the ropes of the cowboy.
6. She *confined* a secret to her best friend.
7. The *taunt* remark embarrassed the person.
8. Sea turtles are many years *longevity*.
9. *Extinguished* flames fed by dried wood made a hot fire.
10. Niagara Falls *spectacular* tourists from all over the world.

Games are still another way in which teachers provide students with opportunities to use their words in active and generative ways. Board games like Taboo®, Password®, Jeopardy®, and Scattergories® are customized with the course vocabulary words. Teachers design their own games as well, with one of the students' favorites becoming known as "the conversation game."

In the conversation game, the teacher selects enough vocabulary words so that each student in the class can be assigned two or three words. Each vocabulary word is written on a separate card, and the cards are passed out to the students. The teacher then begins a "conversation" with the class, saying a sentence or two to introduce a topic. For example, the teacher might say: "I wonder what the world is going to be like in the year 2010. Will schools and workplaces still function in the same ways that we are used to or will everything be different?"

Students raise their hands to request participation in the conversation. After being acknowledged by the teacher, they contribute to the conversation by including one of the vocabulary words on their cards (e.g. "I think that we might see a lot of *innovations* in the field of medicine, like maybe a cure for Aids"). The teacher indicates whether students have used their word correctly and the student who uses all of his or her words first wins the game.

Provide Ongoing Assessment and Communication of Progress

From our experience in teaching students with reading and related learning difficulties, we know the benefits of helping them to see their progress on a frequent and regular basis. Several curriculum-based and standardized test measurements are incorporated into the course to serve that purpose.

Students take multiple choice pre- and post-tests for each unit. For the pre-test, teachers explain that the purpose is to establish what students already know and what they need to learn about the meanings of the words in the unit. A typical item from the test looks like the following one: a persistent worker (i) tires easily, (ii) has a poor attitude, (iii) is independent, or (iv) does not quit.

Students complete the test on their own, without any assistance from the teachers. Pre-test scores are then used by the teacher and students to make decisions about the instructional goals and activities for the unit.

Low pre-test scores indicate the need to focus on instruction designed to increase students' stage three knowledge of the words. High pre-test scores indicate that emphasis should be placed on moving the words from stage three to stage four.

On average students' scores on the weekly pre-test range from 30 to 60 percent. When students have low pre-test scores (i.e. many words were below stage three), teachers place particular emphasis on improving their performance on tasks designed to expand knowledge of word meanings (e.g. the completion activity, the sentence and paragraph clozes, and the read and responds).

When students have high pre-test scores (i.e. many words were at stage three and above), teachers emphasize improvements on tasks emphasizing connections among word meanings (e.g. yes–no–why and analogies) and precision in word use (e.g. writing).

At the end of the unit, students take a multiple choice post-test. The post-test includes as many as five words from past weeks, to facilitate review and generalization. Post-test items always differ from those on the pre-test, and are intended to challenge students' understanding of the words' meaning. The following item is an example: if the child was persistent with his demands he was (i) resilient, (ii) resistant, (iii) insistent, or (iv) consistent.

Grading in the course is based on students' achievement in five areas: analysis of word relationships, response to readings, use of vocabulary words in speaking, use of vocabulary words in writing, and recognition of word meanings. Analysis of word relationships is assessed by completion of the word activities. Response to what was read is assessed by the answers to the questions that follow the readings. Use of the vocabulary words in speaking is assessed by participation in class discussions. Use of the vocabulary words in writing is assessed by the writing assignments. The multiple choice vocabulary post-test score assesses recognition of word meanings.

Whenever possible, teachers meet individually with students at the end of each unit. Students are told how they are doing in all of the areas that affect their grade and they are asked to identify the area in which they will work to improve their performance on the next unit.

Of particular importance during the teacher–student conferences is helping students to understand that their grade on the post-test is only one aspect of their performance in the course. Being able to deal with words in listening, speaking, reading, and writing are all of equal importance in demonstrating their vocabulary growth.

To make time for conferences, teachers assign independent reading activities or use the read-alouds.

Two curriculum-based measures are also administered at the beginning and end of the course. One is a production task in which students are required to write sentences using fifteen of the words, the meanings of which are taught in the course. Students are instructed to use the words in the sentences in such a way that others who read the sentences will be able to figure out the word's meaning.

Students' responses on this task are scored using a sentence production scoring guide that describes how accurately their sentences convey the words' meanings. In the sentence production scoring guide, teachers assign a score of 0, 1, or 2 to each sentence. Focus in scoring is on the content of the sentence rather than spelling, punctuation, or grammar.

A score of 0 is assigned (i) when the use of the target word does not make sense (e.g. "I am very *acclaim*") or (ii) when the meaning of the target word is confused with that of a similar-sounding word (e.g. "I sometimes *demise* my friends and how they act").

A score of 1 is assigned (i) when the word usage is correct but the context is not precise enough to demonstrate knowledge of word meaning ("what is your *destiny?*"), (ii) when the usage is incorrect but the context indicates knowledge of word meaning ("Whitney Houston is my *admiration*, I want to sing just like her"), or (iii) when the sentence defines the target word but does not use it in context (e.g. "to keep something going, to not let go is to *sustain*").

A score of 2 is assigned when the sentence clearly demonstrates knowledge of the meaning of the target word and uses it appropriately (e.g. "I *regret* all my negative behaviors in the past" or "I have a *clever* friend from eighth grade who got straight As every quarter").

The sentence production task is useful for estimating the extent of students' stage four knowledge of words. Before the course begins, they typically earn about 40 percent of the total points possible on the sentence production task. By the end of the course, the mean percentage rises to 75 percent.

The second curriculum-based measure administered pre- and post-intervention is a recognition task consisting of multiple choice items designed to assess knowledge of forty of the course vocabulary words. The multiple choice recognition test is useful for estimating the extent of students' stage three word knowledge. On average, students score about 60 percent correct on the pre-test and 90 percent on the post-test.

In terms of standardized tests, vocabulary and comprehension subtests from tests like the Stanford Diagnostic Reading Test are administered pre- and post-intervention. Data from thirty-nine replications (with an average of twenty-six students in each) have indicated an average gain of about one reading grade level for the 16-week course (from 6.2 to 7.1 on the vocabulary subtest and from 5.7 to 6.7 on the comprehension subtest).

Summary and Conclusions

The instructional activities described in this chapter would be appropriate for promoting vocabulary learning in any classroom—whether it be via the sort of "stand-alone" units we designed or through instruction integrated into a content area. Success in using the activities depends on following some general guidelines, however, which include introducing and activating word meanings, presenting words in a variety of contexts, providing multiple opportunities to learn words in active and generative ways, and providing ongoing assessment.

One area that should warrant careful consideration when doing intensive vocabulary instruction is word selection. In choosing words, the number needs to be limited, allowing for frequent and varied experiences with the words. We have found that a set of ten words at a time works well. Only words that have "high utility" should be selected, that is words which students will be likely to encounter again and again after they have been taught. Words should also be ones that can be applied in many different contexts and content areas (e.g. *persistent* and *vital*).

Words selected for instruction do not need to be limited to ones that appear in students' reading materials. As our results demonstrate, all that is required is that word meanings can be related to what students are reading and that students receive some guidance in their application of those meanings.

Another area for teachers to consider is the kinds of vocabulary assessment to use. The examples described in this chapter can be done at regular intervals throughout a school year (weekly, monthly, or at the end of a semester) or incorporated into existing forms of assessment. Teachers and students may even want to make these decisions together, providing an opportunity to discuss the goals of instruction as well as the purposes of a particular assessment.

The most valuable kinds of assessment, of course, will be the ones that help both students and teachers. Students benefit from consistent feedback about their progress since it allows them to set goals and to keep being motivated. Teachers benefit from knowing what is working so that class time can be spent on tasks that appropriately challenge students.

Many adolescents with reading difficulties find themselves in the same dilemma as the students with whom we worked in developing this curriculum. Their deficits in vocabulary knowledge cause them comprehension problems and their comprehension problems prevent them from improving their vocabulary knowledge on their own.

Intensive and explicit vocabulary instruction can play an important role in turning this situation around (see also Kamil, 2003). What is required, though, is a clear and deliberate focus on facilitating students' creation of meaningful contexts for the word meanings they are learning and a frequent and consistent emphasis on helping them to make connections to what they already know.

Questions and Action Research Assignments

1. What is meant by "high-utility academic vocabulary"? Why is it important for vocabulary instruction for adolescents? Identify a grade level and group of students to whom you might teach vocabulary.

Choose a set of thirty words that you consider high-utility academic vocabulary. You might check your state curriculum word lists for ideas. Check with two of your colleagues to see if they agree on the appropriateness of your word choices.

2. Draw up a plan for introducing ten new vocabulary words to adolescent students using a direct and systematic approach to vocabulary instruction as outlined in this chapter. Develop examples and discussion questions for each word. Role play the lesson with a colleague and then try it out in a classroom. How effective was it? How could you tell? What would you do differently if you were to repeat the lesson?

3. Why is it important that vocabulary words are presented in a variety of contexts? Design your own read and response activity. Select three short informational articles about topics you think will be of interest to adolescent readers. The articles do not have to include the target vocabulary words you will teach, but should lend themselves to application of words, meanings and concepts the students are learning. Write a set of two questions for each article that incorporates some of your target vocabulary (see example questions from this chapter). Have adolescent students read the articles and answer the questions. How well did the students understand the meaning of the vocabulary words based on their responses?

4. Construct multiple choice pre- and post-tests for ten target vocabulary words you will teach (or use the ten words from the sample unit in this chapter). Remember that the post-test items should differ from those on the pre-test and are intended to challenge students' understanding of the words' meaning. According to Dale's (1965) stages of word knowledge, what stage or level of knowledge is assessed by your tests? How can results from your assessment help in designing vocabulary instruction for your students?

5. Why is it important that vocabulary instruction promote active and generative processing? Give examples of how this may be achieved. Create a vocabulary game, either based on a commercially available game or one of your own that reinforces the application of target vocabulary words. Try it out with students and report on your success.

Vocabulary Websites

Academic Vocabulary Games
www.jc-schools.net/tutorials/vocab

Tennessee's Department of Education website contains links to vocabulary games that can be customized as well as graded word lists in language arts, mathematics, and science.

Vocabulary University

www.vocabulary.com

Puzzles and games and activities such as fill-in-the-blanks and Synonym/ Antonym Encounter are provided for sets of pre-selected words.

Merriam-Webster Online

www.m-w.com

A new Word Game of the Day is introduced via different puzzle formats; the site also contains an online student dictionary.

Factmonster

www.factmonster.com

Different types of analogies are shown; an analogy of the day quiz is included, as well as an online dictionary and almanac.

Interweb Schoolhouse: Web Sites for Kids

http://home1.gte.net/sfn1/kids.htm

Provides links to sites containing appropriate nonfiction reading material for struggling adolescent readers.

Note

1. An earlier version of this paper appeared in *Reading Online* (November, 2001), available at www.readingonline.org.

References

Baumann, J. F. & Kame'enui, E. J. (Eds.)(2004). *Vocabulary instruction: Research to practice.* New York: Guilford.

Beck, I. L., Perfetti, C. A., & McKeown, M. G. (1982). Effects of long-term vocabulary instruction on lexical access and reading comprehension. *Journal of Educational Psychology, 74,* 506–521.

Beck, I. L., McKeown, M. G., & Omanson, R. C. (1987). The effects and uses of diverse vocabulary instructional techniques. In M. G. McKeown & M. E. Curtis (Eds.), *The nature of vocabulary acquisition* (pp. 147–163). Hillsdale, NJ: Erlbaum.

Beck, I. L., McKeown, M. G., & Kucan, L. (2002). *Bringing words to life: Robust vocabulary instruction.* New York: Guilford.

Biemiller, A. (1999). *Language and reading success.* Cambridge, MA: Brookline Books.

Chall, J. S. (1983, 1996). *Stages of reading development.* New York: Harcourt Brace.

Corson, D. (1997). The learning and use of academic English words. *Language Learning, 47*, 671–718.

Curtis, M. E. (2006). The role of vocabulary instruction in adult basic education. In J. Comings, B. Garner, & C. Smith (Eds.), *Review of adult learning and literacy* (pp. 43–69). Mahwah, NJ: Erlbaum.

Curtis, M. E. & Longo, A. M. (1997). *FAME: The Boys Town Reading Curriculum.* Boys Town, NE: Father Flanagan's Boys' Home.

Curtis, M. E. & Longo, A. M. (1999). *When adolescents can't read: Methods and materials that work.* Cambridge, MA: Brookline Books.

Dale, E. (1965). Vocabulary measurement: Techniques and major findings. *Elementary English, 42*, 895–901, 948.

Davis, F. (1944). Fundamental factors of comprehension in reading. *Psychometrika, 9*, 185–197.

Gersten, R. & Jiménez, R. (1994). A delicate balance: Enhancing literature instruction for students of English as a second language. *The Reading Teacher, 47*, 438–449.

Graves, M. F. (2006). *The vocabulary book: Learning and instruction.* New York: Teachers College.

Kamil, M. L. (2003). *Adolescents and literacy: Reading for the 21st century.* Washington, DC: Alliance for Excellent Education (available from: www.carnegie.org).

Laufer, B. & Nation, P. (1999). A vocabulary-size test of controlled productive ability. *Language Testing, 16*, 33–51.

Marzano, R. J. (2004). *Building background knowledge for academic achievement: Research on what works in schools.* Alexandria, VA: Association for Supervision and Curriculum Development.

Roswell, F. G., Chall, J. S., Curtis, M. E., & Kearns, F. G. (2005). *Diagnostic Assessments of Reading (DAR)* (2nd ed.). Itasca, IL: Riverside.

Shaughnessy, M. P. (1977). *Errors and expectations: A guide for the teacher of basic writing.* New York: Oxford University Press.

Stahl, S. A. (1999). *Vocabulary development.* Cambridge, MA: Brookline Books.

Sternberg, R. J. (1987). Most vocabulary is learned from context. In M. G. McKeown & M. E. Curtis (Eds.), *The nature of vocabulary acquisition* (pp. 89–105). Hillsdale, NJ: Erlbaum.

Thorndike, E. L. (1917). Reading as reasoning. *Journal of Educational Psychology, 8*, 323–332.

CHAPTER 4

Can You Teach an Older Student to Spell?

LOUISA MOATS

Introduction

Spelling continues to be a neglected aspect of language study, especially for adolescents. This chapter argues that accurate spelling is a foundational subskill for written composition and that older students can improve their spelling through informed instruction. Good instruction links spelling patterns to language history, word meanings, and word use and provides opportunities for extended practice. Concepts are explained directly and systematically, word lists are organized by sound, syllable, and morpheme patterns, and transfer to writing is facilitated through dictation, proof-reading, and structured writing. Learning to spell has positive effects on word recognition in reading and on vocabulary development.

Spelling Counts

Conventional spelling was once called an "ornament of writing" by Noah Webster; accurate spelling, like neat handwriting, was considered a courtesy to the reader. In modern times, good spelling is still important: it is expected in the workplace, in academic settings, and in personal communications. Spelling errors detract from written composition and can lead to embarrassment or worse.

Simultaneously, instruction of spelling is often incidental or non-existent in middle and high school English programs. Some teachers believe that computer spell checkers preclude the need for instruction and that spelling is a low priority on the long list of language arts skills that must be taught. Others feel that good spellers are born, not made and that any time spent in teaching spelling pays off too little for the students who struggle. This chapter argues that spelling is more than a cosmetic concern and that good instruction can benefit students' overall writing skills, vocabulary acquisition, and reading. Further, it is never too late to improve older students' understanding of word structure.

English Spelling *Can* be Explained

If teachers believe that the English spelling system is illogical and irregular, they may convey that attitude to students, who in turn will think that spelling is just a guessing game or a "photographic memory" task. Objective analysis of the English writing system (orthography), on the contrary, suggests that English spelling is pattern based and logical. Prominent linguists who began to analyze English in the late 1960s described the English writing system as "a near optimal system for lexical representation" (Chomsky and Halle, 1968, p. 49). They pointed out that the spelling of a word in English often tells about the word's sound pattern, meaning, and history. Learning to spell, in turn, entails learning about sounds, print patterns, word meanings, and word history.

The first computerized analysis of the sound–symbol correspondences of English found that spellings for speech sounds are quite predictable. There are dominant spellings for almost all of the speech sounds in English, if several properties of words are taken into account. Hanna *et al.* (1966) estimated that nearly 50 percent of English words can be spelled on the basis of predictable phoneme–grapheme correspondences. (A phoneme–grapheme correspondence is the way a single speech sound is spelled. For example, /l/ is written with a single "l", as in *lap*, or double "l", as in *will*.) Another 37 percent of words are almost predictable except for one sound (e.g. *knit* and *boat*). In those words with somewhat less predictable sound-spelling correspondences, spellings for sounds may be determined by the position of a sound in a word. For example, the double "ll" spelling for the sound /l/ occurs after an accented short vowel, in words such as *fell, doll,* and *cull*.

Hanna *et al.* (1966) stressed, in addition, that if other information such as word origin and word meaning are taken into consideration, only 4 percent of English words may be considered truly "irregular." For example, the "kn" spelling for /n/ occurs in a limited family of words handed down from Old English or Anglo-Saxon to Modern English, such as *knot, knight, knack, know,* and *knit* and the "kn" spelling is always in the beginning of those words. Those words could be taught as a group or family and do not have to be memorized entirely in isolation from one another. At least half of the content words in English originated in Latin and/or Greek and retained spellings that give clues as to their language of origin. Greek-based words, the core vocabulary in science and mathematics, often use "ch" for /k/, "y" for /i/, and "ph" for /f/, as in *chlorophyll* or have a special Greek ending, as in *catastrophe/catastrophes*, *crisis/crises*, and *metamorphosis/metamorphoses*. Modern linguists have continued to show that English is a pattern-based language rather than an irregular one (Kessler and Treiman, 2003; Treiman, 2006).

Good Spellers Depend on More Than Visual Memory

When students have trouble spelling, we commonly describe them as having a "poor visual memory," as if good spelling were primarily a function of a photographic image maker in the mind. After all, we use our eyes to look at print: should not spelling have something to do with looking longer and harder at a word or striving to remember the word through visual imaging? Linguists who have studied spelling, however, have demonstrated that one's memory for printed words has much to do with linguistic knowledge and the visual attention and memory processes of good and poor spellers do not explain the differences in their skills. If spelling were a rote visual memory skill, how could the students in the Scripps National Spelling Bee succeed in spelling words they have never seen before? Good spelling is the result of knowledge of language structure, word origin, and word meaning and the memory involved in spelling is memory for linguistic information. This reality implies that asking students to close their eyes and imagine the letter strings in words or asking students to write words in lists many times over may have some value, but these "visual" strategies will be more productive if they are coupled with learning how the words are structured and why they might be spelled the way they are.

The Differences between Good and Poor Spellers

Poor spellers have a much less well-developed sense of the structure of English and are more likely than good spellers to view the task as one of rote visual memory (Lennox and Siegel, 1998). By default, poor spellers try to memorize letter strings, instead of thinking about reasons why words are spelled the way they are. Good spellers try to make sense of spelling and are more sensitive to the presence of letter patterns (Treiman and Bourassa, 2000; Cassar *et al.*, 2005). In a spelling bee, the best spellers figure out words by asking how they are pronounced, what language they came from, and what they mean. Good spellers in English develop (or are taught) knowledge of sound patterns in words, orthographic patterns in print, meaningful parts of words (morphology), and word origin and history (etymology), while poor spellers appear to be indifferent to such information (Moats, 1995, 1996; Ehri, 1998, 2000; Cassar *et al.*, 2005).

How Spelling is Related to Reading

A casual observer of testing practices and language arts curricula in the U.S. would not guess that spelling is closely related to reading. If spelling is tested at all, it is with supplementary, optional tests. Writing instruction, if it is of high quality, tends to emphasize content, ideas, and the writing process, as if spelling will simply take care of itself. Nevertheless, spelling and overall reading skill, as measured by silent passage reading tests, are highly correlated with one another (the coefficient of correlation ranges from 0.66 to 0.90) (Ehri, 1989; Mehta *et al.*, 2005). The nature of that close relationship is of interest, because it should help direct educators toward methods for teaching. The high correlation between silent passage reading and spelling probably reflects a common denominator underlying both. Reading comprehension and spelling both depend on an awareness of language structure and attention to relevant aspects of language at the word and sentence level. If children learn to spell, their conceptual knowledge about words improves; if they are more aware of word structure, in turn, they may be more in tune with word meanings and have larger vocabularies (Ehri, 1997; Joshi and Aaron, 2003; Moats, 2005/2006).

Studies of Spelling Instruction

Reading has been studied much more than spelling and few well-designed and controlled, scientifically conducted studies of spelling instruction have been done. Most recent studies of effective spelling instruction have been conducted with lower elementary students or with students who were poor spellers. Graham (1999) examined five successful spelling instructional approaches for children with learning disabilities and observed that all the successful programs had one criterion in common: they were based on structured, multisensory language teaching. Berninger *et al.* (2000) also found that second and third graders with low skills improved their spelling ability after direct teaching of phoneme–grapheme correspondences or sound–symbol relationships. Analysis of syllables in multisyllable words has also been found to give adolescent students an advantage (Bhattacharya and Ehri, 2004).

Arra and Aaron (2001), working with second graders, compared two methods of spelling instruction: a visual approach or a language-based method that emphasized sound–symbol correspondence. After administering lists of words as spelling tests, these investigators drew the attention of the "visual group" to their errors, wrote the correct spelling on flash cards, and showed the correct spellings. In contrast, the attention of the children who received phonological instruction was drawn to the spelling errors they had committed and they were given instruction on the sound–symbol correspondences involved in their misspellings. Post-tests showed that the group that received phonology-based spelling instruction, emphasizing how sounds were represented by letters and letter sequences, showed significantly greater progress than the visual group.

Moats (1996) examined the response to instruction of adolescent students in a program that emphasized Orton-Gillingham methods. This approach teaches students the common spellings for each sound, how to blend those sounds, and how to analyze the structure of words before writing them to dictation and in compositions. Students with less-severe language deficits responded best to the language-based instruction, making over two years' gain for each year of teaching, while students with more severe phonological difficulties made less than one year's gain for each year of teaching. Proficiency with language at the phonological level determined how well students responded to instruction.

Even though some of the studies cited have been done with younger elementary students, they consistently suggested that learning to spell is a process of understanding word structure and the relationship of word structure to meaning, for the purpose of recalling letter sequences. These factors determine rate of progress more than a vague notion of "visual memory." The more we can teach students to dissect, compare, and think about words, the more likely they are to improve their spelling.

Is Not Spell Checker Enough?

Teachers, parents, and even students often state that the availability of computer spell checkers has made the study of spelling obsolete. Although spell checkers are a very useful tool, students must have about a fifth grade level of spelling ability to use them well (King, 2000) and, even then, the accuracy and usefulness of the feedback given by the programs are limited by technical imperfections. Students must be able to question the results of a spelling search and to verify whether a given spelling is correct. When computer spell checkers were used for the sentence "the bevers bild tunls to get to their loj" the computer yielded the spelling "bevers" for *beavers* and "bild" for *build*. However, for the misspelled word "tunls" the spell check provided these alternate spellings: *tuns, tunas, tunes, tongs, tens, tans, tons, tins, tense, teens,* and *towns* and for "loj " it gave *log, lot, lox, loge, look, lost, lorid, load, lock, lode, lout, lo, lob, lose, low,* and *logs.* Computer spell check is not of very much help if one does not know how to spell "lodge!"[1]

Further, a spell check cannot be relied upon to correct homophone errors. For instance, the computer cannot correct the errors in the sentence "your sure reel glad to no" for "you are sure real glad to know." It would also miss homophone errors such as "meet" and "meat" and "week" and "weak." So, computers may not be much help if one does not have at least some approximate knowledge of correct spelling. Dalton *et al.* (1990) reported a 51–86 percent range of success when computers provided the intended spelling for misspelled words, while studies by MacArthur *et al.* (1996) and Montgomery *et al.* (2001) reported a wider range of about 25–80 percent for spell checkers to identify the correct spelling. If the target word was spelled phonetically, then the spell checker was able to identify the correct spelling about 80 percent of the time and if the target word was not spelled phonetically, then the spell checker was able to identify the correct spelling only about 25 percent of the time. MacArthur (1996) outlined several problems with the spell checker, such as words spelled correctly but used inappropriately (then for them) and an inability of poor spellers to pick the correct word from the list of suggested words.

In the remainder of this chapter, I will briefly explain why knowledge of sound–symbol correspondence, the position of letters within words, the history of English language or word origin (etymology), and the syllable patterns are the meat and potatoes of a good spelling lesson. Spelling lessons can be interesting if they are approached as an exploration of language (Moats and Rosow, 2003, 2005; Bear *et al.*, 2005). After all, we remember most easily that which makes sense to us.

The Basics: Phonemes and Graphemes

Phonemes are the smallest units of speech that distinguish words. For example, *oat* has two phonemes, /o/ /t/. *Boat* has three phonemes, /b/ /o/ /t/. *Bloat* has four phonemes, /b/, /l/, /o/, /t/. The word *float* is distinguished from *bloat* by the initial phoneme only. English has about forty-three phonemes—eighteen vowels, including three vowel-r combinations and twenty-five consonants (see Moats (2005) for detailed listings). Teaching students to be consciously aware of the phonemes in words is a first, very important step in teaching spelling.

The goal of phoneme awareness training is for students to segment the phonemes in any word they want to spell. They can segment a word if they can say each separate sound while putting up a finger for each sound.

Phoneme awareness training is known to help young children in the early stages of learning to spell (Uhry and Shepherd, 1993; Tangel and Blachman, 1995), but may also be necessary to remediate the problems of older poor spellers who are not able to spell phonetically, sound by sound (Carreker, 2005). Phoneme awareness training is easier if the students are directly taught the identity of all consonant and vowel sounds in English, using a chart that shows how each sound is pronounced (Moats and Rosow, 2003). Phoneme awareness activities should be brief, a few minutes in the beginning of the spelling lesson, and can include speech sound identification and isolation (What sound do *once* and *window* start with?), finding examples of words with a given phoneme (Which word ends with /z/, *cats* or *dogs*?), or reversing the sequence of sounds in a word such as *ketch* (*check*).

Simple grid paper or "sound boxes" can be used to show students how many sounds are in a word (Grace, 2006). After the teacher models the activity, students place a chip in a box as they say each phoneme in a word. Saying the sounds orally is very important, because phoneme awareness is developed through the act of articulating sounds overtly.

	.	.	.	.
"sting"	/s/	/t/	/i/	/ng/

Occasionally, older students progress through the grades without knowing letter names, letter forms, and the sequence of the alphabet. Older poor spellers should be asked to write the alphabet in order, accurately, and quickly, until they know it with 100 percent accuracy. Cursive letter formation increases writing speed and fluency and it is never too late to teach older students how to form the cursive letters (Berninger and Graham, 1998).

Phoneme–Grapheme Correspondences

Spelling by explicit phoneme–grapheme mapping (Berninger *et al.*, 1998; Ehri, 1998; Grace, 2006) requires the learner to match the letters/letter combinations in a word to the speech sounds they represent. A grapheme is a letter or letter combination that represents a phoneme. One approach is to use a simple grid wherein each box of the grid represents a phoneme. As these examples show, the teacher selects a word and gives children an empty grid with a box for each phoneme. The teacher says the word: then, the students repeat it, segment the sounds, and write a grapheme in each box.

straight: in this example, the long "a" (/ā/) is spelled with the four-letter grapheme, aigh.

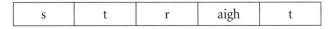

s	t	r	aigh	t

crash: in this example, the "cr" combination stands for two phonemes; the "sh" is a digraph (two letters that represent one sound).

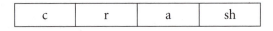

c	r	a	sh

While this technique is an excellent way to teach the phonic code to students of any age, it is especially helpful for older students who need to relearn the code with a novel approach (Grace, 2006). Students who missed the fundamentals in the earlier grades can learn correspondences without feeling as if they are redoing "babyish" material. Boys especially seem to enjoy the approach because the grid paper reminds them of mathematics, a subject with which they may be more comfortable than spelling.

Irregular Anglo-Saxon Words

Because they are often very old words from Anglo-Saxon whose pronunciation—but not spelling—has changed, high-frequency words such as *were*, *was*, and *does* are more often irregular than lower frequency words with a Latin or other romance language base. One of the ironies of spelling instruction is that students who know the regular patterns of sound–symbol correspondence are more likely to learn the irregular words too (Ehri, 2004, p. 155). Poor spellers at every age, on the other hand, make errors on "simple" and "common" irregular words, in part because they are not actively and deeply examining the structure of those words and their orthographic memories are letting them down. Older students have written words such as *they*, *their*, and *too* incorrectly for years and, once a habit is established, the habit is difficult to break.

Some suggested methods for teaching irregular words include (i) grouping words with some memorable similarity (*two, twice, twenty, twilight, twin; one, only, once; their, heir; where, here, there*), (ii) calling attention to the odd part of the word that must be learned by heart (*friend; does*), (iii) using a multisensory memory strategy (Carreker, 2005) that gives the students many ways to repeatedly practice spelling the word (such as copying the word while saying the letters, discussing what is odd about the word, and covering the word and then spelling it aloud), (iv) using mnemonics (*there is a rat in separate; the principal is my pal*); and (v) asking the learner to pay very close attention to the letter sequence by visualizing it and recalling it backwards as well as forwards.

If older, very poor spellers are trying to break habits and learn to spell high-frequency, irregular words, about three to five words per week is all that the students might be able to handle. If students are very poor spellers, concentrate instruction on words they are most likely to write. Graham *et al.* (1994) developed a "spelling for writing" list of about 3000 most commonly used words in English.

Complex, Pattern-based Spellings

Guided discovery with word sorting and teacher questioning is a powerful approach for helping students understand spellings that depend on the position of a sound in a word (Bear *et al.*, 2005) or established conventions (like when to use "-tch"). For example, the "-ge" and "-dge" pattern for the phoneme /j/ lends itself to word sorting and guided discovery. Instead of telling students the pattern (i.e. when a single syllable word ends in /j/, spell it "-dge" right after a short vowel and "-ge" right after a long vowel or other consonant), ask them to sort a list of words by the spellings for /j/ and help them figure out what is going on. Once they see the pattern, they should be ready to learn the rule.

Inflections ("-ed," "-s," "-es," "-ing," "-er," and "-est," which are also called grammatical suffixes) are morphemes that change the number, person, or tense of the word to which they are added, but they do not change its part of speech. The spelling errors in intermediate students' writings frequently concern inflections, especially "-ed" and plural "-s" and "-es" (Moats, 1996; Bryant *et al.*, 1997; Apel *et al.*, 2004; Moats *et al.*, 2006). Although inflections are emphasized (and should be mastered) in third grade, they may need to be retaught and practiced for several years more.

The suffix "-ed" provides an excellent example. Intermediate and older students make many errors on grammatical endings. Begin by making students aware of the sounds the "-ed" suffix makes: /d/ as in "banged," /t/ as in "snacked," and /id/ as in "lifted." Next, sort words according to the sound of the past tense ending and explain that only one of the endings (the "-ed" on "lifted") makes a new syllable. The "-ed" spelling looks as if it spells a whole syllable, but most of the time it does not; thus, those endings are easy to ignore or to misspell. Then, the rules for adding endings must be tackled. There are three major rules in English for adding suffixes to base words: the doubling rule ("hopped"), the drop-e rule ("hoped"), and the change "y" to "i" rule ("studied"). These rules should be introduced one at a time, beginning in second grade, and practiced for several years until they are internalized. To teach them, start by decomposing familiar words with inflections by taking off the ending and finding the base word: "hoping" = "hope" + "ing"; "studious" = "study" + "ous"; "committed" = "commit" + "ed." Then start combining base words and endings.

Multisyllable Words

Students' spelling should be greatly improved if they learn the logic of six basic syllable types (see the Appendix) and how they affect spelling. For example, once they learn about the open, closed, and consonant-le syllable types, students can reliably predict when they should double consonants in words that end with a consonant-le syllable. Open syllables end with a long vowel sound that is spelled with a single vowel letter (as in "*pro*gram"). Closed syllables have a short vowel and end with a consonant (as in "*hos*tel"). Consonant-le syllables are unaccented, only appear at the end of words, and have a consonant, /l/ sound, and silent "e." Here comes the key to doubling: when an open syllable is combined with a consonant-le syllable—as in "cable," "bugle," and "title"—there is no doubled consonant. In contrast, when a closed syllable is combined with a consonant-le syllable—as in "dabble," "topple," and "little"—a double consonant results.

To teach how to spell multisyllable words, consider beginning with compounds (*catfish, hotdog, playground,* and *yellowtail*). Compounds offer two big advantages: students more easily detect their syllables, and the spelling of each base word stays the same.

Multisyllable words bring up the unavoidable problem of schwa (/ə/), the unaccented vowel sound that has been emptied of its identity and can be described as a lazy vowel. Teach students that some vowel sounds have the stuffing taken out of them when they are unaccented. After students spell a word such as *prob-lem, a-dept,* or *com-mit,* they can say the word naturally and mark the syllable that has a schwa. Instruction about schwa helps students understand why some words do not sound the way they are spelled—and reminds teachers not to rely exclusively on "spell it by sounding it out" because that strategy is limited with multisyllable words.

Having already learned the common inflectional endings, students should be ready to move on to other common Anglo-Saxon and Latin suffixes (such as "-en," "-ly," "-y," "-ful," "-less," and "-ness") as well as the most common Anglo-Saxon and Latin prefixes (such as "pre-," "sub-," "re-," "mis-," and "un-"). Students need to learn to recognize these prefixes and suffixes as stable and meaningful word parts and they should begin learning their meanings (Henry, 2003; Ebbers, 2005).

The Latin Layer of English

Direct teaching about the meaningful parts of words begins with the most common inflections, but then extends to prefixes, suffixes, and roots of Latin origin (Henry, 2003; Bear *et al.*, 2005). Prefixes and suffixes have stable spellings and meanings. Suffixes such as "-ly", "-al", "-ment", "-less", "-ness", "-ful", "-ous" also signify the part of speech of the word to which they are added. Roots such as "nat" ("to be born") can be studied through families of words, such as *native, nation, national, multinational, international, nationalistic*, etc. This is especially helpful in the intermediate and middle grades to help students develop a larger vocabulary. Although the relationship between the meaningful parts of a word and the present-day meaning of a word range from transparent, as in "antebellum" (with "ante" meaning "before" and "bellum" meaning "war"), to obscure, as in "apartment" (with "a" meaning "to" or "toward" and "part" meaning "to share" or "part"), the stability of morpheme spellings assists with recall and recognition.

More Complex Derivational Forms

Content words (nouns, adjectives, adverbs, and verbs) in academic text are commonly of Latin origin and composed of prefixes, roots, and/or suffixes. Their study is productive for reading comprehension, spelling, and vocabulary development (Carlisle and Stone, 2005). However, more complex words or word parts derived from Latin often change either the pronunciation or spelling of the prefix and/or root. For example, "collaborate" is related to the root "labor" ("to work"). The prefix "col" is a changed form of "com" ("with"), designed to blend easily into the root. Many other "chameleon" prefixes operate this way. It is best to organize word study around a common root once prefixes and suffixes are recognized (Henry, 2003).

Greek in English

Since the Renaissance, scholars have drawn from the Greek language to name scientific concepts and discoveries. As a result, middle school (and older) students will encounter hundreds of words derived from Greek in mathematics, science, and philosophy texts. Greek word parts work more like compounds than roots. They can be combined more flexibly, as follows: *thermodynamics* and *isotherm, psychobiology* and *neuropsychology,* and *telephone* and *phonogram*. Their spellings are very consistent and often use the correspondences "ch" for /k/, "y" for /ĭ/ or /ī/, and "ph" for /f/.

A Good Spelling Lesson

A language-based spelling lesson has several components. First, students' attention is called to the sounds in words and their pronunciation. Second, individual sound–symbol or phoneme–grapheme correspondences are mapped. This step continues until students reliably spell all the sounds in words and know common within-word patterns. Third, students analyze patterns in print by sorting words, taking them apart, or putting them together by syllable or by meaningful part. Students might draw trees or maps of words related by their root form or their history. Fourth, automatic recall is the goal. Drills might include the location of target words in a list and dictation of words and sentences. Fifth, immediate corrective feedback is given, in which the teacher prompts students to remember what they

TABLE 4.1 Outline of spelling lesson "squalid squid"

Lesson component	Example activities	Examples of words
Sounds and pronunciation	*Identify the number of phonemes in each word*	kick, miss, am, quick, mix, egg, kit, lock, exam, quit
Phoneme–grapheme correspondence	*Sort words by sound– spelling pattern: qu = /kw/, squ = /skw/, x = /ks/, x = /gs/*	quickly, exam, oxen, expect, squad, toxic, quitting, exist, squirted (24 words)
Analyze print patterns	*What always comes after "qu" and "squ"? (a vowel)*	quilted, quizzical, squalid, tranquil, squall, quitting
Build automatic recall of words (fluency)	*Build and write words with given consonant blends*	tranquil, squirted, expressed, reflex, request
	Build words with prefix ex- and given roots; define them	expect, expel, extract, expand, expend
	Locate the origin of "squall" in the dictionary	Exploration of word origin and meaning
Drills with immediate feedback	*Locate and underline all the /k/ spellings in the passage, then read it three times on successive days and time yourself*	"Sid, the squalid squid, lived by the Atlantic coast with a squad of squid. The other squids squawked at Sid because of the sickly sac of toxic ink that Sid squirted when irked . . ."

Spelling concept: review of spellings for /k/ (c, k, ck) and common patterns "-ic," "-ct" from previous lessons and consonant blends with /k/. Introduction of "qu," "squ," and "x" (/ks/ and /gz/).

Lesson 5 from Moats and Rosow (2005)

have been taught, self-correct, or use resources such as dictionaries and word lists.

Spelling is Word Knowledge

Like the prodigies in the national spelling bee, average students can be taught how to think about words and what questions to ask when they do not know a word. Although they may have neither the interest nor the ability to be spelling champions, they can be mindful of word structure, word history, and word pronunciation. Those who come to appreciate what is interesting about language will be more likely to check themselves, use resources such as dictionaries, attend to proofreading, and use language with care. Spelling is a vehicle for touring language—a territory in which many discoveries await the curious.

Assignments

1. Test the spelling ability of students in your class with a developmental spelling inventory. Which spelling correspondences, rules, and patterns do they know and which ones do they need to learn? Does your state or school administer a standardized test of spelling ability? Using these data, can you divide your class into average spellers, good spellers, and poor spellers?

2. Examine the state standards and curriculum guidelines to see if there is a list of words that students should know how to spell at your grade level. Are they arranged by frequency of use in the language? Are they arranged by spelling pattern or by morphological structure? Are only the "demons" listed? Is there an adopted instructional program that is aligned with the standards?

3. If you are to find your own resources for teaching spelling, consult one of the references above that might be appropriate for one group of students you are teaching. After selecting a concept to teach and the example words, design a series of teaching activities for a week (three to four lessons). Give a pre-test and a post-test to measure what your students retain from the instruction.

4. Choose a few interesting words from the week's spelling concept to explore in depth. Ask students to look up one word in the *Oxford English Dictionary* for its full history in the English language. Note how many times the word's spelling has changed, what language it came from originally, and how many meanings are listed.

5. Select one common Latin or Greek root morpheme. Ask students to generate or find as many words as they can that have that root (for

example, "fer" (to carry), or "vers"/"vert" (to turn)). Ask students to make a tree diagram or a graphic organizer that shows how many related words there are in English that have the root.

Appendix: Common Syllable Patterns in English Spelling

TABLE 4.1A Six types of syllables in English orthography

Syllable type	Examples	Definition
Closed	*Dap*ple *Hos*tel *Bev*erage	A syllable with a short vowel, ending in one or more consonants. The vowel is spelled with one vowel letter
Open	*Pro*gram *Ta*ble *Re*cent	A syllable that ends with a long vowel sound, spelled with a single vowel letter
Consonant-le	Bi*ble* Bea*gle* lit*tle*	An unaccented final syllable containing a consonant before /l/ followed by a silent *e*
Vowel team and diphthong	A*we*some *Trai*ner Con*geal* *Spoil*age	Syllables with long or short vowel spellings that use a vowel combination. Diphthongs *ou/ow* and *oi/oy* are included in this category
R-controlled (vowel-r)	*Spur*ious Con*sort* *Char*ter	A syllable in which a single vowel is followed by an /r/. Vowel pronunciation often changes before /r/
Vowel-C-e (magic e)	Com*pete* Des*pite*	Syllable has a long vowel spelled with a vowel-consonant-silent *e*

Some unstressed and odd syllables do not fit into these categories, such as -age in verbiage, –ture in sculpture, and –tion in adoration.

Spelling Rules for Adding Endings

There are four major orthographic rules that operate when endings are added to words. They are important for both reading and spelling. They are much easier to learn and teach if syllable constructions are already understood.

1. Consonant doubling. When a one-syllable word with one vowel ends in one consonant, double the final consonant before adding a suffix beginning with a vowel (*wettest, sinner, crabbing*). Do not double the consonant if the suffix begins with a consonant.
2. Advanced consonant doubling. When a word has more than one syllable and if the final syllable is accented and has one vowel followed by one consonant, double the final consonant when adding an ending

beginning with a vowel (*transferred* versus *remitted*; *imbedded* versus *signaling*).

3. Drop silent *e*. When a root word ends in a silent *e*, drop the *e* when adding a suffix beginning with a vowel. Keep the *e* before a suffix beginning with a consonant (*blaming*; *confinement*; *extremely*; *pasted*).

4. Change *y* to *i*. When a root ends in a *y* preceded by a consonant, change *y* to *i* before a suffix, except *-ing*. If the root word ends in a *y* preceded by a vowel (*ay, ey, uy, oy*), just add the suffix. Note that *y* changes to *i* even if the suffix begins with a consonant.

Note

1. Experiment reported by Professor Malateshi Joshi at Texas A & M University, reported by personal communication.

Teacher Resources on the Structure of English Spelling

Ayers, D. M. (1986). *English words from Latin and Greek elements* (2nd ed.). Tucson, AZ; University of Arizona Press.

Balmuth, M. (1992). *The roots of phonics: A historical introduction.* Baltimore, MD: York Press.

Bryson, B. (1990). *The mother tongue: English and how it got that way.* New York: Avon Books.

Moats, L. C. (2004). *LETRS Module 3: Spellography for teachers.* Longmont, CO: Sopris West.

Sacks, D. (2003). *Language visible: Unraveling the mystery of the alphabet from A to Z.* New York: Broadway Books.

Venezky, R. L. (1999). *The American way of spelling: The structure and origins of American English orthography.* New York: Guilford.

Webster's *Dictionary of Word Origins* (1992). New York: Smithmark Publishers.

References

Apel, K., Masterson, J. J., & Niessen, N. L. (2004). Spelling assessment frameworks. In C. A. Stone, E. R. Silliman, B. J. Ehren, & K. Apel (Eds.), *Handbook of language and literacy: Development and disorders* (pp. 644–660). New York: Guilford.

Arra, C. & Aaron, P. G. (2001). Psycholinguistic instruction on spelling development. *Psychology in the Schools, 38,* 357–363.

Bear, D. R., Invernizzi, M., Templeton, S., & Johnston, F. (2005). *Words their way: Word study phonics, vocabulary, and spelling instruction* (3rd ed.). Upper Saddle River, NJ: Merrill Publishing Co.

Berninger, V. & Graham, S. (1998). Language by hand: A synthesis of a decade of research on handwriting. *Handwriting Review, 12,* 11–25.

Berninger, V. W., Vaughan, K., Abbott, R. D., Brooks, A., Abbott, S., Reed, E., Rogan, L., & Graham, S. (1998). Early intervention for spelling problems: Teaching spelling units of varying size within a multiple connections framework. *Journal of Educational Psychology, 90,* 587–605.

Berninger, V. W., Vaughan, K., Abbot, R. D., Brooks, A., Begay, K., Curtin, G., Byrd, K., & Graham, S. (2000). Language-based spelling instruction: Teaching children to make multiple connections between spoken and written words. *Learning Disability Quarterly, 23,* 117–135.

Bhattacharya, A. & Ehri, L. (2004). Graphosyllabic analysis helps adolescent struggling readers read and spell words. *Journal of Learning Disabilities, 37* (4), 331–348.

Bryant, P., Nunes, T., & Bindman, M. (1997). Children's understanding of the connection between grammar and spelling. In B. Blachman (Ed.), *Foundations of reading acquisition and dyslexia* (pp. 219–240). Mahwah NJ: Erlbaum.

Carlisle, J. F. & Stone, C. A. (2005). Exploring the role of morphemes in word reading. *Reading Research Quarterly, 40* (4), 428–449.

Carreker, S. (2005). Teaching spelling. In J.Birsh (Ed.), *Multisensory teaching of basic language skills* (2nd ed.) (pp. 257–295). Baltimore: Paul Brookes.

Cassar, M., Treiman, R., Moats, L. C., Pollo, T. C., & Kessler, B. (2005). How do the spellings of children with dyslexia compare with those of nondyslexic children? *Reading and Writing: An Interdisciplinary Journal, 18,* 27–49.

Chomsky, N. & Halle, M. (1968). *The sound pattern of English.* New York: Harper & Row.

Dalton, B., Winbury, N. E., & Morocco, C. C. (1990). "If you could just push a button": Two fourth grade boys with learning disabilities learn to use a computer spelling checker. *Journal of Special Education Technology, 10,* 177–191.

Ebbers, S. (2005). *Vocabulary through morphemes.* Longmont, CO: Sopris West.

Ehri, L. C. (1989). The development of spelling knowledge and its role in reading acquisition and reading disability. *Journal of Learning Disabilities, 22,* 356–365.

Ehri, L. C. (1997). Learning to read and spell are one and the same, almost. In C. A. Perfetti, L. Rieben, & M. Fayol (Eds.) *Learning to spell* (pp. 237–269). Mahwah, NJ: Lawrence Erlbaum Associates.

Ehri, L. C. (1998). Grapheme–phoneme knowledge is essential for learning to read words in English. In J. L. Metsala & L. C. Ehri (Eds.) *Word recognition in beginning literacy* (pp. 3–40). Mahwah, NJ: Lawrence Erlbaum Associates.

Ehri, L. C. (2000). Learning to read and learning to spell: Two sides of a coin. *Topics in learning disorders, 20* (3), 19–49.

Ehri, L. (2004). Teaching phonemic awareness and phonics. In P. McCardle & V. Chhabra (Eds.), *The voice of evidence in reading research* (pp. 153–186). Baltimore: Brookes Publishing.

Grace, K. (2006) *Phonics and spelling through phoneme–grapheme mapping.* Longmont, CO: Sopris West.

Graham, S. (1999). Handwriting and spelling instruction for students with learning disabilities: A review. *Learning Disability Quarterly, 22,* 78–98.

Graham, S., Harris, K. R., & Loynachan, C. (1994). The spelling for writing list. *Journal of Learning Disabilities, 27* (4), 210–214.

Hanna, P. R., Hanna, J. S., Hodges, R. E., & Rudorf Jr., E. H. (1966). *Phoneme–Grapheme correspondences as cues to spelling improvement* (USDOE Publication No. 32008). Washington, DC: U.S. Government Printing Office.

Henry, M. K. (2003). *Unlocking literacy: Effective decoding and spelling instruction.* Baltimore, MD: Paul H. Brookes Publishing Co.

Joshi, R. M. & Aaron, P. G. (2003). A new way of assessing spelling and its classroom applications. In R. M. Joshi, B. Kaczmarek, & C. K. Leong (Eds.), *Literacy acquisition, assessment and instruction: The role of phonology, orthography, and morphology* (pp. 153–161). Amsterdam: IOS Press.

Kessler, B. & Treiman, R. (2003). Is English spelling chaotic? Misconceptions concerning its irregularity. *Reading psychology, 24,* 267–289.

King, D. (2000). *English isn't crazy.* Baltimore: York Press.

Lennox, C. & Siegel, L. (1998). Phonological and orthographic processes in good and poor spellers. In C. Hulme and R. M. Joshi (Eds.), *Reading and spelling: Development and disorders* (pp. 395–404). Mahwah, NJ: Lawrence Erlbaum Associates.

MacArthur, C. A. (1996). Using technology to enhance the writing processes of students with learning disabilities. *Journal of Learning Disabilities, 29,* 344–354.

MacArthur, C. A., Graham, S., Haynes, J. B., & DeLaPaz, S. (1996). Spell checkers and students with learning disabilities: Performance comparisons and impact on spelling. *Journal of Special Education, 30,* 35–57.

Masterson, J., Apel, K., & Wasowicz, J. (2007). *SPELL: Spelling Performance Evaluation for Language and Literacy – 2.* Evanston, IL: Learning by Design.

Mehta, P., Foorman, B. R., Branum-Martin, L., & Taylor, P. W. (2005). Literacy as a unidimensional construct: Validation, sources of influence, and implications in a longitudinal study in grades 1 to 4. *Scientific Studies of Reading, 9* (2), 85–116.

Moats, L. C. (1995). *Spelling: Development, disability, and instruction.* Baltimore: York Press.

Moats, L. C. (1996). Phonological spelling errors in the writing of dyslexic adolescents. *Reading and Writing: An Interdisciplinary Journal, 8,* 105–119.

Moats, L. C. (2005). *Language essentials for teachers of reading and spelling (LETRS), module 2, the speech sounds of English: Phonetics,phonology, and phoneme awareness,* and *module 3, spellography for teachers.* Longmont, CO: Sopris West.

Moats, L. C. (2005/2006). How spelling supports reading: And why it is more regular and predictable than you think. *American Educator, 29,* 12–22, 42–43.

Moats, L. C., Foorman, B. R., & Taylor, W. P. (2006). How quality of writing instruction impacts high-risk fourth graders' writing. *Reading and Writing: An Interdisciplinary Journal, 19,* 363–391.

Moats, L. C. & Rosow, B. (2003). *Spellography: A student road map to better spelling.* Longmont, CO: Sopris West.

Moats, L. C. & Rosow, B. (2005). *Spellography: A student road map to better spelling, Book A Advanced.* Longmont, CO: Sopris West.

Montgomery, D. J., Karlan, G. R., & Coutinho, M. (2001). The effectiveness of word processor spell checker programs to produce target words for misspellings generated by students with learning disabilities, *Journal of Special Education Technology, 16,* 27–41.

Tangel, D. & Blachman, B. (1995). Effect of phoneme awareness instruction on the invented spelling of first grade children: A one year follow-up. *Journal of Reading Behavior, 27,* 153–185.

Treiman, R. (2006). Knowledge about letters as a foundation for reading and spelling. In R. M. Joshi & P. G. Aaron (Eds.), *Handbook of orthography and literacy* (pp. 581–599). Mahwah, NJ: Lawrence Erlbaum Associates.

Treiman, R. & Bourassa, D. (2000). The development of spelling skill. *Topics in Language Disorders, 20,* 1–18.

Uhry, J. K. & Shepherd, M. J. (1993). Segmentation and spelling instruction as part of a first-grade reading program: Effects on several measures of reading. *Reading Research Quarterly, 28,* 219–233.

Meeting Reading and Literacy Challenges for Diverse Students

Edy Stoughton's "'I am Never Going to Be a Reader': Issues of Literacy in the Upper Grades" incorporates a very human touch in the opening chapter of this section. She paints a picture of a struggling adolescent reader and how that influences behavior and attitude towards school. Keeping the student in mind provides the context for the strategies offered in this chapter. She harkens us back to a Church and Newman article wherein the premise is based upon instructionally induced reading failure. Though the tone of the chapter lends itself toward a meaning-centered approach, Stoughton pulls the reader back to the center with critical teaching and learning strategies and ideas to support struggling readers in how best to navigate through narrative and expository text. She believes wholeheartedly in contextualized support that will help students become independent readers, writers, and thinkers.

Irene Nares-Guzicki's chapter "Promoting Reading and Language Proficiency for English-Language Learners in Secondary General and Special Education Programs" addresses English-language learners who struggle to read. She provides the reader with a comprehensive background starting with the basic question of who are English-language learners. This fundamental question shapes the chapter giving the reader the context to finally understand why instruction in the way it is outlined in this chapter meets the needs of these marginalized students in our secondary schools. Too often instruction for English-language learners is based solely on re-segregation, placing students from linguistic and language minority groups in a row of trailers, isolated classroom blocks, or large open space environments to be taught with a watered-down curriculum by teachers with little or no training. After Nares-Guzicki builds the context for the chapter she goes on to offer cogent strategies on how best to teach adolescent English-language learners who struggle to read. The chapter sensitizes educators to a very complex and highly politicized field of study. Her level-headed approach to teacher-oriented methods dovetails nicely with both Edy Stoughton's and Vicki Lord Larson's chapters.

One of the most difficult areas to understand when working with adolescents who struggle to read is when they seem to give you that blank stare as if nothing is getting through. **Vicki Lord Larson**'s chapter "Adolescents with Language Disorders as Partners in the Learning Process: Empowerment through Strategy-based Intervention" unearths some of the reasons why some adolescents give you that blank stare. It may be that there is a language-based disorder that disrupts their ability to receive, send, process, and comprehend verbal and non-verbal concepts. According to Lord Larson, adolescents who exemplify these conditions have problems in developing literacy skills. Her chapter uncovers the reasons for these difficulties and then combines a slate of academic and social solutions that are very practical. One will be drawn to the section on referential communication activities where she extols the virtues of this very interesting approach. Through an example, Lord Larson brings the method to life.

All three chapters delve into the very human side of reading challenges at the secondary level. Over the years method upon method has been heaped on the proverbial educational pile without much of it sticking to an educator's ribs, let alone making a difference in instruction at the secondary level. Instead of seeing diversity as something to run from, these authors ask us to embrace diversity and then help us with ideas and instructional approaches to do just that.

CHAPTER 5

"I am Never Going to Be a Reader": Issues of Literacy in the Upper Grades

EDY HAMMOND STOUGHTON

The harsh metallic blast of a buzzer announced the beginning of sixth period and the students began straggling into the classroom for their daily dose of tenth grade English. The nine students were assigned to this particular class on the basis of their special education designation. They were all labeled emotionally and/or behaviorally disturbed, which had the effect of positioning them as among the "hardest kids to teach" in the school.

After 15 minutes spent vainly attempting to locate missing worksheets that students insisted they had turned in and dealing with procedural matters such as where a student had been hiding for the past week instead of being in class when the official attendance records indicated that he was in school, the rather flustered young teacher stepped to the front of the room and wrote on the blackboard "context clues," "denotation," and "connotation."

She asked if anyone knew the definitions of these words, but her question was met by a blank silence. After an agonizingly long "wait time" it was apparent that no answer was forthcoming, so she gamely filled in the definitions herself. Two boys were draped face down across their desks, apparently asleep, and a third had put on a stocking cap that he pulled down over his face. One of the girls was brushing her hair and the other was deeply absorbed in folding a piece of paper into smaller and smaller squares.

The teacher optimistically, if somewhat frantically, plowed ahead even though with each question she asked it became more apparent that no one had the slightest idea what a context clue was, much less what could possibly be meant by such unfamiliar words as "denotation" and "connotation." Further, it was equally apparent that no one was particularly interested in finding out as none of this appeared to have much to do with them.

The lesson continued. Several students who had been called upon to read the definitions on the chalkboard aloud made an attempt, but then gave up in frustration after stumbling over each word. When a written class assignment over the material was announced, there was generalized confusion as to what they were to do. Without further explanation newspapers were distributed to the students along with worksheets asking them to find four unfamiliar words in a newspaper article, make a guess as to the meaning from context clues, find the word in a dictionary, write the dictionary definition, give the connotation of the word, and indicate whether the connotation was positive or negative.

Although the majority of the students gave up before they began and either joined the ranks of their sleeping classmates, talked and joked among themselves, or, as with the group in the back of the room, began a rap song accompanied by the intricate drumming of a rhythmic beat on their desks, one or two students doggedly attempted the assignment. It was tough going. A girl who had been looking up words in the dictionary and carefully writing the definitions on her paper called out "I do not know what to do with that 'conno' word." A few minutes later, seeing that no help was forthcoming, she slammed her paper down saying "I am done. I do not get this." There were, somewhat surprisingly, no instances of challenging behavior or outbursts of angry frustration. The overall atmosphere was rather a feeling of weary passivity.

Finally, seemingly to everyone's relief, the buzzer blared again signaling the end of the class period, although the class had actually ended 10 minutes earlier as the students began gravitating to the door. Those students who had slept through class were handed the worksheet and a newspaper to take home for homework and the nine young people wandered aimlessly out the door having spent 50 minutes in an apparently practiced exercise in not learning. The fact that no learning had occurred did not seem to be of much concern to any of the participants. The idea seemed to be that, if the students refrained from causing trouble, the teacher would not enforce any expectations—even that they would stay awake. They had, in short, been given "tacit permission to fail" (Ladson-Billings, 2005).

The teacher explained that any attempt to come up with a meaningful lesson was complicated by the fact that the majority of the students in the class could not read above a third or fourth grade level indicating that, although it was above their ability, her hope was that they might "pick something up" by being exposed to the material. She added with resignation that she had to teach this lesson because it was mandated by the State Standards. In further discussion, however, she admitted that the possibility of any real learning occurring as a result of being "exposed" to a newspaper that they could not read and an assignment that they did not understand was quite remote. Yet she contended that it would be impossible to do a more interesting activity with "those kids" because it would be too hard to control their behavior.

The classroom scene brings into focus several of the major problems with literacy instruction for students who struggle with reading and writing in the upper grades. Positioned as failing students, they do not believe that they will ever become successfully literate, they do not have a sense of the purposes of literacy, why it is important and how it connects to their lives, and they have not learned effective strategies to help them engage in such school-based literacy activities as constructing meaning from written texts. They are "locked in a losing battle with reading that has affected not only their reading progress, but their self-image as well" (Mueller, 2001, p. 66). Too many young people in our schools are caught in a cycle of failure, falling farther behind in academic skills and becoming increasingly discouraged and disconnected to the learning process. Many of these students see reading as a tedious exercise that is both generally incomprehensible and lacking in purpose and meaning.

This dynamic is dishearteningly common for students who have gone through years of schooling without gaining the ability to read and write successfully and who have either given up in resignation—simply putting in time until they can drop out of school—or have become classified as behavior problems in the belief that it is better to be seen as noncompliant than incompetent.

According to Kletzien and Hushion (1992) increasing at-risk students' motivation to read requires not only teaching reading strategies, but encouraging thoughtful interaction with what they are reading and helping them to see that reading is a pleasurable, useful activity.

This is certainly a tall order for students who are steeped in negative ideas about reading. If we are to make that kind of a difference for struggling readers in the upper grades we will need to address both their disidentification with literary activities and their lack of effective skills and strategies. It is crucial to provide young people—even and, perhaps most importantly, remedial students—with rich opportunities to learn to read for comprehension, increased accuracy in decoding strategies and recognition of sight words, and plenty of pleasurable recreational reading (Underwood and Pearson, 2004). Work with struggling readers tends to deal most heavily with the mechanics of reading and yet, as important as those are, we must simultaneously work to connect students to reading as a pleasurable activity. Although teaching students to read is about teaching them skills and strategies, it cannot be *only* about skills and strategies. Students will be impervious to our most sophisticated, research-based strategies if they believe that reading is something they hate and will never master.

How can we as educators change this situation? How can we help students who have struggled with reading for years learn to decode language, make sense of what they read, and transform their perceptions both of reading and themselves? What will we need to do to meet the challenge voiced by Sharer *et al.* (2005) to "not only ensure acquisition of basic skills, but also to guarantee high levels of comprehension and a positive emotional response to reading"? (p. 28). In short, how can we convince students that they really can become "readers"?

Clearly a crucial element in their struggle with written material is a lack of the basic skills of reading and writing. However, of equal importance is their lack of interest in literacy learning and frequent disengagement with the purposes of schooling in general. Young people who have difficulty with reading and writing have had years to build up a resistance to literacy, an aversion to any tasks that require them to read, and a hatred of school as a result of repeated feelings of failure and inadequacy. They have little confidence in their ability to read well and with understanding and they also generally have extremely negative attitudes toward reading as a result of early failure and marginalization (Mueller, 2001, p. xviii; Sadoski, 2004). For many students there is a "snowballing negative set from early middle grades to middle school, to high school" (O'Brien, 1998, p. 29). It is crucial, therefore, to understand the important balance in learning between the cognitive domain and the affective domain. Students who have struggled with reading throughout their school lives have problems in both of these domains with social, affective, cognitive, and environmental factors all playing a role.

If we are to begin to conceptualize how to construct an effective literacy program that has the potential to make a difference in the disheartening trajectory of struggling readers in the upper grades we must take into account the following.

1. Their limited and inaccurate idea of the purposes and goals of literacy including a perceived lack of connection between literacy and their lives, their interests, and the knowledge that they bring to the school environment.

2. Their positioning as inadequate and ineffective learners and their internalizing of that positioning resulting in decreased motivation and self-efficacy.

3. Their inability to apply helpful and appropriate strategies to literacy tasks. In the upper grades this is increasingly important.

The Growing Importance of Secondary Literacy

Changes need to be made in the ways we approach literacy learning for at-risk readers in the upper grades. We can no longer afford the high costs in terms of students' educational lives of the "benign neglect" of struggling adolescent readers (Underwood and Pearson, 2004, p. 137). According to the Alliance for Education, we must place a new priority on the literacy needs of adolescent learners. In addition, both the National Council of Teachers of English and the National Middle School Association have published policy statements urging more support and attention for secondary literacy programs (Anders and Guzzetti, 2005). The balance seems to be shifting from an almost exclusive emphasis on early grade reading and writing to a growing recognition that we must thoughtfully reconsider adolescent literacy (Reed *et al.*, 2004). A recent editorial in *Education Week* (May 24, 2006) stated that "after a decade of state- and federal-level attention to improving reading instruction in the early grades, the challenge of strengthening adolescents' literacy skills has shifted to older students." The conventional wisdom that there is little practical reason to teach literacy beyond elementary school is changing as our understanding about the necessity for the need to increase comprehension in older students grows. The philosophy that it is too late to make a difference by the time a student reaches the upper grades and that all that we can do is simply help them "get through" the assigned work, is no longer viable.

Disconnection From Literacy

> It was clear to us that unless students could develop their own authentic reasons for reading, there was little chance that anything they learned would have a lasting impact.
>
> (Schoenbach *et al.*, 1999, p. 59)

One of the major obstacles in teaching struggling readers is that they have become convinced by the accumulation of years of reading failure not only that they are poor readers, but also that there is no reason to put in the effort to improve. They frequently see the world as populated by two types of people: those who can read and those who cannot (Mueller, 2001). They see little point in the reading process itself viewing it as a meaningless round of word-calling activities. In short, they have an inadequate idea of the purposes of literacy and fail to see why they should struggle to become successfully literate. As Mueller (2001) pointed out "One of the biggest problems we face in working with struggling adolescent readers is their total disengagement from text . . . they see reading as a dead end, a pointless process that goes nowhere" (p. 44).

What can students' lack of interest tell us about how we teach or fail to teach literacy in secondary school? How does the lack of opportunities to interact with interesting and relevant material cause them to decide that reading is "boring"? How do their limited choices and lack of control over their own reading influence the disidentification and decreased motivation of so many adolescent readers?

Young people bring their interests, abilities, and literacies with them to class. Yet we often fail to build on these elements in our literacy programs and what happens in classrooms often is isolated from their lives. The students in the class at the beginning of this paper certainly had many experiences in their everyday social experiences in which they learn to understand about the importance of context and connotation and yet their out-of-school literacies were not utilized in the classroom assignment. Their lives outside of school were considered irrelevant to instruction leading to apathy.

Apathy, in fact, was the word for what I felt as I watched a one-on-one tutorial session in an adolescent prison facility. Brandi, 17 years old, incarcerated and operating at a very low level academically, was struggling through a lesson on finding the main idea with her remedial reading teacher. She was hunched over a printed sheet of short paragraphs followed by a list of possible main ideas from which to choose. In a barely audible monotone Brandi attempted to read the paragraphs. She worked her way through the passages in a dispirited manner, punctuating her reading aloud with complaints that she was hot, thirsty, and tired. Her frequent stumbling over words was met by the unvarying response to "sound it out." If she was unsuccessful in sounding out the words, the teacher supplied the missing word for her. No alternative strategies were suggested. Her strategy for finding the main idea consisted of guessing each choice until she hit upon the correct one. As an observer I was unsure how much Brandi had comprehended of what she had read as the teacher did not initiate any discussion with her that would indicate what she understood or how she might be helped to understand future passages more fully.

After Brandi had been released from her session, I had the opportunity to talk with Dena, the teacher. Dena expressed frustration with the nature of the lesson she and Brandi had just completed, a required prepackaged curriculum module. She said that she knew it was boring and far from high-level learning. She also expressed the fear that lessons like that were turning Brandi off from reading. But then her face lit up as she began to share with me a very different reading experience that had occurred recently. She explained to me that the principal had asked her to tutor Anthony, a 16-year-old boy in the same locked facility. Anthony had scored at the first grade level on the standardized Test for Adult Basic Education reading assessment that was administered to all students upon entry. Because Dena was also the librarian at the facility, they met for their sessions in the library surrounded by books. One day she called Anthony's attention to the book, *Lonesome Dove.* As Dena explained:

> I told him it was a Western with killing, hangings, bad guys, wild scenes, and ladies of questionable reputation. Now I had his attention and he developed a sudden interest in a book he would never have taken off the shelf, much less consider reading. We started into the book and he found that old Westerns had value and he liked them. What drew him was the discussion of guns, hangings, the salty language of the times, and the interaction between the characters. After a few weeks into our reading sessions we met with the principal to discuss his progress. During the meeting he admitted he had blown off the TABE test, intentionally doing poorly because he did not like to read. I asked him, "Why the great interest in *Lonesome Dove*? It's a high level reading book and your scores say you can't read this." He said, "It had stuff in it that interested me."
>
> He is a young, black, gang member, and the regular literature that he had been forced to read in school bored him. He wanted action and material he could relate to. After we talked, I made sure to steer him towards books that had what he was looking for in reading material. One thing, before I let him have any more books, I made him retake the TABE test. He tested kindergarten—1.5 grade before. On the re-test he tested at tenth grade. I now have a reluctant reader who has "stuff" that interests him and that he wants to read about.

Dena concluded the story by saying with obvious pleasure that Anthony now "follows me around asking for more books like that one."

My conversation with Dena led me to wonder if connecting Brandi to interesting, pleasurable reading materials would have been a more worthwhile reading lesson. Would reading a book that aligned with her interests have been a richer and more authentic context for learning how to locate main ideas than the printed worksheet? When I overhear kids talking enthusiastically about the latest Harry Potter book or even a teen magazine they are involved with, I rarely hear them struggling to explain the main idea. It seems odd that we so frequently tend to separate interest and literacy learning in the name of remediation.

This disconnection does not need to happen. Students bring much knowledge to our classrooms constructed from cultural and family funds of knowledge and popular texts such as magazines, popular books, and technology. These sources can serve as a rich resource to build upon in connecting out-of-school literacy with school literacy (Moje, 2000). Obadiah (1998) contended that

> When teachers make spaces for dialogues that include students' literate currency, it begins a reciprocal process of learning between them and their students, with an end product of higher levels of student engagement, interest, and desire to acquire new knowledge as its benefits to their lives are made clear.
>
> (p. 56)

The Effects of Positioning Students as Inadequate Learners

> Adolescents who have not been successful—have failed—in tradi-tional classrooms are at risk. Unless we find ways to engage them, they will shut down. If we continue to focus only on identifying deficits and devising sterile remedies, these students will surely use their energy and talent for unproductive purposes—or not at all.
>
> (Krogness, 1995, p. 1)

Literacy plays a crucial part in the construction of identity, both in positive and negative ways. What and how we teach students depends upon how we construct them as learners (Ladson-Billings, 2005). Remedial programs are frequently based on the assumption that skills deficits must be corrected as a prerequisite for higher-level learning. This thinking effectively restricts students' access to literacies that allow them to succeed in secondary level educational tasks. As these young people increasingly see themselves as incompetent, they become disengaged. Disengagement is a redefining process that protects one's self-image from feedback that is perceived as being damaging and demeaning. According to Reed *et al.* (2004), "dis-identification and disengagement are concepts used to describe what happens when individuals relinquish their personal connections to a domain and lower their motivation for its purpose" (p. 262).

It is crucial for us to realize in our efforts to improve teaching and learning that many struggling readers are actually learning what we ourselves demonstrate to be important by the learning activities we present. According to a Web-based source devoted to literacy "Reading and writing not only involve skills, but are meaning making processes that are developed in communities of readers engaged in purposeful activities" (www.literacymatters.org). However, numbers of young people in remedial reading programs typically have little experience of learning communities organized around meaning making. There also tends to be a serious dearth of purposeful activities in classes like the one highlighted at the beginning of this chapter where, rather than learning about context clues in the pursuit of authentic activities, students are exposed to segmented tasks that lack both interest and purpose. Two assumptions have traditionally tended to guide remedial reading instruction: that reading needs to be broken down into simple skills and, if students learn these skills in sequence, they will emerge fluent readers. As a consequence too many struggling readers in remedial contexts are socialized into seeing reading as composed of highly structured and irrelevant skill activities.

Church and Newman (1985) examined what they called "instructionally induced reading failure" in a case history of a student they called Danny. Danny's reading profile throughout his years of schooling was marked by severe deficits in comprehending what he was reading. Grounded in a mode of instruction that emphasized word analysis and identification skills, his teachers believed that his low comprehension abilities stemmed from an inability to deconstruct sound–symbol relationships. They maintained this stance even though testing indicated that his phonics skills were actually quite adequate—in fact his strongest area was decoding. As Danny proceeded through the grades in remedial programs, his instruction became more constrained and more focused on a phonics/skills accuracy model. According to the authors, "all of the extra assistance he received focused on words and parts of words. The drills, exercises, accurate oral reading all served to direct his attention away from the important business of reading—that of making sense" (Church and Newman, 1985, p. 178). In short, Danny was not being taught what reading really involves. What was the overall effect on Danny of all the years of remedial help that he had received? When he was interviewed, Danny made it clear that he "disliked reading, never read at home, and really did not want any more help" (Church and Newman, 1985, p. 175).

This leaves us with questions about what can be done about students who struggle with the basics of reading. As Mueller (2001) pointed out

"At-risk readers have poor decoding and spelling skills, possess a weak vocabulary, and are unable to read strategically and actively" (p. xv). It would be a mistake to minimize the difficulty that many students have with the mechanics of reading. Certainly authentic and engaging literature and a degree of choice over texts are extremely important. However, we must also teach strategies to help them access texts.

Strategic Learning

There are a whole lot of other things besides decoding of words that affect kids' literacy at the high school level.

Although a creative, concentrated, holistic literacy program containing the elements described above will go a long way toward changing the learning trajectory of many children, we are still left with the haunting question of what can be done to help students who reach the higher grades without basic reading and writing skills or who repeatedly say "I read it, but I just do not get it." What can we do for students, like Brandi, who have reached the upper grades unequipped with word attack skills, phonological awareness, or cognitive strategies? Problems for these students can stem from deficits in phoneme awareness, difficulty in translating words from print to speech, and an inability to analyze multisyllabic words. Another problem area is an over-reliance on "sounding out" as the strategy of choice coupled with a lack of other strategies such as context clues and sight word knowledge (Curtis, 2004). There is a temptation to give up on teaching these students to read, choosing instead to fill in the cracks, simply working to help them "get by" academically.

Strategies to help students with deficiencies in word attack skills are different from those needed for younger students. Reading problems in upper grades are generally not, as is commonly assumed, a result of a lack of knowledge of symbol–sound relationships. Furthermore, research is quite clear that explicit phonics instruction is not particularly effective after second grade (Pikulski, 1994; Allington & Walmsley, 1995).

Certainly a number of older struggling readers have trouble with identifying unfamiliar, complex words and there are a number of strategies that have been shown to be effective in helping older students decipher words. One is word identification by analogy, in which familiar words that rhyme with unfamiliar ones are used to help in word identification. Increasing semantic and syntactic knowledge through analysis of elements of language structure such as spelling and grammatical patterns has been shown to be successful.

The use of syntactic cue systems (Newman, 1985) can help students with word recognition as they learn to predict, confirm, and integrate information on the basis of prior knowledge of how words work and the context of the text. Readers are encouraged to substitute something that makes sense for the unknown word in order to help them organize semantic and synctatic information (Newman, 1985).

Older students most need strategies to make sense of what they read and how to retain that information. Comprehension—getting meaning from text—is the purpose of reading, a purpose that becomes increasingly important in the upper grades as students are required to gain increasing amounts of information from more complex texts. However "the predominant focus on transmitting phonics rules in isolation that has come to be the norm in many classrooms fails to develop the foundations for strong reading comprehension" (Cummins, 2005, p. 287). Many students enter the upper grades with adequate skills in decoding, yet they cannot comprehend what they read. This leads to the familiar "grade 4 slump" when reading comprehension takes precedence over decoding in standardized tests of reading and subject area academic tasks and getting the words right simply is not enough (Underwood and Pearson, 2004; McCarty, 2005). Decoding and fluency are certainly necessary for comprehension and there is no doubt that students need word attack skills. Yet the almost exclusive focus on these skills may actually increase the problems of struggling adolescent readers as students come to believe that phonics is synonymous with reading (Mueller, 2001; Underwood and Pearson, 2004). The emphasis is too frequently on reading every word correctly rather than on higher order, more holistic strategies that have a much greater effect on understanding. Too many students have relied so long on "drilled strategies that they have lost the notion of reading as making meaning" (Mueller, 2001, p. 33).

The most effective instructional models are based on an interactive approach between skills acquisition and active construction of meaning in a literacy-rich environment. Reading instruction is best absorbed in a full communicative context rather than centering on isolated sounds, letters, or words (Pikulski, 1994; Sadoski, 2004; Ash, 2005; Glynn et al., 2006). As Adams (1995) contended, skills such as phonological awareness and spelling patterns must be developed "in concert with real reading and writing and with deliberate reflection on the forms, functions, and meanings of texts" (p. 422). Students must be engaged in thinking about and discussing interesting and absorbing reading materials from the very beginning if they are to have access to the full range of opportunities to develop their knowledge and language strategies. They also need to see reading as a way of sharing ideas and connecting to the thoughts of others through text. We need to design remediation to maximize the amount and quality of time adolescents spend directly engaged in reading and writing (O'Brien, 1998).

Revisiting the stories of Brandi and Anthony in light of our emerging understanding of current research leads us to see that student needs, as well as some solutions to their reading problems are not as disparate as conventional wisdom would assume. A number of studies have shown that both those who refuse to read and those who struggle to read are helped a great deal by simply doing more reading (Allington and Walmsley, 1995; Curtis, 2004). Word recognition skills are strongly related to the amount of time one spends reading by increasing familiarity with words and Curtis (2004) reported that "differences among adolescents in word-identification skill appear to be strongly related to the extent of their experiences with print" (p. 123). One of the major problems is the limited transfer of skills learned in isolation to other contexts. Students build their capacity to comprehend by reading more widely, according to Underwood and Pearson (2004) who cited data from National Assessment of Educational Progress testing to show that

> Students in 8th grade who reported reading more than 11 pages per day scored roughly 25 points higher than students who reported reading fewer than 5 pages per day; 12th grade students who reported reading more than 11 pages per day scored roughly 30 points higher than students who reported reading fewer than 5 pages per day.
>
> (p. 138)

It appears that, depending upon a student's reading level and interests, whether one reads *Lonesome Dove* or less challenging texts, the opportunity to interact with whole texts in meaningful ways seems to make the difference.

What Do "Expert" Readers Do?

> The most important thing we can teach our students is how to learn. Or put another way, the most powerful thing we can teach is strategic knowledge, a knowledge of the procedures people use to learn, to think, to read, and to write. The most effective way to introduce students to how to use these tools is to model them in the contexts of meaningful tasks and then to assist students in their own use of these strategies.
>
> (Wilhelm, 2001, p. 7)

Teachers find that successful strategies for students who struggle with literacy have certain commonalities.

1. They teach specific strategies in a rich context of authentic, engaging materials that connect to students' interests and motivate students to learn and employ the skills that are taught.
2. They have high expectations of what students are capable of doing.
3. They model what "expert" readers do through dialogue and example.

If we consider that becoming a proficient reader means learning what "expert" readers do, the key is to teach and model specific strategies intentionally that lead to that end. In general, strategy instruction for secondary students promotes deep thinking about text and metacognitive thinking about what one does and does not understand (Nokes and Dole, 2004). Older students need metacognitive strategies in which they monitor their own thinking and become aware of how they interact—or fail to interact—with text.

Some metacognitive strategies that are used by proficient readers are connecting to prior knowledge, determining importance, asking questions, drawing inferences, synthesizing, and using fix-up strategies when comprehension is inaccurate (Keene and Zimmerman, 1997; Ivey and Fisher, 2005). However, research has shown that these are seldom used effectively by struggling readers (Fisher et al., 2004b; Ash, 2005). Successful teachers create a classroom culture that devotes time in explicit instruction of particular strategies and thoughtful discussion of why particular ones are effective and others less effective (Anders and Guzzetti, 2005).

What is it that good readers generally do? According to Anders and Guzzetti (2005), they read actively, monitoring their learning and are able to recognize when they are confused. They have a repertoire of "fix-up strategies when they find themselves struggling" (Anders and Guzzetti, p. 68). These strategies include asking questions as they read, anticipating what is to come, and reflecting on what they have read. Nokes and Dole (2004) provided additional information on the elements of successful reading when they wrote that good readers use relevant prior knowledge to make sense of text, determine what is important in the material, and make inferences and ask questions as they read.

If we are to teach reflectively and intentionally, Wilhelm (2001, p. 89) posed certain key questions that can clarify our purpose.

1. How can I build background knowledge of important concepts, procedures, and vocabulary necessary to successfully comprehend this text?

2. How can I help students summarize important information and text cues?
3. How can I help students make predictions that will help drive their reading?
4. How can I help students make personal connections with the text?

I choose two specific strategies to discuss from among those that have been proven to be most successful in accomplishing these purposes. I highlight activating prior knowledge and creating mental representations because they are basic to making text accessible and comprehensible and, also, because they do not require extensive training, expensive materials, or massive changes in the curriculum making them relatively easy to implement.

Using Prior Knowledge as an Aid to Understanding

This cognitive strategy is based on the idea that, if new learning is hooked to something that is meaningful and makes sense to the student, this new learning will be understood more thoroughly and will be retained more effectively. The importance of this strategy was referred to by Anders and Guzzetti (2005) as they wrote that "The research related to reading comprehension convinces us that a reader's prior knowledge is directly related to the quality of the reader's reading comprehension" (p. 65). By connecting with something they already know, readers are able to make sense of their reading. We use what we already know to make meaning from new information and to connect personally to the material being read. Having background knowledge about a topic helps readers "draw on and build schemas before, during, and after reading" (Underwood and Pearson, 2004, p. 142).

The following are some ways to use prior knowledge in expanding reading.

1. Brainstorm a topic before it is read so students are made aware of the knowledge they already possess. This helps focus students and make connections between different areas of knowledge.
2. Provide practical experiences before reading through concrete, hands-on activities. For example, a simple experiment can be engaged in before reading a section in the science book.
3. Pre-read a simpler passage or watch a video about the subject first to build up students' funds of knowledge, confidence, and interest.
4. Conduct a pre-reading discussion to show students how their interests and experiences connect to the reading assignment. This also has the added advantage of setting a purpose for reading.

Visualization

> The strategy of visual imagery is not employed spontaneously by many students, can be taught relatively easily, and can be an effective tool for improving comprehension. Struggling students should be introduced to and trained in this basic strategy.
>
> (Nokes and Dole, 2004, p. 7)

Visualization is an extremely important tool in comprehension particularly in terms of seeing text as a whole rather than simply disconnected parts. Students who see reading as "just words," who must re-read several times to get the "gist" of a passage, and who have great difficulty recalling what they have read generally are found to have a hard time producing mental images of what they read. A holistic image is necessary in order to process higher level comprehension skills such as discerning the main idea, inferring, drawing conclusions, and predicting. Wilhelm (2001) wrote that "my data demonstrated that if students did not visualize and participate in a textual world, they were then unable to do all of the other kinds of things expert readers often do with text during or after their reading" (p. 114).

This ability can be developed through modeling as the teacher talks through his or her own visualization process while the class works on a text together. Conversation about what "we see in our mind's eye" while reading, comparing different conceptions, and connecting to text or pictures to show why particular images occur can be quite enjoyable as well as extremely enlightening for students. Some other ways to practice visualization skills include picture mapping and "mind movies." Simply having students draw and discuss a scene from their reading and then discussing their different portrayals can be helpful.

Becoming a Reader

> One important way in which children achieve understanding and skill is through participating in contexts where there is regular and sustained interaction with more skilled individuals around genuinely shared activities.
>
> (Glynn *et al.*, 2006, p. 173)

Literacy learning at its best is a form of apprenticeship. Students learn how to be good readers through being actively involved as learners with peers and adults who demonstrate and talk about what is involved in the process of making sense of text. Therefore, if we are to help struggling students become successfully literate, we must initiate them into the community of

readers, providing opportunities for demonstration and thoughtful discussion of what successful literacy entails. Skills learned in isolation are not
smoothly or easily translated to real-life settings.

Three research-proven methods of helping students learn successful
strategies that are based on the above principles are reciprocal teaching
(Palincsar and Brown, 1984), think-alouds (Wilhelm, 2001), and directed
reading and thinking (Fisher *et al.*, 2004b). These strategies have been
shown to be effective, taking into account the crucial communicative
function of literacy rather than focusing on isolated skills and are quite
accessible for teachers without extensive training.

The dialogic basis for these three programs is significant in terms of the
disconnection from learning tasks and activities that at-risk readers feel. In
looking for ways to reconnect these students to literacy while at the same
time helping them learn essential comprehension skills, programs such as
these can be extremely effective. In reciprocal teaching and think-alouds
student voices are heard and their opinions are respected as they participate
in literate conversations. There is a sense of shared control and efficacy on
the part of students as they become active participants in constructing
meaning. As Fisher *et al.* (2004a) pointed out "reciprocal teaching is an
important (and highly effective) strategy for students who are at risk in the
traditional classroom either through disaffection or even oppositional
attitudes to direct instruction" (p. 155).

Directed Reading and Thinking

This program has been used successfully for a number of years to teach
metacognitive awareness. Based on a three-step process of predicting,
reading, and proving, students are instructed to stop after designated
chunks of text and ask themselves the following questions: "What do I think
about this?," "Why do I think so?," and "How can I prove it?" (Fisher
et al., 2004b, p. 67). The sequence of instruction of directed reading and
thinking begins with activation of background knowledge and making
predictions to establish a purpose for reading. In addition, prior to beginning to read, vocabulary is developed and unfamiliar words are discussed
and analyzed. After reading the text and asking themselves the monitoring
questions noted above, students typically share their initial predictions
and how and why they revised those predictions if they did. This form of
improving comprehension and engagement with text has the added
advantage that it is relatively easy to understand and apply.

Reciprocal Teaching

One of the most widely used and highly regarded comprehension strategies
is reciprocal teaching (Palincsar and Brown, 1984). Reciprocal teaching is

a strategy in which students use prediction, questioning, clarifying, and summarizing to guide and monitor their understanding. Each of these elements has been shown to play a significant role in comprehension (Fisher *et al.*, 2004a). The strategies are taught in a dialogical manner. The strategies highlighted in reciprocal teaching serve to focus student attention, promote active and thoughtful engagement, and focus on the content of the reading. Predicting activates background knowledge and provides a purpose for reading. Questioning helps students focus their attention and hone in on main ideas in the reading passage, while clarifying helps children monitor their own comprehension and become aware of what they are not understanding. Summarizing provides an overall check on cognition.

The teacher models the strategies, monitors student understanding, scaffolds student learning, and provides feedback (Slater, 2004). Active involvement is encouraged with the teacher first modeling and drawing students into the dialogue. Then students take increased responsibility for leadership of the discussion.

Reciprocal teaching has a strong record of research support (Sadoski, 2004, p. 114). There is a great deal of data that reciprocal teaching increases positive affect toward reading, particularly among disaffected and resistant readers. It has also been shown to increase standardized test scores and has been shown to be particularly highly effective for students who struggle to read (Fisher *et al.*, 2004a). A significant body of research has shown excellent results in a number of grade levels including first, sixth, and seventh grades as well as high school. Slater (2004) noted that research results of reciprocal teaching are extremely promising. Improvement has been noted on almost all measures, particularly for poor readers who, in a number of studies, went from below average to average on comprehension tests.

Think-alouds

> A think-aloud of reading is creating a record, either through writing or talking aloud, of the strategic decision-making and interpretive processes of going through a text, reporting everything the reader is aware of noticing, doing, seeing, feeling, asking, and understanding as she reads. A think-aloud involves talking about the reading strategies you are using and the content of the piece you are reading.
>
> (Wilhelm, 2001, p. 19)

Think-alouds are a particularly effective way for a teacher to share strategic knowledge with students by modeling and dialogue. They help to "make otherwise invisible reading practices apparent to struggling readers who would otherwise lack strategic knowledge" (Nokes and Dole, 2004, p. 169).

In using this method of teaching, the teacher demonstrates a particular strategy such as inference, visualizing, asking questions, making predictions, or summarizing and explains why that strategy is important and useful in that particular situation. He or she discusses when the strategy is used in actual reading and models how to use it in a specific context by talking through his or her thinking processes while reading. Then students are given guided practice in the use of the strategy—again using authentic texts. Wilhelm (2001) cautioned that texts should be used that are of immediate interest so that modeling is always done in the context of reading that is meaningful.

Think-alouds generally follow the pattern that the teacher reads a text aloud with the students following along in their books. He or she stops frequently to talk about what she is thinking, spotlighting specific strategies that she is using. The teacher names certain features of the text that are used strategically. After the reading is completed, a list is made of the signals that prompt the use of each strategy and students are asked to identify when they think they would use that strategy. Follow-up lessons with teacher scaffolding and then at a gradually more independent level reinforce transfer of knowledge.

Not only are think-alouds extremely helpful for students as they let them in on the thinking processes of the cognitive and visual processes that proficient readers do naturally, they can be very useful for teachers themselves. Frequently the process of reading is so automatic for good readers that it is hard to explain the process we go through naturally. Think-alouds force us to slow down and analyze our own reading process so we can be more aware of what students are doing or not doing (Wilhelm, 2001).

Conclusion

We can help the struggling students in our schools become "readers." We have the understanding and the tools we need to teach both those who refuse to read and those who are unable to read successfully. However, before we can teach them they must want to learn from us. We have not always made the effort required very appealing. As Mueller (2001) pointed out "In our ongoing and unsuccessful attempts to teach these at-risk students to read, the very point of reading has been lost for them" (p. 67). Adolescents who struggle with literacy need an enlarged view of the purposes of reading and an altered view of themselves as learners.

A balanced program that takes into account both the cognitive and affective domains by connecting reading and writing to the lives and interests of students, that teaches them strategies through which they can experience success and that actively engages them in the joys and benefits of literacy that can make a significant difference in their educational trajectories. It is necessary both to work with students to develop their confidence in themselves and to show them that learning to read well is worth their while.

We can go beyond mechanized "skill and drill" instruction to create engaging curriculum that connects to students' interests and lives and opens their minds to reading as worthwhile and personally meaningful. We can re-emphasize the notion of reading as making meaning, and then teach in that way. We can also teach our students specific strategies in real contexts. Those strategies must be the ones older students most need in order to comprehend content, not a repetition of worksheets and drills that have been unsuccessful for these students for years. Through instruction in metacognition, we can teach students how to learn and how to improve their learning. We can give contextualized support that will help students become independent readers, writers, and thinkers. We can say with Sharer *et al.* (2005) that "We want to make two promises to every student: we will teach you to read, and we will help you become a reader—a literate person who experiences the power and joy of comprehending" (p. 24).

Questions

1. In the example of the class at the beginning of the chapter, the young teacher was struggling with meeting the required standards and yet also designing a lesson that was engaging for her students and that contained tasks they could accomplish and learn from. Can you design a lesson or a series of lessons built around the standards you must meet in your class that balances affective and cognitive domains?

2. In the same introductory story, how did the teacher's beliefs about the behavioral issues and low reading levels of her students influence her choice of teaching methods? Many educational experts believe that one of the major causes of poor behavior is boredom and low expectations. How could she have created a context that would make behavior concerns less of a problem?

3. When you examine your overall literacy program do you find that the mechanics of "how to read" are overshadowing creating in students an understanding of reading as a pleasurable and meaningful activity? How could you alter the balance to "hook students on reading?"

4. This chapter describes several strategies to help students comprehend what they read. Pick one of those areas: background knowledge,

visualizing what is read, summarizing important information and text cues; making predictions; and making personal connections with the text. Develop a creative lesson featuring that strategy surrounding a high-interest text.

5. Do you use your students' out-of-school literacies and their experiences to help you plan your curriculum? What could you do to find out more about their interests and use those interests to connect them to reading?

6. How could you accomplish the goal of helping students understand that reading is important to their lives and their futures? What reading materials would you choose? What teaching methods would you employ? What would your curriculum look like?

7. Action Research Project: survey your students about their out-of-school interests and their out-of-school literacy activities. Design a way to incorporate these into your classroom lessons.

Suggested Websites

www.readingonline.org/articles/art_index.asp?HREF=ash

Ash, G. E. (2002). Teaching readers who struggle: A pragmatic middle school framework.

www.literacymatters.org

www.nchd.nih.gov/publications/nrp/smallbook.htm

Report of the National Reading Panel: teaching children to read.

References

Adams, M. (1995). *Beginning to read: Thinking and learning about print.* Cambridge, MA: MIT Press.

Allington, R. L. & Walmsley, S. A. (1995). *No quick fix: Rethinking literacy programs in America's elementary schools.* New York: Teachers College Press.

Anders, P. L. & Guzzetti, B. J. (2005). *Literacy instruction in the content areas* (2nd ed.). Mahwah, NJ: Erlbaum.

Ash, G. E. (2005). What did Abigail mean? *Educational Leadership, 63* (2), 36–41.

Church, S. & Newman, J. M. (1985). A case history of an instructionally induced reading problem. In J. M. Newman (Ed.), *Whole language theory in use* (pp. 169–180). Portsmouth, NH: Heinemann.

Cummins, J. (2005). Can schools effectively challenge coercive power relations in wider society? In T. L. McCarty (Ed.), *Language, literacy, and power in schooling* (pp. 283–296). Mahwah, NJ: Erlbaum.

Curtis, M. E. (2004). Adolescents who struggle with word identification: Research and practice. In T. L. Jetton & J. A. Dole (Eds.), *Adolescent literacy research and practice* (pp. 119–134). New York: Guilford.

Frey, N. & Fisher, D. (2004). Read-alouds and shared readings: Not just for elementary anymore. In D. Fisher & N. Frey (Eds.), *Improving adolescent literacy: Strategies at work* (pp. 37–57). Upper Saddle River, NJ: Pearson.

Fisher, D., Frey, N., & Fehrenbacher, T. (2004a). Reciprocal teaching: Giving responsibility to students. In D. Fisher & N. Frey (Eds.), *Improving adolescent literacy: Strategies at work* (pp. 153–168). Upper Saddle River, NJ: Pearson.

Fisher, D., Frey, N., & Johnson, C. (2004b). Questions, questions, everywhere. In D. Fisher & N. Frey (Eds.), *Improving adolescent literacy: Strategies at work* (pp. 59–81). Upper Saddle River, NJ: Pearson Publishing Co.

Glynn, T., Wearmouth, J., & Berryman, M. (2006). *Supporting students with literacy difficulties: A responsive approach.* Berkshire: Open University Press.

Ivey, G. & Fisher, D. (2005). Learning from what doesn't work. *Educational Leadership, 63* (2), 8–15.

Keene, E. & Zimmerman, S. (1997). *Mosaic of thought.* Portsmouth, NH: Heinemann.

Kletzien, S. & Hushion, B. (1992). Reading workshop: Reading, writing, thinking. *Journal of Reading, 35* (6), 444–451.

Krogness, M. M. (1995). *Just teach me Mrs. K.: Talking, reading and writing with resistant adolescent learners.* Portsmouth, NH: Heinemann.

Ladson-Billings, G. (2005). Reading, writing, and race: Literacy practices of teachers in diverse classrooms. In T. L. McCarty (Ed.), *Language, literacy, and power in schooling* (pp. 133–150). Mahwah, NJ: Erlbaum.

McCarty, T. L. (2005). Reclaiming critical literacies. In T. L. McCarty (Ed.), *Language, Literacy, and power in schooling* (pp. 297–303). Mahwah, NJ: Erlbaum.

Moje, E. B. (2000). "All the stories that we have": Adolescents' insights about literacy and learning in secondary schools. Newark, DE: International Reading Association.

Mueller, P. N. (2001). *Lifers: Learning from at-risk adolescent readers.* Portsmouth, NH: Heinemann.

Newman, J. M. (1985). What about reading? In J. M. Newman (Ed.), *Whole language theory in use* (pp. 99–110). Portsmouth: Heinemann.

Nokes, J. D. & Dole, J. A. (2004). Helping adolescent readers through explicit strategy instruction. In T. L. Jetton & J. A. Dole (Eds.), *Adolescent literacy research and practice* (pp. 162–182). New York: Guilford.

Obadiah, J. E. (1998). Black-mystory: Literate currency in everyday schooling. In D. E. Alverman, K. A. Hinchman, D. W. Moore, S. F. Phelps, and D. R. Waff (Eds.), *Reconceptualizing the literacies in adolescents' lives* (pp. 51–72). Mahwah, NJ: Erlbaum.

O'Brien, D. G. (1998). Multiple literacies in a high school program for "at risk" adolescents. In D. E. Alverman, K. A. Hinchman, D. W. Moore, S. F. Phelps, & D. R. Waff (Eds.), *Reconceptualizing the literacies in adolescents' lives* (pp. 27–50). Mahwah, NJ: Erlbaum.

Palincsar, A. S. & Brown, A. L. (1984). Reciprocal teaching of comprehension and monitoring activities. *Cognition and Instruction, 1* (2), 117–175.

Pikulski, J. J. (1994). Preventing reading failure: A review of five effective programs. *The Reading Teacher, 48* (1), 30–39.

Reed, J. H., Schallert, D. L., Beth, A. C., & Woodruff, A. L. (2004). Motivated reader, engaged writer: The role of motivation in the literate acts of adolescents. In T. L. Jetton & J. A. Dole (Eds.), *Adolescent literacy research and practice* (pp. 251–282). New York: Guilford.

Underwood, T. & Pearson, P. D. (2004). Teaching struggling adolescents to comprehend what they read. In T. L. Jetton & J. A. Dole (Eds.) *Adolescent literacy research and practice* (pp. 135–161). Mahwah, NJ: Lawrence Erlbaum.

Sadoski, M. (2004). *Conceptual foundations of teaching reading.* New York: Guilford.

Schoenbach, R., Greenleaf, C., Cziko, C., & Hurwitz, L. (1999). *Reading for understanding: A guide to improving reading in middle and high school classrooms.* San Francisco: Jossey-Bass.

Sharer, P. L., Pinnell, G. S., Lyons, C., & Fountas, I. (2005). Becoming an engaged reader.*Educational Leadership, 63* (2), 24–29.

Slater, W. H. (2004). Teaching English from a literacy perspective: The goal of high literacy for all students. In T. L. Jetton & J. A. Dole (Eds.) *Adolescent literacy research and practice* (pp. 40–58). Mahwah, NJ: Lawrence Erlbaum.

Wilhelm, J. D. (2001). *Improving comprehension with think-aloud strategies.* New York: Scholastic.

CHAPTER 6

Promoting Reading and Language Proficiency for English-language Learners in Secondary General and Special Education Programs

IRENE NARES-GUZICKI

Ruben is a typical tenth grade boy, the oldest of three siblings. He lives in a Spanish-speaking home with his parents, siblings, grandmother, and aunt. He was born in the U.S. and has participated in various bilingual programs throughout his elementary grades while migrating with his family during the agricultural seasons. In fifth grade, he was identified with a specific learning disability and qualified for special education services. Since fifth grade, Ruben has been receiving help from the special education resource specialist for approximately 2 hours daily. Despite the additional service, Ruben continues to struggle, especially in reading and oral and written language. Coupled with limited English proficiency skills and a learning disability, he frustrates easily and often demonstrates a lack of self-esteem. His teachers and counselors at the high school are concerned about Ruben and his poor grades. In addition, they are troubled that Ruben will have difficulty passing the mandatory California High School Exit Examination, which requires all students (including English-language learners in general or special education) to pass an examination in order to receive a California high school diploma.

This is a common scenario that many general and special educators teaching adolescents encounter in an ever rapidly changing U.S. demographic public school system, especially within the traditional immigration states which include California, Texas, New York, Florida, and Illinois (Batalova *et al.*, 2005). The purpose of this chapter is to address the critical issues regarding language and literacy and impart practical interventions teachers can implement in the classroom to meet the needs of English-language learners in secondary education. In California's K-12 school population, 40 percent of students speak a language other than English at home with over 90 percent of those speaking one of five languages: Spanish, Vietnamese, Filipino, Hmong, or Cantonese (California Department of Education, 2005). Only 39 percent of high school English learners were able to pass the English language arts section of the California High School Exit Examination in 2004, compared with 81 percent of their English-only peers (Gándara *et al.*, 2005). In the U.S., more than 3000 students drop out of high school every day, primarily due to their lack of literacy skills to keep up with the complex curriculum (Alliance for Excellent Education, 2003; Kamil, 2003). In addition, there are 8 million struggling readers in grades four to twelve in the U.S. (National Center for Educational Statistics, 2003). Compounding this alarming statistic is the fact that 53 percent of all high school graduates enroll in remedial courses in college (National Center for Educational Statistics, 2001). These problems are exacerbated if the student is an English learner, a recent immigrant, and/or has a learning disability. Therefore, the withholding of high school diplomas due to reading and writing below grade-level standards is a cause for alarm for those professionals who address educational policy issues and for teachers who educate English-language learners in our high schools on a daily basis (Nares-Guzicki, 2005b).

Without a doubt, there is a need to improve literacy skills for all students. Literacy demands are increasing as the technological requirements of our society continue to expand. According to Barton (2000) the average literacy requirements for all American occupations was projected to rise by 14 percent between 1996 and 2006. He also noted that the fastest growing professions have far greater than average literacy demands compared to the declining professions which have lower than average literacy demands. As educators, especially in diverse states such as California, we need to continually make robust improvements in literacy so our youth can learn to be economically competitive and lead successful lives.

This chapter will address these and other alarming statistics and propose effective methods and strategies teachers can implement in their classrooms to assist English-language learners in general and special education programs. Specific emphasis will be on practical suggestions for vocabulary development, for improving comprehension skills, and for strengthening written language skills.

Who are our English-language Learners?

Since the passage of the 1998 Bilingual Education Act, Title VI of the Civil Rights Act, and the Equal Education Opportunities Act of 1974, the federal government has had a special obligation to ensure that states and local districts take appropriate action to provide equal educational opportunities to limited English-proficient children (Baca and Cervantes, 1998). Federal laws prohibit discrimination against students based on languages, so school districts are required to take steps to overcome language barriers.

The 1974 U.S. Supreme Court decision in *Lau v. Nichols*, as codified in the Equal Education Opportunities Act, requires that each educational agency "take appropriate action to overcome language barriers that impede equal participation by its students in its instructional programs" (*Lau v. Nichols*, 1974). Although federal law still requires bilingual education, it does not require primary language instruction or any other specific methodology unless a state educational agency chooses to do so. "Appropriate action" is determined using an analysis developed in *Castaneda v. Pickard* (5th circuit 1981) court ruling which requires school districts to (i) use instructional practices which are based on sound educational theory, (ii) implement effective programs that provide the procedures, resources, and personnel necessary to apply the theory in the classroom, and (iii) achieve results after a reasonable period of time, demonstrating that the English-language barriers were overcome, and the English-language learners were not left with "substantive academic deficits" (Reutter, 1994).

In addition to adhering to federal laws like other states, California implemented state bilingual education laws written in California's Education Code. The programmatic provisions of California's "bilingual education" program became inoperative in June 1987. However, for funding purposes, the "bilingual education" program continues as specified in the operational provisions in the Education Code requiring public school districts to develop fluency in English for each student as efficiently and effectively as possible. In June 1998, Proposition 227 added Chapter 3 to California's Education Code clearly stating that the purpose of the new law is to teach English to English-language learners as rapidly and effectively as possible.

Much remains to be learned about the most effective and efficient ways to teach English, as directed by Proposition 227 in California. Unless parents request an alternative bilingual education program through a waiver, English-language learners are required under Proposition 227 to be educated through a sheltered/structured English immersion process during a temporary transition period before placement in an English-only classroom. This structured immersion process must include (i) special curriculum designed for English-language learners, (ii) teachers trained in the methods of second-language acquisition, and (iii) instructional strategies designed for students learning a second language (Californian Department of Education, 1999). California's K-12 public school teachers now play a critical role in developing English-language learners' oral language and literacy skills to meet the requirements for high school graduation.

English-language learners is a term that refers to students who come from language backgrounds other than English and whose English proficiency is not yet developed to a point where they can profit fully from English-only instruction (Baca and Cervantes, 1998). Commonly these students are labeled limited English proficient. Many California school districts also use "English learners." For our purposes, second-language learners will be referred to as English-language learners and the limited English proficient label will only be used when quoting from or citing other sources, or referring to issues rather than students.

According to Handscombe (cited in Rigg and Allen, 1989), English-language learners in our educational system fall into four major subgroups.

1. Immigrants. These students have been attending school in their country of origin and arrive in the U.S. accompanied by a family member to join other family members after a separation period. They experience stages of adjustment during the first years in the new country, especially with economic, social, and language factors.
2. Refugees. These students had to leave their homeland and come to the U.S. to avoid serious political conflict and unequal citizen rights. Leaving behind most of their possessions, these students feel a sense of loss. Most of these English-language learners not only need academic remediation from educators, but someone to listen to the traumatic events that propelled them to their new home.
3. International students. These students come from overseas on a student visa to have an education in the U.S. Although most of the English-language learners have adequate English conversational skills, they encounter difficulties when higher levels of proficiency are needed to be successful in school.
4. Second-generation immigrants. These students are born in the U.S. and raised with family members that predominately speak a language other than English and who identify solely with the values and customs of the culture of that language. Many of these English-language learners experience stages of cultural and social adjustment especially if there is a mismatch between the language home culture and the culture language of the school. In 2005, according to Batalova et al. (2005), 27 percent of second-generation immigrants and 30 percent of third-generation immigrants are adolescent English-

language learners that were born in the U.S. That means that over half of our English-language learner adolescents in the middle and high schools were born in America, yet continue to lack proficiency in English. In addition, the remaining 43 percent of adolescent English-language learners that are foreign-born have more obstacles if they enter U.S. schools at the secondary level. Not only do they have to master the English language in a shorter time period, but they also have to learn the American school system (with fewer resources in reading at the secondary level) while mastering content-area subjects (Capps *et al.*, 2005).

Implementation of the Bilingual Education Act among school districts varies from state to state. In the California public school system during school registration, the parents/guardian complete a home language survey consisting of four questions to determine the language spoken at home. This California Education Code requirement provides essential information for schools to provide meaningful instruction. If the parents reply with an answer "other than English," the student must be administered a state-approved language proficiency test in their first and second languages. The scores on these examinations determine how limited or fluent the student is in the home and second languages and in what stage of second language acquisition development they are functioning. It also monitors their progress in learning English and how quickly they can be reclassified from non- or limited English proficient to fluent English proficient. These assessment tools are of even greater importance since the passage of the No Child Left Behind Act of 2001, reauthorizing the Elementary and Secondary Act of 1965. This act includes a stronger educational accountability principle which mandates disaggregate assessment results by significant categories including English-language proficiency and disabilities, among others (Alliance for Excellent Education, 2003). In California, the California English Language Development Test was developed for the state language proficiency test, but each state differs on their selection of tools to measure language proficiency. For example, North Carolina uses the Individuals with Disabilities Education Act Proficiency Test, in Illinois it is the ACCESS for ELLs Placement Test, and in Colorado, the Colorado English Language Assessment was adopted (Short and Fitzsimmons, 2007).

No matter what language proficiency measure is utilized, the overall scores tend to rank the English-language learner as a non- or limited English-proficient beginning level English-language learner, intermediate English-language learner, or advanced English-language learner, culminating with fluent English proficient status. These English-language learner levels of English proficiency are aligned with theorists Krashen and Terell's

(1983) natural approach of overlapping stages of second language acquisition: (i) comprehension/pre-production, (ii) early speech production, (iii) speech emergence, and (iv) intermediate fluency. Beginning level English-language learners tend to function at the pre- and early production stages; intermediate level English-language learners tend to overlap in the early production and speech emergence stages, and the advanced level English-language learners tend to function at the speech emergence and intermediate fluency stages (Richard-Amato, 1996). Therefore, as an educator it is critical to adhere to the English-language learner's stage of second-language acquisition development to aid in the alignment of instruction. In addition, an educator of English-language learners should have an awareness of the various oral language behaviors the student can and cannot do so as to ensure success in the classroom. Samples of possible student oral language behaviors and responses that are aligned to the levels of English proficiency and second-language acquisition stages are given in Table 6.1. Other language development profiles specifically related to reading (including fluency and vocabulary development, comprehension, and writing) and based on grade level are available in many published curriculum resources (Herrell and Jordan, 2008) and in some state-developed English-language development and English-language arts standards for English learners.

Who are our Special Needs Learners?

The development of the right to education policy has its roots in the Fourteenth Amendment to the Constitution. The Fourteenth Amendment provides that no state may deny any person within its jurisdiction the equal protection of the law. Case law has advanced a series of interpretations of the Fourteenth Amendment preventing government from denying governmental benefits to people because of age, sex, race, or disability (Reutter, 1994).

The Fourteenth Amendment is very important because of the major role it has played, not only in general education, but in the history of bilingual education and special education as well. If a state agrees to provide a free and appropriate public education to all school-aged children, it cannot exclude those with disabilities and/or students with limited English-proficient skills (Baca and Cervantes, 1998).

In 1975, the federal government decided to bring the various pieces of state and federal legislation into one comprehensive law regarding the education of students with disabilities by enacting PL 94–142, Education for All Handicapped Children Act. Despite this landmark law and its requirements, Congress found that nearly half of the students with

Table 6.1 Levels of English proficiency, second-language acquisition stages, and sample behaviors

Levels of English proficiency	Second-language acquisition stages	Samples of oral-language student behavior	Samples of student responses
Beginning	Pre-production/ comprehension	• The student is an avid listener and tends to be silent • The student gives non-verbal responses • The student listens to stories read aloud • The student draws picture of main idea • The student has minimal comprehension	Nod, point, touch, circle, draw, cut out, mime, match, choose, listen
Beginning	Early speech production	• The student uses one or two word responses • The student uses short fixed phrases ("How are you?") • The student has limited comprehension • The student uses few word responses to factual comprehension questions • The student draws/labels pictures of characters and setting	Say, name, list, label, recall, fill in, sort, group, recite, repeat, categorize
Intermediate Advanced	Speech emergence	• The student speaks in longer simple sentences with limited descriptive vocabulary • The student engages in conversation • The student tends to make some errors in grammar, syntax, and pronunciation • The student will attempt to communicate messages in academic situations with good comprehension • The student identifies literary elements of a story • The student can write short sentences and paragraphs with assistance	Describe, retell, explain, complete, compare, contrast, define, order, summarize, recall, role play
Advanced	Intermediate fluency	• The student implements content area information in conversations to respond to questions and talks about other topics • The student has close to native oral fluency • The student makes inferences and conclusions • The student makes predictions and story summaries • The student writes short narratives with more detail and fewer grammatical errors	Give opinions, analyze, create, design, defend, justify, examine, simplify, conclude, infer, organize, take apart, rearrange, debate, evaluate
	Fluent		

Source: Adapted from Williams and Cary (1985).

disabilities were not receiving an appropriate education. According to Turnbull and Turnbull (1990), this denial of an appropriate education is "functional exclusion" by which the student is included in a school program in name only and not truly benefiting from it. This amounts to being "excluded" from the "function" of the program. In response to this exclusion, Congress amended PL 94–142 in 1990 and again in 1997. It is now called the Individuals with Disabilities Education Act. In 2004, the law was reauthorized as the Individuals with Disabilities Education Improvement Act with alignment to the 2001 No Child Left Behind Act signed by President Bush which promotes excellence, accountability, and equity to all students (Turnbull *et al.*, 2004).

This federal law, Individuals with Disabilities Education Act, ensures all students with disabilities in the U.S. receive a free, appropriate public education in the least restrictive environment. This includes specially designed instruction, individualized to the student's needs, written into an individualized education plan by a multidisciplinary team. Although there are specific eligibility requirements for each of the thirteen disability categories, specific learning disability is the largest category under Individuals with Disabilities Education Act. Students with learning disabilities accounted for nearly 5 percent of the U.S. school population (Smith *et al.* 2006). Special education services are provided in classrooms (including special day class and resource specialist program settings), special schools, hospitals and residential facilities, and other various settings where services are needed.

There is a shortage of research on English-language learners who are identified as students with disabilities (Nares-Guzicki, 2000). The federal statutes under the Education for All Handicapped Children Act (PL 94–142) and its reauthorization, Individuals with Disabilities Education Act (PL 105–17) supersede any state code sections and its accompanying regulations. With the passage of PL 94–142, a student is not eligible for special education services unless an individualized education plan was written by the individualized education plan team for the student with a disability. According to Individuals with Disabilities Education Act 1997, "the individualized education plan team shall consider as a special factor, if the child is of limited English proficiency, the language needs of the child as they relate to the individualized education plan" (Special Education Division, California State Department of Education, 1997). If the individualized education plan team determines that instruction in the student's primary language is necessary to meet the individualized education plan goals, linguistically appropriate services must be provided. In addition, the individualized education plan must include the English-language learner's level of English proficiency, which language each goal and objective will be accomplished, and a plan for comprehensible instruction in English and/or primary language support (Special Education Division, California State Department of Education, 1997).

In addition, English-language learners who are special education students need English-language development services. The individualized education plan team needs to determine if the special education or the general education teacher will provide these services and then document it on the individualized education plan. The teacher providing the English-language development services must possess the appropriate credential and certification or undergo training to receive it (Special Education Division, California State Department of Education, 1997).

English-language learners with disabilities are sometimes referred to as culturally–linguistically diverse exceptional students (CLDES). Culturally and linguistically diverse exceptional students are individuals whose native or primary language is not English, who are not native members of the Euro-Caucasian base currently dominant in the U.S. (Salend, 1994) and are enrolled in a special education program.

The educational needs of language-minority students with disabilities is a new area of research. Although knowledge about bilingual special education practices has grown in recent years, there is still a paucity of empirical research examining the issues of bilingualism in exceptional children and effective instructional strategies. Much of the evidence is deductive, generalized from studies in special education or bilingual education (Baca and Cervantes, 1989). The heavy, double demands of students learning academic content while learning a second language in a context of coping with language-learning disabilities are often disheartening for both students and educators (Gersten *et al.*, 1998).

Suggested Guiding Principles on English-language Learners in General and/or Special Education Programs

Whether you are a middle or high school general or special educator with students who have individualized education plans and/or are English-language learners, there are a few general guidelines to keep in mind before effective instruction with English-language learners can be implemented (Nares-Guzicki, 2005a).

1. *Determine each level of language proficiency for the first and second language.* This usually involves studying the student's folder for language proficiency scores or requesting this information from your bilingual resource teacher. It is helpful if you can obtain and study the student's work samples from the test.

2. *Analyze results and determine the stage of second-language acquisition.* Once you have obtained the level of English proficiency, determine the stage of second-language acquisition development and what it entails (see Table 6.1).

3. *Study any prior assessment results, including formal and informal achievement measures.* If the student is receiving special education services, read also the present level of performance page of the individualized education plan and the psycho-educational report. Consult with the special education teacher(s) or individualized education plan team for any clarification of the data.

4. *Determine the stage of reading development the student is currently functioning in school.* There are various stages of reading development. Chall's (1987) stages of reading development extend to adulthood (see Table 6.2).

5. *Prioritize needs from the student's present level of performance data.* This involves studying the student's areas of strength and areas of need from various sources of assessment data. Priority on survival skills for life success is crucial. If the student is receiving special education services, read the individualized education plan goals and objectives.

6. *Confirm that the educational needs/goals are aligned to the academic content standards and the student's second-language acquisition stage.* Ensure that your goals include outcome-based performance standards in addition to the content standards that need to be met.

7. *Implement research-based pedagogical methods and strategies that are aligned to the specific stage of second-language development and learning style.* Reflect on your own teaching style and evaluate how closely aligned you are to your student's learning style. Establish and nourish a collaborative dialogue with all your students' service providers that focuses on goal attainment and not the barriers to goal attainment.

Instructional Methods and Strategies for English-language Learners

Many of the common instructional methods and strategies used to teach English-language learners are aligned with the theories of second-language acquisition and language development stages (Richard-Amato, 1996). However, there is not one instructional method or strategy that is effective for all English-language learners given the complexity of variables each English-language learner brings into the classroom (Genesee *et al.*, 2005).

There are three well-known models of second-language acquisition that have had a significant impact on our understanding of how second-language learners function in academic contexts and have greatly influenced pedagogy. The first model was developed by Cummins (1978) and was termed the basic interpersonal communication skills (BICS) and cognitive academic language proficiency (CALP) model. Cummins (1978) postulated that educators can misjudge a student's total language proficiency when relying primarily on observation of students' ability to participate in

Table 6.2 Stages of reading development

Stage and designation	Reading grade level	Essential learnings
Stage 1 Early literacy or pre-reading	Below grade one reading level	Early literacy learnings. Awareness of print. Phonological awareness. Reads commons signs and labels. Can write one's name.
Stage 2 Decoding	Reading grade levels one and beginning two	Letter–sound correspondences. Knowledge of the alphabetic principle and skill in its use. Identifies about 1000 of the most common words in the oral language. Can read very simple texts.
Stage 3 Fluency	Reading grade levels two to three	Integrates knowledge and skills acquired in Stages 1 and 2. Relies on context and meaning as well as on decoding (phonics for identifying new words). Reads with greater fluency. By the end of Stage 2, can recognize about 3000 familiar words and derivatives.
Stage 4 Uses reading for learning	Reading grade levels four to eight	Can use reading as a tool for learning new information, ideas, attitudes, and values. Growth in background knowledge, meaning vocabulary, and cognitive abilities.
Stage 5 Multiple viewpoints	High school reading grade levels nine to twelve	Ability to read widely a broad range of complex materials, expository and narrative, from a variety of viewpoints and at a variety of levels of comprehension: inferential and critical as well as literal.
Stage 6 Construction and reconstruction	College and beyond	Reading for one's own needs and purposes (professional, personal, and civic) to integrate one's knowledge with that of others and to create new knowledge.

Source: Adapted from Chall (1987) with permission of the International Dyslexia Association.

everyday social conversation (the BICS). Educators need to allow 5–7 years for students to develop the deeper levels of language proficiency which entails higher order cognitive processes including the academic language such as synthesis and evaluation. Once CALP is developed, the cognitive dimensions are common or interdependent across languages (Cummins, 1978, 1984, 1991).

The second model, Krashen's (1981) Monitor Model of second-language acquisition, consists of five central hypotheses: first, the acquisition learning hypothesis. Krashen (1981) believed that language is acquired sub-consciously where the focus is on meaning, rather than learning language formally. Second, the natural order hypothesis. This hypothesis affirms that grammatical structures are acquired in a predictable order. Third, the monitor hypothesis. Learners use a "monitor" as a learning device to edit their language performance. Fourth, the input hypothesis. This states that language acquisition results from the learner receiving input that is a little beyond the current level of competence ("comprehensible input"). Finally, the affective filter hypothesis. Learners with high motivation, high self-confidence and low anxiety have low filters and develop language faster (Krashen, 1981; Krashen and Terrell, 1983).

Some effective teaching practices developed from Krashen's (1981) hypotheses include (i) conveying meaning is more important than drill and practice, (ii) curriculum need not be organized around grammatical structures since there is a natural order to language development, (iii) teachers need to simplify language by making instruction relevant and meaningful, and (iv) teachers should lower the "affective filter" by creating a spirit of mutual respect, high expectations, and cooperative learning (Diaz-Rico and Weed, 1995).

The third model of second-language learning compliments Krashen's (1981) and Cummins' (1978) models. Wong-Fillmore's (1985) model in-cludes three components necessary for second-language learning that interact with three types of processes. The necessary components are the learners, the speakers of the target language, and a social setting that allows second-language learners and proficient speakers to interact. The processes identified in this model are social, linguistic, and cognitive. The three processes and components are interrelated. Wong-Fillmore (1985) noted that differences in the rate and level of second-language learning are due to the involvement of general cognitive processes, especially those that are important in language learning (Wong-Fillmore and Valdez, 1986; O'Malley and Chamot, 1990; Wong-Fillmore, 1991; Richard-Amato, 1996).

There are numerous methods and strategies of instruction for second-language learners in general education. The research remains inconclu-sive regarding the most effective, appropriate instructional approaches.

Fortunately, many of the commonly used methods are consistent with the second-language acquisition stage the student is functioning (Richard-Amato, 1996). For example, the total physical response is used often at the beginning stages of second-language acquisition (Asher, 1972). A student's oral production is delayed until the student's listening comprehension has been developed and they speak when they are ready. For students at the intermediate stages of second-language learning, the natural approach works well (Krashen, 1981). According to Krashen and Terrell (1983), the foundation of the natural approach is based on four principles: (i) comprehension precedes production, (ii) production must be allowed to emerge in stages, (iii) instruction must be based on communicative goals, and (iv) the activities must produce low anxiety when speaking. For students at the advanced stages of second-language learning, the sheltered instruction approach, often referred to as specially designed academic instruction in English, and cognitive acquisition language learning approach are two effective instructional methods that combine English language development with content-specific information and with instruction in special learner strategies in order to help students understand and remember concepts (Chamot and O'Malley, 1989). Designed for general education students, both of these methods can be adapted for those with disabilities.

Although English as a second language (ESL) has been practiced for many years, ESL for children with disabilities began in the early 1980s when a few special educators began to experiment with ESL instructional techniques for teaching disabled second-language learners. They found that the principles of effective ESL instruction could be applied to students with disabilities as well. It was also discovered that educators were successful when materials and instructional approaches were adapted to the students' learning, cognitive, and sensory disabilities (Grossman, 1995). Therefore, for students with mild disabilities, programs paralleled general education ESL programs and focused on both oral language instruction and literacy development in English. Instruction was modified to account for the child's disability by using specialized teaching strategies, providing abundant practice, and applying positive reinforcement and behavior management techniques (Winzer and Mazurek, 1998).

According to Winzer and Mazurek (1998), bilingual education and English-language learner instruction should be modified for the exceptional learner by weighing three factors for each student: the degree of disability, the level of language proficiency in English and the primary language, and the student's intellectual capacity. In addition, Gersten et al. (1998) identified several principles for second-language learners in special education programs. Some of the most salient ones included (i) stress acquisition, not learning, (ii) use assessment results carefully, (iii) target language development skills realistically, (iv) stress functional communication and pragmatic skills, and (v) use comprehensible input when teaching.

Whether bilingual education is appropriate for bilingual children with disabilities remains an area of considerable debate. Some educators point out that, while retention of the first language is to be encouraged, children who are already at risk with severe language difficulties (deafness and multiple disabilities) may find the use of two systems simply too confusing. Others hold that the language of instruction, particularly for students with mild–moderate disabilities, should be the language through which the child learns more effectively. If that language is other than English, placement must be with a teacher fluent in that language, knowledgeable about the student's cultural background and values, and trained in the process of instructing in a second language (Winzer and Mazurek, 1998). Language-learning disabled bilingual children, however, are likely to always have language problems in both first and second languages. Therefore, the individualized education plan team may have to select one language to help the student become functionally communicative (Grossman, 1995; Baca and Cervantes, 1998).

Although knowledge about bilingual special education practices has grown slightly in recent years, there is still limited empirical research that has attempted to examine the issue of bilingualism in exceptional students and effective instructional methods and strategies. However, it is ultimately the classroom teacher who draws from knowledge, experience, and high expectations, coupled with the combination of many methods and strategies, to make learning effective for students.

A preliminary study (Nares-Guzicki, 2000) examined commonly used methods and strategies for English-language learners taught in teacher preparation pathways that can be implemented by both general and special educators. Methods were defined as effective approaches to support students in their acquisition of a new language and content knowledge (e.g. the language experience approach and cognitive academic language learning approach). Strategies were defined as specific techniques that increase the amount of active engagement in academic learning and the quality and quantity of feedback provided to students during lessons (e.g. comprehensible input strategies and scaffolding/cognitive strategies). Both the methods and strategies used in this study were aligned with theories of second-language development. These instructional practices have been supported in the small body of available research by the theorists and linguists to optimize learning of English-language learners across all subjects at various stages of second-language acquisition development. The definitions for each of the commonly used methods and strategies are summarized below.

Commonly Used Instructional Methods for English-language Learners

1. *English-language development (ELD).* Teaching English language, literacy, and academic development.
2. *Specially designed academic instruction in English.* Promoting second-language instruction while teaching cognitively demanding, grade-level appropriate material.
3. *Total physical response.* Combination of visual, auditory, kinesthetic learning modalities students receive while following commands.
4. *Natural language approach.* Communicative-based acquisition of second language in a supportive, meaningful environment.
5. *Cognitive academic language learning approach.* Learning strategies and language functions used in content area curriculum.
6. *Language experience approach.* Students' dictated experiences become the reading and language curriculum activities.
7. *Thematic unit approach.* Use of literature-based curriculum/activities under one theme.
8. *Process writing approach.* Systematic steps from brainstorming, drafting, to completion of a final written product.
9. *Functional–Notional approach.* Language functions and the different ways of expressing the meaning of those functions.

Commonly Used Instructional Strategies for English-language Learners

1. *Active student participation strategies.* Cooperative learning, peer tutoring, and learning centers.
2. *Scaffolding/cognitive strategies.* Think-aloud tasks, learning techniques, and story mapping.
3. *Mediation/feedback strategies.* Frequent monitoring of student progress and learning.
4. *Comprehensible input strategies.* Connecting prior knowledge to new information in concrete, meaningful manner using various modalities.
5. *Functional communication strategies.* Use of clear, consistent acquisition of pragmatics.
6. *Modeling and visual organization strategies.* Use of visual aids and graphic organizers.
7. *Guided practice strategies.* Multiple examples presented with multiple opportunities to practice new concepts and language.
8. *Cultural diversity instructional strategies.* Incorporating diversity, language, and respect for students' culture.

9. *Targeted stage of second-language acquisition development strategies.* Use of appropriate, realistic lessons matching students' language development stage.

General Suggestions in Reading and Language Arts for English-language Learners in General and/or Special Education Programs

There is a plethora of effective practices for teaching English-language learners of all ages in general education (Rothenberg and Fisher, 2007; Short and Fitzsimmons, 2007). Some important practices for English-language learners in special education should include the following.

1. Make content understandable and meaningful—comprehensible input.
2. Generalize the new information learned to real-life situations and explain why the information is important to learn in relation to future life skills.
3. Connect new information to prior knowledge and experiences when announcing lesson objectives.
4. Teach critical literacy skills for narrative and expository texts.
5. Set daily routines, use cooperative learning and give students a chance to teach each other.
6. Frequently use a variety of engaging visuals and graphic organizers in all subjects.
7. Modify the curriculum based on essential concepts and key vocabulary and use direct instruction.
8. Explicitly teach essential functional living skills in connection to the content area subjects.
9. Teach a learning strategy or study skill whenever possible.
10. Teach self-monitoring and self-evaluation skills to instill goal achievement.
11. Establish behavioral and academic goals as a class and instill partnerships in learning.
12. Continuously review, through weekly summaries, essential information learned to foster mastery.
13. Continue to build pragmatic and academic language and skills by scaffolding from actual to potential achievement.
14. Summarize frequently the key information learned using partner and group activities.
15. Model, praise, and identify appropriate academic behavior often while maintaining a low anxiety environment.

Utilizing these important practices, coupled with the commonly used methods and strategies, effective instruction can occur in all subjects. Most specifically, for vocabulary development, there is a wealth of research-based instructional methods educators can implement into their lessons. Specifically, for adolescent English-language learners in general or special secondary education, the eclectic vocabulary method would be ideal for students at various stages of second-language acquisition development. Functional common vocabulary words are listed first, followed by a few relevant content or unit vocabulary words. For each vocabulary word, a word study page in a semantic mapping format is developed. This creative page would always include (i) the definition in the student's own words, (ii) a graphic symbol or visual representation of the word, (iii) a list of synonyms or related words that almost mean the same as the target vocabulary word, (iv) a morphemic analysis in which the root is circled and the affixes (prefix-suffix) underlined, and (v) a phrase or sentence using the target vocabulary word. If the vocabulary word was taken directly from their text, the student could also add to this creative word study page the word clues from the text paragraph that surrounded the vocabulary word, which helped give away the meaning of the word. A weekly review activity can entail a partner or group technique in which the students self-select one of their creative word study pages and take turns acting out the definitions. This follow-up activity, in addition to the word study page, can easily be modified depending on the disability and/or the stage of second-language acquisition development.

In the area of narrative and expository text reading comprehension, there exists a multitude of effective evidence-based methods that aid in the development of this critical skill. However, for adolescent English-language learners at various stages of second-language acquisition development, including students receiving special education services, a modified version of the question–answer relationship method (Pearson and Johnson, 1978) would be an effective practice for differentiated instruction. Whether it is from a narrative text or expository text, the content needs to be modified first by using advance organizers (i.e. outlines, one-page summaries, preview questions, etc.). Then make it a practice to include students from all stages of English-language development when reviewing the concepts and information from their reading. After modeling and explicitly teaching the three types of questions (literal, inferential, and evaluative) and the relationship to where the answers could be found, have the students at first find the answers and, later in the academic year, have them (as a class, then independently) develop the questions. Nevertheless, to ensure participation from all your English-language learners, assign the answering and development of the literal questions to your beginning-level English-language learners, the inferential type comprehension questions to your intermediate English-language learners, and, for your advanced English-language learners, assign the implicit, evaluative type comprehension questions. Eventually, they can exchange questions and work collaboratively in partners or groups to answer the questions.

The development of oral and written language skills, especially for English-language learners, varies depending on many variables, including the adolescent's stage of English-language development. Keeping this in mind, especially when you have English-language learners with individualized education plans, an effective writing instruction technique is the language experience approach (Lee and Allen, 1963) with modifications. With the language experience approach the students' dictated experiences become the reading and language curriculum activities. In other words, after much class discussion on a common experience, the teacher models sentence and paragraph structure by writing on the board (or chart paper) the students' dictated experiences of sequential events. During this activity, the teacher encourages the use of complete sentences with extensive vocabulary while demonstrating the appropriate use of capitalization and punctuation. Following this, numerous reading language lessons and projects are designed from this approach.

The language experience approach can be modified in many ways to match the individual English-language learner's needs, including students receiving special education services. After discovering a couple of very common interests (e.g. cars and dating) shared by your class members, utilize an anticipatory set strategy by creating a grade-level-appropriate scenario for each interest. Read aloud the two different scenarios and have the individual students choose a scenario and write "what happens next" until the end of the story. Students at the beginning English-language learner level will most likely need to dictate the entire story and later use the story to practice oral reading and fluency among other skills. Students at the intermediate and advanced levels of English proficiency should rely less on the dictation approach and write their story using the writing process method. After much practice, they learn to self-correct, revise, and edit into the final form. As a follow-up activity, each student showcases their story in a pamphlet format using various artistic materials to design a creative front cover to depict the story theme. This culminating art project illuminates other strengths that English-language learners, with and without disabilities, possess that are not always valued in today's academic-driven world. While exchanging and reading each other's high-interest stories, students' morale and self-esteem are renewed and invigorated.

Summary

This chapter has highlighted the complexity of promoting reading and language proficiency for English-language learners in secondary general and special education programs. Serving the individual needs of these students requires specialized knowledge and skills associated with (1) understanding the characteristics of English-language learners and special needs learners, (2) knowing the stages of reading development, and the stages of second-language acquisition development, and (3) providing instruction using methods and strategies known to be effective for adolescent English-language learners in general and special education programs. In addition, responsible instruction also requires an awareness of the laws pertaining to bilingual education and special education, and the guiding principles to keep in mind before any effective instruction can be implemented with English-language learners with or without individualized education plans. Lastly, general suggestions in reading and language arts have been presented and specific methods to improve vocabulary, comprehension, and written language skills for adolescents at various levels of English proficiency have been described and discussed. It is now up to educators to accelerate the empowerment of English-language learner adolescents, especially in language and literacy, so as to ensure that they are not left behind in today's global society.

Discussion Questions

1. From the four major subgroups of English-language learners, where do most of your English-language learners fall? What factors assisted you in determining this conclusion? Do any of your English-language learners have an individualized education plan?
2. For each class you teach, make a list of your English-language learners and determine each student's level of English proficiency, stage of reading development, and specific strengths and needs in reading. Discuss what will be your next steps in instruction.
3. Discuss instructional methods and strategies that you feel are particularly effective in language arts for English-language learners with disabilities. Why did you choose those practices?
4. Identify one student in your class who is an English-language learner with an active individualized education plan. After studying your student's level of proficiency in both languages, his/her interests, his/her strengths, and overall needs, determine the most effective methods and strategies that are best aligned to the academic content standards and the individual needs of this student. What is your implementation plan using the specific methods and strategies chosen for this student?

5. Website resource: Instructional Methods and Program Models for Serving English Language Learners: An Overview for the Mainstream Teacher (www.nwrel.org/request/2003may/instructional.html). Share your favorite methods that best parallel your student population.

References

Alliance for Excellent Education (2003). *Left out and left behind: NCLB and the American high school.* Washington, DC: Alliance for Excellent Education.

Asher, J. (1972). Children's first language as a model for second-language learning. *Modern Language Journal, 56,* 133–139.

Baca, L. M. & Cervantes, H. T. (1989). *The bilingual special education interface* (2nd ed.). Columbus, OH: Merrill Publishing Company.

Baca, L. M. & Cervantes, H. T. (1998). *The bilingual special education interface* (3rd ed.). Columbus, OH: Merrill Publishing Company.

Barton, P. E. (2000). *What jobs require: Literacy, education, and training, 1940–2006.* Washington, DC: Educational Testing Service.

Batalova, J., Fix, M., & Murray, J. (2005). *English language learner adolescents: Demographics and literacy achievements. Report to the Center for Applied Linguistics.* Washington, DC: Migration Policy Institute.

California Department of Education (1999). *Education in California: Looking through the prism.* Sacramento, CA: California Department of Education.

California Department of Education (2005). *Educational Demographics Unit.* Retrieved from: www.cde.ca.gov, November 4, 2005.

Capps, R., Fix, M., Murray, J., Ost, J., Passel, J. S., & Herwantoro, S. (2005). *The new demography of American schools: Immigration and the No Child Left Behind Act.* Washington, DC: Urban Institute.

Chall, J. (1987). Reading development in adults. *Annals of Dyslexia, 37,* 240–251.

Chamot, A. U. & O'Malley, J. M. (1989). The cognitive academic language learning approach. In P. Rigg & V. Allen (Eds.), *When they don't all speak English* (pp. 108–125). Urbana, IL: National Council of Teachers of English.

Cummins, J. (1978). Bilingualism and the development of metalinguistic awareness. *Journal of Cross Cultural Psychology, 9,* 131–149.

Cummins, J. (1984). *Bilingualism and special education: Issues in assessment and pedagogy.* San Diego, CA: College-Hill Press.

Cummins, J. (1991). Interdependence of first- and second-language proficiency in bilingual children. In E. Bialystok (Ed.), *Language processing in bilingual children* (pp. 70–89). Cambridge: Cambridge University Press.

Diaz-Rico, L. T. & Weed, K. Z. (1995). *The cross-cultural language, and academic development handbook. A complete K–12 reference guide.* Needham Heights, MA: Allyn & Bacon.

Gándara, P., Maxwell-Jolly, J., & Driscoll, A. (2005). *Listening to teachers of English language learners: A survey of California teachers' challenges, experiences, and professional development needs.* Santa Cruz, CA: The Center for the Future of Teaching and Learning.

Genesee, F., Lindholm-Leary, K., Saunders, W., & Christian, D. (2005). English language learners in U.S. schools: An overview of research findings. *Journal of Education for Students Placed At-Risk, 10* (4), 363–385.

Gersten, R., Baker, S. K., & Marks, S. U. (1998). *Teaching English-language learners with learning difficulties: Guiding principles and examples from research-based practice.* Eugene, OR: Eugene Research Institute.

Grossman, H. (1995). *Special education in a diverse society.* Needham Heights, MA: Allyn & Bacon.

Herrell, A. L. & Jordan, M. (2008). *Fifty strategies for teaching English language learners.* Columbus, OH: Pearson Merrill Prentice Hall.

Individuals with Disabilities Education Act Amendments of 1997. PL 105–17, 105th Cong., 1st session.

Kamil, M. (2003). *Adolescents and literacy: Reading for the 21st century.* Washington, DC: Alliance for Excellent Education.

Krashen S. (1981). *Second language acquisition and second language learning.* Oxford: Pergamon.

Krashen, S. & Terrell, T. (1983*). The natural approach: language acquisition in the classroom.* Englewood Cliffs, NJ. Alemany/Prentice Hall.

Lau v. Nichols (1974). *Free appropriate public education: Law and interpretation.* Denver, CO.: Love Publishing Co.

Lee, D. M. & Allen, R. V. (1963). *Learning to read through experience.* New York: Meridith.

Nares-Guzicki, I. (2000). *Teacher roles, certification routes, and instructional methods and strategies used by general and special educators certified in second language acquisition.* Unpublished doctoral dissertation, University of San Francisco, California.

Nares-Guzicki, I. (2005a). *English language learners and special education: Promoting language and reading proficiency.* Paper presented at the Leading Best Practice in Language and Reading Conference, California State University, Monterey Bay.

Nares-Guzicki, I. (2005b). Promoting literacy and policy issues: A shared responsibility. *New Waves—Educational Research and Development Chinese-English Quarterly, 10* (4) 4–8.

National Center for Education Statistics. (2001). *The condition of education* (Appendix 1, Tables 29–30). Washington, DC: US Government Printing Office.

National Center for Education Statistics. (2003). *Nation's report card: Reading 2002.* Washington, DC: US Government Printing Office.

Pearson, P. D. & Johnson, D. (1978). *Teaching reading comprehension.* New York: Holt, Rinehart & Winston.

Reutter Jr, E. E. (1994). *The law of public education* (4th ed.). Westbury, NY: The Foundation Press.

Richard-Amato, P. A. (1996). *Making it happen: Interaction in the second language classroom* (2nd ed.). New York: Longman.

Rigg, P. & Allen, V. G. (Eds.). (1989). When they don't all speak English: Integrating the ESL student into the regular classroom. Urbana, IL: NCTE.

Rothenberg, C. & Fisher, D. (2007*). Teaching English language learners: A differentiated approach.* Columbus, Ohio: Pearson Merrill Prentice Hall.

Salend, S. J. (1994). *Effective mainstreaming: Creating inclusive classrooms.* New York: Macmillan.

Short, D. & Fitzsimmons, S. (2007). *Double the work: Challenges and solutions to acquiring language and academic literacy for adolescent English language learners—A report to Carnegie Corporation of New York.* Washington, DC: Alliance for Excellent Education.

Smith, T. E., Polloway, E. A., Patton, J. R., & Dowdy, C. A. (2006). *Teaching students with special needs in inclusive settings.* Boston: Allyn and Bacon.

Special Education Division, California Department of Education. (1997). *Guidelines for Language, Academics, and Special Education Services required for limited-English-proficient students in California public schools, K–12.* California Department of Education, Sacramento.

Turnbull, A. P. & Turnbull III, H. R. (1990). *Families, professionals, and exceptionality: A special partnership* (2nd ed.). Columbus, OH: Merrill Publishing Company.

Turnbull, R., Turnbull, A., Shank, M., & Smith, S. (2004). *Exceptional lives: Special education in today's schools.* Columbus, OH: Pearson Merrill Prentice Hall.

Williams, B. & Cary, J. (1985). Educating the ESL Student. Workshop presented at Monterey County Office of Education, Monterey, CA.

Winzer, M. A. & Mazurek, K. (1998). *Special education in multicultural contexts.* Columbia, OH: Prentice-Hall.

Wong-Fillmore, L. & Valdez, C. (1986). Teaching bilingual learners. In M. C. Wittrock (Ed.), *Handbook of research on teaching* (pp. 648–685). New York: Macmillan.

Wong-Fillmore, L. (1991). When learning a second language means losing the first. *Early Childhood Research Quarterly, 6,* 323–346.

CHAPTER 7

Adolescents with Language Disorders as Partners in the Learning Process: Empowerment through Strategy-based Intervention

VICKI LORD LARSON

Introduction

This chapter will focus on general intervention guidelines that motivate adolescents with language disorders to be partners in the learning process. General strategies of the class meeting, mediation, and bridging, will be presented. More specifically, two selected strategy-based approaches to assist the student to learn aspects of speaking, listening, thinking, reading, and writing will be discussed.

All intervention tasks should be designed noting which stage of adolescence development (i.e. early, middle, or late) that the student is in (Larson and McKinley, 2003). In early adolescence, the emphasis should be on learning language that assists in enhancing academic progress and in developing personal–social interactions. In middle adolescence, the emphasis should be on learning language that assists not only in enhancing academic progress and developing personal–social interactions but also assists the student in reaching vocational potential. In late adolescence, the emphasis for those not going on to post-secondary education should be on learning language that assists the adolescent in developing personal–social interactions and reaching vocational potential. Adolescents with language disorders often have problems in developing literacy skills. The term language disorder is defined as "impaired comprehension and/or use of spoken, written and/or other symbol systems. The disorder may involve:

(1) the form of language (phonology, morphology, and syntax), (2) the content of language (semantics), and/or (3) the function of language in communication (pragmatics) in any combination" (American Speech–Language–Hearing Association, 1993, p. 40). Reference is also made to communication disorders, which is a broader term than language disorder. "A communication disorder is an impairment in the ability to receive, send, process, and comprehend concepts or verbal, nonverbal graphic symbol systems" (American Speech–Language–Hearing Association, 1993, p. 40). Again the American Speech–Language–Hearing Association (2001) defines literacy as "an individual's ability to read, write, and speak in English and compute and solve problems at levels of proficiency necessary to function on the job and in society, to achieve one's goals, and to develop one's knowledge and potential" (p. 6). It is obvious from these definitions, that adolescents with language disorders have a more difficult time in developing their literacy skills and language abilities to achieve academic progress, enhance personal–social interactions, and reach their vocational potential.

General Intervention Guidelines

Larson and McKinley (2003) presented six guidelines that they considered to be important in motivating and empowering adolescents with language disorders to be partners in the learning process. Those six guidelines are (i) determine the purpose of intervention, (ii) establish responsibility for the problem, (iii) be prepared to counsel, (iv) adjust to the social–cognitive developmental level of the student, (v) be cognizant of adult learning theory, and (vi) establish ground rules for intervention sessions. Each of these six guidelines will now be discussed in greater depth.

Determine the Purpose of Intervention

As a result of the assessment protocol, the student's strengths and challenges should have emerged. It is critical that, during assessment, the student was made aware of the language/communication disorder and the impact it has on academic achievement, personal–social interactions, and vocational potential. Thus, the student should be fully aware of the need for intervention and be prepared to engage in mutual planning of the learning goals to be undertaken. There must be no "hidden agenda" when providing services to adolescents with language disorders. As educators, we must communicate openly, honestly, and frequently about what needs to be accomplished and why it is important that certain strategies and skills be learned. Adolescents need to be involved in the goal-setting process; this will help them to be more active and cooperative learners during intervention. As educators, we should help them establish priorities and what goals will be most beneficial for long-term success. Students need to help determine what is most relevant and meaningful for their particular lives. They need to see the relevancy of individualized education plan goals or benchmarks to be partners in the learning process. The outcome of the goals should result in improvement in academic progress, personal–social growth, and/or vocational potential. These goals need to be authentic, meaningful, and relevant from the student's perspective, not just from the professionals' or parents' viewpoint.

Establish Responsibility for the Language/Communication Disorder

With adolescents, it is important to establish that they are responsible for taking charge of their disability and changing behaviors that will result in improvement. Until students recognize their language/communication disorders, and take ownership of them, they will not be motivated to make behavioral changes. One of the ways to have students take responsibility for their language/communication problems is to use contracts. Some students seem to be more motivated and focused to learn specific goals and timelines for accomplishing specific outcomes when they sign a contract. The contract should appear adult-like and official and the content should be developed jointly between the student and the educator. Larson and McKinley (2003) stated that students tend to take the contract more seriously when it is notarized.

Be Prepared to Counsel

Counseling should be specific to problems associated with the language/communication disorder. The focus should be on giving information to the student about the impact of the language disorder on academic progress, personal–social interaction, and vocational potential. It is important to obtain information about the students' perspective of the problem and how the adolescents believe that it may be impacting on their life. This information will allow the educator to provide release and support for the students' frustrations, lack of confidence or lowered self-esteem. By knowing the students' perspective of the problem, it will help the educator to ensure that goals are relevant and meaningful to what the student believes is important. Counseling about the language/communication disorder should be an integral part of the intervention/learning process.

Adjust to the Social–Cognitive Development of Students

It is during adolescence that major transitions in social–cognitive skills occur. Early adolescents are intellectually and socially different from middle adolescents, who are different from late adolescents. Adolescence, regardless of the stage, is significantly different than other periods of development.

Adolescents are too old to show up for intervention simply for a trivial reinforcer and too young to come because they realize the lifelong importance of having good communication skills. It is during the late part of early adolescence and into middle adolescence and beyond that the student begins to develop a meta-awareness, i.e. meta-cognitive ability or the ability to think about their thinking, or meta-linguistic ability or the ability to talk about their talking. Thus, this new cognitive development and meta-awareness may allow them to learn behaviors that previously eluded them. It is also a time when socially they are very sensitive to peer pressure and may do better learning in small groups where they can interact and learn from one another through group discussions.

Be Cognizant of Adult Learning Theory

There is a body of information available on the topic of adult learning theory (Knowles, 1973; Vella, 1994; Knowles *et al.*, 1998). Although adolescents are not yet adults, they are not children either and, therefore, it is important to be aware of adult learning theory information. One of the basic tenets of adult learning theory is that adults learn what they want and when they want to learn it. This is particularly important with middle and late adolescents who need to feel they are learning what is meaningful to them and what they want to learn. Vella (1994) noted that intrinsic motivation is magically enhanced when we teach the older learners about the topics relevant to them.

Establish Ground Rules for Intervention Sessions

It is important that the educator establish ground rules for adolescents to follow during the intervention/learning sessions. This allows the student to know the schedule, routines, and rules that are expected in the classroom and, ultimately, this will lead to the student feeling more comfortable because they know what to expect. It is also important to establish rules of confidentiality because students need to feel secure that what they say and do will remain private. They need to know when adults are legally obligated to report illegal activities and child abuse/neglect. Ground rules may best be established and maintained through a class meeting, which will be discussed more specifically in the next section.

General Intervention Approaches

Regardless of the skill or strategy to be learned, three general intervention approaches should be considered, which are class meeting routines, mediation, and bridging. Each contributes to the adolescents being partners in the learning process and increasing their meta-awareness.

Class Meeting Routines

When opening each intervention session with "class meeting" routines, it can serve as a medium for keeping the six intervention guidelines in the forefront. The class meeting contains three parts.

1. The self-report time of the class meeting targets two or three behaviors the student and educator have agreed upon that were learned during the intervention/learning process and now are being worked on outside the intervention setting. Students are to self-report on how successfully they have used these newly learned skills in situations such as the home and community. This is a meta-communication task and it is important that students think about their communication behaviors and how they are doing outside the intervention/classroom sessions. Generalization outside the intervention/classroom session is more likely to occur when students spend time reflecting on where and when they used the behavior and evaluate how well they did.

2. Issues and/or problem time of the class meeting allows for students to express their concerns to other students and the professionals about how the language/communication disorder impacts on their lives. This is an excellent time to discuss feelings and how to solve problems that arise using a systematic problem-solving approach (i.e. defining the problem, stating alternative solutions, selecting the best solution, implementing the best solution, and evaluating the solution).

3. Reinforcement of compliments time of the class meeting allows for students to reinforce themselves for achievements and to compliment others. Many adolescents who have language/communication disorders have received few if any compliments and therefore adults may need to model compliments for them. As much as possible get student compliments to focus on actions (e.g. I like the way you said hi to me) rather than on physical attributes (e.g. I like your shirt). Many times adolescents will feel uncomfortable giving and receiving compliments but as they become more comfortable they make more positive comments about themselves and their peers and self-esteem increases. Once they feel more comfortable with one another, group cohesiveness and cooperative learning often becomes stronger and their emotional support of each other may become evident inside and outside of the intervention/classroom session.

In summary, the class meeting time should not take more than 5–10 minutes depending on the number of self-reports, issues or problems, and compliments. It is important that the self-reports, issues, and compliments are appropriate for the group discussion and are intertwined with intervention goals and skill outcomes.

Mediation

Feuerstein (1979) posited that mediated learning experiences account for much of human learning, especially by students who either do not have or cannot make sense out of direct experiences they have been exposed to in daily life. For example, much of what we know about history is acquired through mediation, not direct exposure. Mediation is different from direct exposure in that some human—a teacher, a parent, a sibling, or a friend—comes between the stimulus and the organism (i.e. student) and/or between the organism and the response. The human involved in mediation frames, filters, and schedules the stimuli. The mediator may cause certain aspects of the stimuli to be more salient and others more suppressed. For example, when teaching writing, the educator serving as the mediator might provide a critique of the content and deliberately ignore spelling and punctuation errors or vice versa.

Also, in mediation there is an intention to transcend the immediate teaching situation (Feuerstein, 1980; Feuerstein et al., 1997). Even something as simple as asking a student to close the door can be mediated by saying "Please close the door because there's a strong draft in the hallway and your art projects may blow away." By giving an explanation or reason for closing the door you have just transcended the immediate situation. You have also established a relationship between closing the door and preventing a problem (destruction of the art projects) and have modeled how to anticipate predictable mistakes. According to Feuerstein (1980), the more mediation students have the more capable they become to learn independently through direct exposure.

To apply mediation consistently, no matter what specific goals are being taught, during intervention common questions and statements should be used by the educator. Assume that you have given the student a workbook page with a series of words in pairs and two columns with same and different such as

	Same	Different
Bread Butter	_____	_____
Sun Moon	_____	_____
Man Woman	_____	_____

When using mediation, you would focus and frame the activity by asking the adolescent the following questions.

- What do you see on this page?
- What do you think we are supposed to do on this page?

Or

- What do you think the problem to be solved is?
- What were the cues that helped you figure out what we are supposed to do?
- What strategy (ies) do you think you could use to complete the tasks on this page?

The prevalence of meta-cognition and meta-linguistics in these mediation questions is apparent. Students are constantly being asked to think about their thinking and talk about their talking during mediation activities. Intervention for adolescents with language disorders should focus and frame their activities so that they think meta, plan meta, and do meta.

Bridging

Bridging is another essential aspect of general intervention that should occur concurrently with mediation (Feuerstein, 1980). Bridging involves the application of an idea, concept, or skill being used in one situation to a different situation. For example, assume that you have been teaching and practicing the rules of conversation and have been emphasizing when you might topic shift or interrupt politely as part of a conversation during an intervention session. Before the students leave, ask them where else they might use these skills of topic shifting and interrupting politely in the home, in the community, or in the classroom. It should be noted that educators mediate but students bridge. You cannot bridge for your students. Rather you guide students to do the bridging through asking questions and allowing time for discussion of where the new behavior has been used. It is through bridging that students apply new behaviors and strategies learned to novel academic, personal–social, or vocational situations. Bridging might also be thought of as "transferring" or "generalizing." Larson and McKinley (2003) preferred the term bridging because it provides a visual image for adolescents.

To apply bridging consistently no matter what specific intervention goal is being taught ask the student the following questions.

- Where else have you seen_____?
- Where else have you ever had to_____?

- You used this strategy:_____. When else have you used that strategy in school? At home? In the community?
- Who might use this strategy at his or her place of work? Give examples.
- What mistakes might you make if you did not use a strategy (plan)?

Remember only the student can bridge for themselves but the educator can help the student to focus and think about their bridging by asking these types of questions when appropriate.

A word of caution should be considered here. Expect dead silence when first asking these types of questions of adolescents. Many have never been asked these types of questions as they are learning new behaviors. So the student may resist answering these questions. Larson and McKinley (2003) noted it may take several months to get total student engagement. However, once the student does begin and continues to use these types of question/answer schema, you will note that the students' ability to engage in meta-tasks increases. Larson and McKinley (2003) emphasized that students older than 10 years should be learning meta-activities such as (i) thinking about their thinking, (ii) thinking about their talking, (iii) talking about their thinking, (iv) talking about their talking, (v) thinking about their writing, (vi) writing about their thinking, and (vii) writing about their writing.

This ability to engage in higher level cognitive discussions and tasks should be routinely incorporated into intervention/classroom sessions as students learn how to learn. We as mediators help students select meaningful skills to learn, structure questions and activities so students understand why the skills are important, and provide opportunities to bridge the skills to relevant academic, personal–social, and/or vocational situations.

Strategy-based Approach

Overview

For nearly 25 years professionals have discussed and researched a strategy-based approach to intervention for students with special needs (Alley and Deshler, 1979). For the majority of adolescents, the learning strategies approach is the most appropriate. Emphasis is on how to learn (i.e. process) rather than what to learn (i.e. product). "Learning strategies are defined as techniques, principles, or rules that will facilitate the acquisition, manipulation, integration, storage, and retrieval of information across situations and settings" (Alley and Deshler, 1979, p. 15). Young people who attain competence in learning strategies maximize their learning efficiency; they use their meta-cognitive abilities successfully in both academic and non-academic settings (Ehren, 2002; Ehren and Jackson, 2004). A strategy-based approach has been proven to be successful with a wide array of students with disabilities (Beckman, 2002; Larson and McKinley, 2003; Ehren and Jackson, 2004; Kaufman and Larson, 2005).

Beckman (2002, p. 2) provided an excellent list of outcomes that can be expected with a strategy-based approach as follows.

- Students trust their minds
- Students know there is more than one right way to do things
- They acknowledge their mistakes and try to rectify them
- They evaluate their products and behavior
- Memories are enhanced
- Learning increases
- Self-esteem increases
- Students feel a sense of power
- Students become more responsible
- Work completion and accuracy improve
- Students develop and use a personal study process
- They know how to try
- On-task time increases; students are more engaged.

It is obvious that a strategy-based approach empowers students to engage in the learning process and to become independent learners.

Basic Steps in Teaching a Strategy-based Approach

Beckman (2002) recommended a five-step approach to teaching students how to use a strategy-based approach.

1. Describe the strategy. Discuss with the student the value of learning the strategy, i.e. why the strategy is important, when and where the strategy can be used, and how to use the strategy.
2. Model the strategy. Use the strategy yourself so that the student sees it in action and how you are using it.
3. Provide ample practice. Monitor, provide cues, scaffold, simplify, and mediate the strategy in order for the student to experience it over and over again. Give feedback to the student as they practice the strategy, constructively assisting them to perfect and make the strategy more automatic for them.
4. Promote student self-monitoring and evaluation of the strategy. Have the student monitor and evaluate how they are using the

strategy, where they are using it, and, if they feel they can do even better to perfect their ability, to use the strategy at school, at home, and in the community.

5. Encourage students to use the strategy in new and different situations. Using the strategy across and within multiple situations will help in knowing when, why, how, and where to use a strategy and integrate it within the student's repertoire.

A strategy-based approach is time-consuming but once learned it can and will be generalized across and within situations and helps the student to learn to learn and, thus, empower them to be their own teacher.

Selected Strategy-based Approaches

Although numerous activities could be selected to illustrate how to use a strategy-based approach during the learning process, two will be presented. The first will be on how to give (speaking) and get (listening) information using referential communication activities. The second will be on how to learn expository text skills to assist in achieving academic success.

Giving (Speaking) and Getting (Listening) Information

Referential communication activities, also known as barrier activities, emphasize the communication functions of giving and getting information. Thus, to perform these functions, adequate speaking and listening skills are required when exchanging information orally, and reading and writing skills when using a written medium. Although speaking and listening is performed many times during daily communication, students with language disorders often have difficulty in speaking in a clear, concise, and precise way as well as listening specifically to what and how something is said. Referential communication activities improve this precision. Referential communication activities require a minimum of one speaker and one listener (or one writer and one reader). They should be seated near each other with a physical barrier between them. The speaker and listener have identical sets of materials that are concealed from each other by a screen. Materials for referential communication activities may be either two- or three-dimensional. The critical aspect is that the materials should be sophisticated enough for the adolescent and not perceived as babyish. The educator conducting the learning process should explain to the student that the model constructed with the materials is secondary to the communication process occurring. The purpose of the activity is to be a clear, concise, precise speaker and an active listener.

During the activity, the speaker explains to the listener how to use the materials to construct identical models that only the speaker can see. Obviously multiple listeners could be involved as well as having one listener and one speaker with multiple observers. The observer(s) could study the model that the speaker is describing and observe the responses of the listener. Observers could record communication breakdowns and later discuss how to repair them. Many times adolescents will listen to the comments of a respected peer over an adult. Whatever combination of participants is used during barrier activities, the outcome is natural communication. There is a reason for the speaker (writer) to convey a message and a reason for the listener (reader) to understand it. All participants, including any observers (editors), are given the opportunity to observe the effects of adequate and inadequate communication.

Referential communication activities can be altered in content and level of difficulty by modifying the following variables (Schreiber and McKinley, 1995).

1. Clarification questions versus no questions. Allowing the adolescent to ask questions usually makes the task easier as opposed to not being able to ask questions during the activity.
2. State versus state–restate. Allowing the adolescent to have the speaker state–restate the message makes the referential communication activity easier since it provides for the identification of the sources of any communication breakdowns and permits repair.
3. Gestures versus no gestures. Allowing the adolescent to see gestures that aid spatial activities in particular should assist in understanding of the referential communication activity.
4. Partial message versus complete message. Allowing the student to receive partial messages in sequential order makes the task the easiest. Often a complete/comprehensive message may overload the memory skills of the adolescent with a language disorder.
5. Information questions versus clarification questions. This variation requires the listener (reader) to ask questions for information rather than clarification. The speaker (writer) supplies responses to selected questions rather than initiating the content of the message. For example, only "wh-" questions would be allowed such as, What shape is it? What size is the triangle? Where it is placed on the page?.
6. Time limit versus no time limit. This variation introduces the impact of time pressure. Usually adolescents with language disorders do better if there is no time pressure.

These variations when controlled and manipulated allow the task to be made easier or more difficult. Too frequently, the classroom demands and curriculum make learning the most difficult by not allowing questions, the stating and restating of the information, or allowing no gestures. In addition, messages may be too long and given as a complete directive rather than breaking it up into steps, and having a time limit which is too short can be frustrating for the adolescent with the language disorder. Referential communication activities provide opportunities for the educator to mediate when these variations occur in daily situations and to accommodate them. For example, if the speaker (writer) knows no questions for clarification are allowed, the message should be delivered after more planning and perhaps with a slower rate of speech (or with a step-by-step list in writing).

As the teacher, you might specifically use a referential activity as follows. John (age 16 years) will work on giving information and Mary (age 17 years) will work on getting information or following directions to complete a drawing. As the teacher, have John and Mary sitting across from one another with a barrier or divider between them. First, you might give John a drawing on a piece of paper of a large rectangle with a square in the center of it. You tell John to tell Mary how to draw the same design on her piece of paper. As the teacher, you tell Mary to listen to John's directions and draw on her blank piece of paper the exact drawing that John is describing to her. You tell Mary that she may ask one question for information after each of John's directions. As the educator, observe if John's directions are clear, concise, and precise. Observe to determine the quality of Mary's questions. Once the task is complete, then take down the barrier and determine if Mary's drawing looks like John's. If not, why not? Ask John and Mary to describe what went well and what went wrong with both the speaking and listening strategies they used.

A partial list of strategies to mediate for adolescents during referential communication activities may include the following.

1. Visualizing the information being spoken or listened to (seeing the model in your mind).
2. Using a plan to organize the information (i.e. what is most important to say (write) first, next, last?).
3. Concentrating attention on the speaker when in the role of a listener (i.e. blocking out distractions).
4. Knowing how and when to ask a question for clarification.
5. Using appropriate concepts (e.g. spatial, quantity, and quality) to make messages concise.

6. Taking the listener's (reader's) perspective when producing a message.

The educator may wish to consider asking these types of bridging questions during or after referential communication activities.

1. In what other situations has it been important to communicate a message clearly?
2. Tell me about a time when you were talking and a breakdown in communication occurred (i.e. when you, as a speaker, were the cause of the breakdown). What were the consequences?
3. Tell me about a time when you were listening and a breakdown in communication occurred (i.e. when you, as the listener, were the cause of the breakdown). What were the consequences?
4. Give an example of when you asked a question for clarification. Did it prevent a communication breakdown?
5. You have just been restricted from using gestures and eye contact when saying your message. When else might you be prevented from using gestures or non-verbal communication?
6. You are not allowed to look at the speaker and therefore cannot see any gestures or non-verbal communication. When else might you be prevented from observing the speaker's non-verbal communication?

In summary, referential communication activities allow the adolescent to experience the value of giving and getting information in a clear, concise, and precise way. Also, it illustrates that, by changing certain characteristics (variables), it changes the dynamics of the speaking and listening situation and how we as both speakers and listeners need to alter our behavior.

Expository Text

According to Nelson (1993) expository discourse is defined as "discourse that conveys factual or technical information" (p. 358). As educators, we use expository text as follows: when the rules of a game or routine are explained, when how to make something is delineated, when characteristics of an object are described (Larson and McKinley, 2003). Success in school relies heavily on being competent in expository discourse because it is used in most content textbooks and teacher lectures (Nelson, 1998; Ehren and Jackson, 2004). Ehren and Jackson (2004) noted that expository text is used about 60 percent of the time in the middle school curriculum and 70 percent or more of the time in the high school curriculum. When students understand expository text structures, they can follow the outline of a teacher's lectures, organize their notes, apply mnemonic strategies, and prepare their own papers more efficiently. Adolescents are at risk for school failure when they do not understand the complex language of expository discourse (e.g. direction, predictions, facts, specifications, dates, and conclusions).

Expository discourse involves both comprehension and production of language. Adolescents are simultaneously expected to listen to lectures, to derive main ideas and relevant details from textbooks while reading, to write expository texts of their own (e.g. answer essay questions or write book reports), and to give oral reports (e.g. book reports, scientific experiments, or give directions).

Intervention strategies might include teaching adolescents to recognize different expository text structures and the key words associated with each structure. Table 7.1 lists the nine text structures and the key words or phrases associated with each.

These key words are often in the form of conjunctions and logical connectors and serve as text cohesion devices. Intervention should focus on students comprehending these key words, stressing them during oral exchanges, highlighting them during reading, and editing them during writing.

When teaching expository discourse skills, educators should use the students' textbooks, supplemental reading, handouts, and tests as the materials to be analyzed for key words. Likewise, video or audio taped teachers' classroom lectures or directions could be analyzed.

A partial list of strategies to mediate for adolescents during expository discourse activities might include the following (Larson and McKinley, 2003).

1. Organizing information by several characteristics simultaneously (e.g. chronologically and by problem and solution) and seeing how text structure would alter accordingly.
2. Using relevant information once a text structure is chosen and ignoring irrelevant information.
3. Looking for relationships among separate objects, events, and experiences, then selecting the expository discourse macrostructure that can reflect these relationships.
4. Using logic to defend the text structure chosen for spoken or written discourse assignments.
5. Taking sufficient time to think through the text structure that is to be comprehended or produced.

Table 7.1 Key words for different expository text structures

Text structure	Key words
Comparing and contrasting	Same, different, however, but, on the contrary, similar, dissimilar, yet, still, common, alike, rather than, instead of, compare, contrast
Problem and solution	One problem, the problem is, the issues are, a (some) solution(s) is (are)
Cause and effect	If, then, because, reason, affected, influenced, resulted in, therefore, since, thus, hence, consequently, cause, caused, effect, net effect, result, consequence
Chronological sequence (episodic sequence)	First, second, third, after that, antecedent, before that, preceding, next, last, in order, subsequent, proceeding, finally, eventually, gradually
Order of importance (hierarchical)	First, second, third, most, least, all, none, some, always, never, more, less, +er, +est, frequent, infrequent
Category (topical cluster or list)	Group, set, for instance, another, an illustration of, such as, an example of, like, category, class
Physical location	Here, there, left, right, above, below, north, south, east, west, around, on top, under, bottom, front, back, forward, backward, side
Description	Defined as, called, labeled, refers to, is someone who, is something that, means, can be interpreted as, describes, procedure, how to
Matrix	Interpret, intersection, come together, overlap, influenced by, simultaneously, at the same time, converge

Sources: Nelson (1993), Larson and McKinley (1995), and Schreiber and McKinley (1995). Reprinted with permission from Larson and McKinley (2003).

The following bridging questions might be asked during or after expository discourse activities (Larson and McKinley, 2003).

1. We just analyzed a section in your textbook and decided it fit the organizational structure called _____. When else have you heard or read information organized by that structure?
2. We have been reading information organized by category. Now you have been given some new information. How would you fit the new information into the existing categories?
3. Your teacher has given you an assignment to write about some aspect of the Second World War. What are some choices of text structure and how would what you write change with the structure? (For example, a student could write about the major chronological events of the Second World War or focus instead on the causes of the war

and the net effects or compare and contrast the First World War and Second World War.)
4. You need to organize a 3-minute speech in which you introduce yourself to the class. You decide to organize your speech using a 'comparing and contrasting' structure. What are some of the questions you could ask yourself to prepare for your speech?
5. Sometimes reports are organized by describing the problem and then giving solutions. What are some topics you could organize that way? Sometimes it is easier to organize reports by the order of events (i.e. first, next, last). What are some topics you could organize that way?

In summary, expository discourse permeates the curriculum and classroom at the middle school and secondary level. Thus it is critical that our students with language disorders know how to use and understand expository text.

Summary

This chapter, adapted from the work of Larson and McKinley (2003), emphasizes applying intervention guidelines and using a strategy-based approach, which encourages adolescents to be partners in the learning process. Using class meeting routines and applying mediation and bridging procedures, adolescents' meta-abilities are enhanced. It is through thinking meta, planning meta, and doing meta that adolescents direct and evaluate their own learning and become their own self-advocates. A strategy-based approach is recommended because it empowers adolescents to be partners in the learning process. Two selected approaches: first, giving/getting information and second, developing expository text and vocabulary illustrate how to use mediation and bridging procedures.

Discussion Questions

1. What additional intervention guidelines should be considered to empower adolescents with language disorders during the learning process?
2. When teaching adolescents with language disorders to understand and use expository text and vocabulary what mediation and bridging strategies will you use?
3. Using referential communication activities, how can adolescents with language disorders be taught better listening/reading (getting information) and speaking/writing (giving information) abilities?

What strategy(ies) must the adolescent with a language disorder apply to be successful?

4. In a small group, discuss the following:

(i) What are the advantages or disadvantages to using a strategy-based approach to enhance learning with adolescents with language disorders? What additional procedures should be used to empower adolescents with language disorders to direct and evaluate their own learning?

(ii) How do we as educators assist adolescents with language disorders to be their own self-advocate in their learning?

(iii) What would you teach and how would you teach adolescents with language disorders to think meta, plan meta, and do meta?

Websites

www.KU-CRL.org: details strategy-based approaches.

www.ncte.org: details development of the National Adolescents Literacy Coalition.

www.reading.org: insights on literacy development.

www.asha.org: provides a paper on the role and responsibilities of the speech–language pathologist in language and literacy.

References

Alley, G. & Deshler, D. (1979). *Teaching the learning disabled adolescent: Strategies and methods.* Denver, CO: Love Publishing.

American Speech–Language–Hearing Association. (1993). Definitions of communication disorders and variations. *American Speech–Language–Hearing Association, 35* (Suppl. 10), 40–41.

American Speech–Language–Hearing Association. (2001). *Role and responsibilities of speech-language pathologists with respect to reading and writing in children and adolescents.* Rockville, MD: American Speech–Language–Hearing Association.

Beckman, P. (2002). *Strategy instruction* (ERIC Report No. E638). Retrieved March 3, 2005 from the Council for Exceptional Children's Information Center on Disabilities and Gifted Education: http//www.ericec.org/digest/c639.html.

Ehren, B. (2002). Speech–Language pathologists contributing significantly to the academic success of high school students: A vision for professional growth. *Topics in Language Disorders, 22* (2), 60–80.

Ehren, B. & Jackson, J. (2004). *Curriculum-based language intervention with adolescents.* Rockville, MD: American Speech–Language–Hearing Association.

Feuerstein, R. (1979). *The dynamic assessment of retarded performers: The learning potential assessment device: Theory, instruments and techniques.* Chicago: Foresman.

Feuerstein, R. (1980). *Instrumental enrichment.* Chicago: Foresman.

Feuerstein, R., Feuerstein, R., & Schur, Y. (1997). Process as content in education of exceptional children. In A. L. Costa and R. M. Lieberman (Eds.), *Supporting the spirit of learning: When process is content* (pp. 1–22). Thousand Oaks, CA: Corwin Press.

Kaufman, N. & Larson, V. L. (2005). *Asperger syndrome: Strategies for solving the social puzzle.* Greenville, SC: Thinking Publications/Super Duper Publications.

Knowles, M. (1973). *The adult learner: A neglected species.* Houston, TX: Gulf.

Knowles, M., Holton III, E., & Swanson, R. (1998). *The definitive classic in adult education and human resource development* (5th ed.). Houston, TX: Gulf.

Larson, V. L. & McKinley, N. (1995). *Language disorders in older students: Preadolescents to adolescents.* Eau Claire, WI: Thinking Publications.

Larson, V. L. & McKinley, N. (2003). *Communication solutions for older students: Assessment and intervention strategies.* Greenville, SC: Thinking Publications/Super Duper Publications.

Nelson, N. (1993). *Childhood language disorders in context: Infancy through adolescence.* New York: Merrill.

Nelson, N. (1998). *Childhood language disorders in context: Infancy through adolescence* (2nd ed.). Boston: Allyn and Bacon.

Schreiber, L. & McKinley, N. (1995). *Daily communication: Strategies for the language disordered adolescent* (2nd ed.). Greenville, SC: Thinking Publications/Super Duper Publications.

Vella, J. (1994). *Learning to listen–learning to teach: The power of dialogue in educating adults.* San Francisco, CA: Jossey-Bass.

Systemic Change Around Reading and Literacy at the Secondary Level

The authors in this section address activities related to literacy improvement through systemic change. The issues include the implementation, persistence, fidelity, and institutionalization of change in literacy instruction in secondary schools. If schools have been found deficient in their pursuit of literacy for all students and, in particular, in their support of students with poor literacy skills, how is this situation to be corrected?

Three different but complementary approaches to literacy improvement are described in this section. The chapter by **Guerin and Denti** is focused on teacher-initiated and teacher-supported actions to bring about improvement in literacy at the classroom, department, and school levels. The emphasis is on active and sustained teacher involvement. Change strategies revolve around actions that teachers can take to create a positive school climate for literacy, to support teacher development, and to increase student involvement.

Davidson's chapter examines the use of response to intervention as a central process for literacy improvement through differentiated and multitiered instruction. The response to intervention process involves professional development, student screening and progress monitoring, research-based interventions, data-driven decisions, and increased intervention, as needed. The model provides for systematic reading support for students at-risk for reading failure and increases the intensity of instruction when needed to overcome failure.

Carnine and Grossen describe a literacy program that addresses five "pillars" of successful intervention, namely focused leadership, scientifically based instruction, adequate time allocation, professional development, and data-based decisions. The program REACH is a combination of three reconfigured instructional methods that include corrective reading, spelling through morphographs, and reasoning and writing. Instruction is explicit and systematic and has been validated through controlled studies. Once students have reached upper level goals within the REACH program, they move into more specific content-area literacy instruction that incorporates strategies to optimize curriculum access.

These three chapters propose class and school changes that concentrate resources on improving student literacy. Each involves professional development, data-based instructional decisions, researched-supported methods and strategies, and progress monitoring. Each, separately or in combination, should lead to significant improvements in student literacy skills.

CHAPTER 8

Let's Get Serious About Literacy in High School!

GILBERT GUERIN AND LOU DENTI

Implementing change is like crossing a stream on slippery rocks—
it requires boldness and risk taking, confidence and balance,
judgment and luck.

This chapter encourages all high school teachers to take a proactive stand
to improve student literacy in their classrooms, in their departments, and
in their schools. The chapter examines three approaches to literacy improvement that include assessment of instructional methods, curriculum,
and school climate. The chapter also considers literacy improvement at the
classroom, department, and school levels. The teacher's role is pivotal,
requiring committed, persistent, and informed action.

The role of teaching literacy is often overlooked in the preparation of
teachers in subjects other than English. This neglect results in teachers who
feel ill prepared to teach literacy and who question their responsibility in
this area of instruction. The neglect also means that little attention has
been given to determining "What is literacy?" within the context of various
content areas. In actual practice, literacy is the legitimate responsibility of
all teachers and is critical to improving student performance in all academic
school subjects (Vacca and Vacca, 2005).

It is easy for a teacher in a classroom to lose sight of the totality of the
effort that goes into educating a single student. It is easy to undervalue the
joint effort necessary to reach the optimal setting and experience for

learning. Statewide mandatory tests, however, focus on performance of schools as single units and not on their separate classrooms. Teachers are judged collectively as well as individually. Working in isolation, teachers can feel powerless to influence change in their classrooms and in their schools. Whether that sense of powerlessness is real or imagined, it can be a serious obstacle to class and school improvement.

Literacy Improvement in All Subjects for All Students

In middle and high school, students encounter academic discourses and disciplinary concepts in such fields as science, mathematics, and the social sciences that require different reading approaches from those used with more familiar forms such as literary and personal narrative.

(National Council of Teachers of English, 2007)

The key elements to literacy improvement in all academic subject areas include understanding student skill levels, employing content-specific literacy instruction, and creating a class, department, and school culture that fosters literacy. Literacy, within the context of academic disciplines, requires the development of fluency within content area texts (broadly defined), in the language and form of discourse, and in the expression of knowledge, discovery, and product (Draper and Siebert, 2004). A schoolwide culture of literacy can increase literacy awareness and support, improve teacher and student skills, increase student motivation, and reward progress.

Donahue (2003) and Draper and Siebert (2004) discovered different goals and applications of literacy instruction in different departments. These findings supported a deeper appreciation for the unique perspectives of different disciplines, caused improvements in content-area literacy, revealed that strategies are not universally applicable, and acknowledged that cross-discipline literacy improvement is a work in progress.

A change in a single classroom is not likely to spread to other classrooms or to be sustained over time without collaboration among teachers and without administrative support. Significant school improvement requires the involvement of at least one academic department and, at best, the whole school. This chapter examines three levels of high school structure and the teaching skills and actions that support literacy improvement at each level— level 1: the classroom, level 2: the department, and level 3: the school.

Level 1: The Classroom: Assessment, Instruction, and Motivation

Growth in literacy occurs in environments where teachers understand the range of literacy skills that exist in their classrooms and adjust instruction to elevate those skill levels. Often, the range of student skills in a high school classroom spans the grades from mid-elementary through to post-high school. Frequently, there are class members who are second-language learners at various stages of English-language development and there are students with general reading disabilities. At the other extreme are students with skills far advanced of their grade level. Unadapted texts, materials, and curriculum can overwhelm some students while bore others. Either or both student extremes represent a large segment of many classrooms.

In order to make significant improvements in student literacy, the in-class activities must have an explicit focus on the application of reading skills (e.g. words, symbols, graphs, formulas, etc.), problem solving, and communication skills (written and oral) as they relate to the content area of instruction (e.g. mathematics, science, and social science). Key components of this focus are provided in Table 8.1 and a discussion of the elements in each component follows.

Table 8.1 Literacy components: assessment, instruction, and motivation

Assessment	Instruction	Motivation
Reading/writing	Vocabulary	Extrinsic and intrinsic
Readability	Comprehension	Teacher and peers
Listening/speaking	Speaking/discourse	Rewards and tests
Progress monitoring	Products/skill demonstrations	Interest and challenge
Test taking	Access Standards	Success and satisfaction

Assessment

READING AND WRITING

While assessment of academic performance is an ongoing practice in effective teaching, group test data can provide invaluable information on individual and group proficiency in literacy. Allington (2002) believed that effective teachers know their students, know where to begin appropriate instruction, and monitor student progress. The results of group tests can provide a class overview and student-specific information that is otherwise unavailable to high school teachers who teach large groups of students and whose time with students is limited.

At the high school level, the process of student assessment needs to be efficient, accurate, and transparent. It needs to be reported in a form that assists teachers in making instructional decisions and informs students about their skills and needs. Ideally, test data can provide common information to both teacher and student that results in a shared plan of assistance and commitment to improvement.

Often, information on student skills is not available to teachers early enough to assist in the development of instruction. Brozo and Hargis (2003) described a literacy project where appropriate data was not available to project teachers. As a result, the teachers selected tests that would provide them the data they needed to make instructional decisions in a timely manner. In their study, teachers selected the Gates–MacGinitie Reading Test (2000/2006) and the Nelson–Denny Reading Test (1993) in order to determine more precise estimates of individual students' reading skills. Reading, writing, and discipline-specific test scores can be helpful in the selection of texts, resources, and instructional strategies that are appropriate to a range of student skills. A teaching staff needs to determine the tests that will provide them with useful assessment data. A listing of middle and high school tests by the National Association of Secondary School Principals (2005) is provided in the Appendix.

An added challenge to teachers in content areas is that test results can mislead teachers into believing that failures in content skills at lower levels will preclude students from learning the subject at a higher level. This assumption can lead to erroneous tracking decisions. For example, problems with computational skills do not necessarily lead to problems with the abstractions needed to master algebra. Earlier computational problems, however, may interfere with algebraic problems that involve large number computations, as poor reading skills may interfere with the understanding of advanced word problems. In both situations, skillful teaching and adaptations may produce a successful algebra student in spite of earlier problems in mathematics and reading. Test results do alert a teacher to potential hurdles within specific content learning.

Testing at the classroom level can often be accomplished using oral or demonstration strategies. However, preparation for mandated tests, except in the case of a few young people with disabilities, requires responding on written tests. This often means that a teacher must use a two-level class assessment design where non-written procedures are used to determine actual knowledge and skill. Teacher assistance is then provided to assist students develop group testing skills so that the students can demonstrate their knowledge on written mandated tests.

READABILITY

Students' level of reading can significantly impact on their ability to access information in narrative, descriptive, persuasive, and expository texts and materials. Their reading level, however, does not necessarily reflect their ability to learn content information. The challenge in teaching is to increase student access to written material so that they can demonstrate their comprehension ability.

Text Reading The word "text" has somewhat different meanings in different content areas. The differences in written genre (i.e. narrative and expository) are fairly apparent. However, the forms of writing and expression can vary widely depending on the academic discipline. The use of graphs, charts, tables, formulas, examples, etc., requires different reading skills and understanding. Each content area (e.g. mathematics, science, and economics) also has a "different way of thinking" that requires an understanding of information within the context of the content area. As a result, there is a general reading and writing "literacy" as measured on a reading test and, also, there are various content "literacies," each with its own vocabulary, comprehensions, and goals. The tasks are to establish students' general level of literacy and also to determine, develop, and monitor literacies in the relevant content areas.

Textbooks are designed to provide information to their readers. In some texts, authors provide minimal help in understanding the text to students and teachers, while in others the help is extensive. Poor readers and low-achieving students often require added instruction to understand the structure and features that text authors use to communicate information and understanding. This may mean guiding students through a book's table of contents to help students gain an overview of a book's content, its sections, and its chapters. It may mean reading aloud to students at the beginning of a text section in order to provide a focus and help clarify misunderstandings. It may mean pointing out the authors' efforts to assist student understanding, such as the use of headings, highlights, tables, definitions, examples, and focus questions. When the author does not provide appropriate support for students, the teacher needs to provide that assistance. When the match between student entry skills and text requirements is insurmountable, texts will require modification or alternate texts or materials should be provided.

Readability Readability is a measure of the reading level required to understand the content of a text. Formulas used to determine the level of reading difficulty are often based on sentence length and the number of syllables per 100 words. Both the Fry Readability Formula and the Flesch–

Kincade Reading Ease and Grade Level provide readability formulas. The formulas of both authors are available free on the Internet. Readability formulas provide useful but limited understanding of readability and can be used to compare texts.

The weakness of commonly used formulas lies in their inability to judge conceptual difficulty, familiarity with vocabulary, and student interest. In another readability procedure, the cloze method, the teacher selects several 200- to 250-word passages that provide a representative sample of the material to be read. The first and last sentences are left intact, but otherwise, every fifth or ninth word is replaced by a blank. Proper names, numbers, or colors are not deleted. Students are asked to fill in the blanks with a word that best fits in each blank. Reasonable answers are accepted, while inappropriate words and verb tenses are not. A success rate of 50–70 percent suggests a text that can be read independently. Passages with every fifth word removed are the more difficult to complete.

The concept of readability can be a useful tool in selecting texts, constructing word problems, and choosing supplementary materials. Whatever method of measure of readability is selected the teachers must seek to answer the following array of questions about written materials.

1. Is the text readable and understandable to the students in the classroom?
2. Are concepts, activities, and outcomes sequenced appropriately to prepare students to meet state standards?
3. What text adaptations and what supplementary and advanced materials are needed to assure growth in achievement by all students in the class?

LISTENING AND SPEAKING

Listening and speaking activities demonstrate the oral face of literacy. The keys to effective student discourse and oral reporting are adequate preparation, opportunity to practice, supportive coaching, and guidance in the "way of thinking" within the content area. The assessment of listening and speaking is usually performed informally. Teachers operate with concepts about what are accurate, appropriate, and effective listening and speaking skills and base their evaluation on changes in student performance.

In order to monitor improvements more closely and accurately, written notations need to be made on the quality of the content of oral discussions and reports. These notations should inform the teacher about specific needs for specific instruction and coaching. Table 8.2 provides examples of evaluation and instructional activities designed to improve student listening and speaking skills.

Table 8.2 Assessment to improve listening and speaking skills

- Use a class roster to record quality and quantity of instances evidencing listening and speaking; introduce activities, such as those in Table 8.6.
- Listen for vocabulary, fluency, comprehension, logic, approximations, applications, response to questions or challenges, etc.
- Record changes in individual and class performance based on pre- and post-records of student responses

PROGRESS MONITORING

An example of progress monitoring in the area of listening and speaking is provided in the first and last items in Table 8.2. Tests and demonstrations are often used to measure progress in content areas. Frequent measures of growth toward goals and objectives, transparency in the purpose and results of the measurement, redetermining individualized new goals/objectives, and an instructional plan for achieving success are important features of progress monitoring at the high school level.

In a literacy-focused classroom, tests should be both a method of determining progress and the opportunity to adapt instruction to improve growth. A less loaded and perhaps more accurate term than "test" would be "probe" or "sample." This is especially true if the "probes" are used to reset the course of instruction rather than assign grades. In this way, the intention is to measure instructional effectiveness rather than student ability. Probes that result in learning strategies tailored to students' needs provide some assurance that, with effective effort, the student will reach or approximate the standard. See component—instruction, element—standards and Table 8.9 for more discussion on monitoring.

TEST TAKING

A literate student understands the language of testing and the language that is unique to the content area. Success on a test requires an understanding of test purpose, test vocabulary, and test formats, as well as the knowledge or skills under evaluation. Low-achieving students often need help understanding the purpose and focus of the tests they take. They need to know, in advance, if the test is being used to measure short-term classroom growth, a semester's growth, or a general level of knowledge. This information can help students focus on the type of content that they need to remember.

Students also need to understand both the vocabulary of the subject being tested and specific subject-related meaning for words such as *list, classify, estimate, order, most accurate, most appropriate,* and *alike* or *not*

Table 8.3 Ongoing evidence of student progress in literacy

- Student entry data provides a baseline for considering growth
- Assessment data can provide students with an understanding of their skill levels and, when paired with appropriate instructional plans, can result in reachable objectives
- Daily or weekly assessment can monitor growth and may indicate the need for more effective interventions
- Assessment activities can provide natural opportunities for students to learn test-taking strategies useful in other test situations
- Students can participate in test item preparation as a part of instructional activities, providing an opportunity for student engagement in instruction
- Students can evaluate their responses and self-select activities to improve performance
- Teachers can design alternative forms of measurement that allow students to demonstrate a wide range of knowledge and skills

alike. Teachers can help students by using the test language and format in their classrooms that is expected on mandatory testing and by helping students successfully navigate the "language of testing." Willoughby (2005, p. 2) recommended that science teachers prepare their students in the following test-taking skills: practiced in problem solving, comfortable with timed tests, and experienced with general test-taking skills. With the latter, she recommended answering every question, regardless of difficulty, making educated guesses by eliminating all known wrong answers, and checking their work.

The use of statewide testing and exit examinations has focused new attention on student assessment and teacher accountability. At its best, assessment can help students and teachers monitor progress, identify strengths and weaknesses, and provide alerts when growth is stagnant. At its worst, assessment can put unreasonable pressures on both teachers and students, result in a narrow approach to instruction, and focus on limited short-term gains. The positive use of assessment results can recognize student growth and suggest the sequence of learning experiences needed to reach objectives and standards. Teachers need to select instructional experiences that make progress likely. Table 8.3 provides examples of assessments used in the service of effective instruction and student improvement.

The drawbacks of a narrow focus on the assessment of objectives and standards include the loss of the "big picture," inadequate ties to the relevance for the future, and a restriction in the scope or depth of the subjects learned. Teachers are challenged to strike the balance between "teaching to tests" and providing broad, useful, and motivating learning experiences. Professional staff conversations can help teachers achieve this balance.

Instruction

Vocabulary

Explicit and direct vocabulary and comprehension instruction are among the most powerful literacy interventions that teachers can provide to students (Carnegie Report, 2004). Vocabulary building strategies, either word learning or semantic learning, are more effective than teaching through incidental learning. Semantic instruction, such as mapping and semantic feature analysis, generally is more effective than word learning. (Blachowicz *et al.*, 2006). Teachers in each content area need to examine vocabulary and comprehension strategies to determine those that are most appropriate for their discipline. Examples of explicit vocabulary instruction are provided in Table 8.4.

Table 8.4 Examples of explicit vocabulary instruction

- Graphic representation of the relationships between words (e.g. mapping) as they occur within a content area.
- Study of prefixes and suffixes commonly used within the content area
- Study words with specific contextual meaning and key words within a discipline
- Analysis of words by features, such as categories of words
- Use of mnemonics that links a key word to the target word by story, sound, or visual image

Comprehension

The Carnegie Report (2004) provided examples of strategies for direct and explicit comprehension instruction at middle and high schools. One example recommends a reciprocal teaching approach where the teacher models the strategies and the students are responsible to implement and then "teach" each strategy to other students. The strategies include the following: (i) posing questions based on a portion of a text that has been read, (ii) clarifying words, phrases, or concepts, (iii) summarizing the content of the text, and (iv) predicting what will happen next in the text. This model is designed to build student mastery and independence. Other examples include (i) the strategic instruction model, (ii) text-based collaborative learning, (iii) strategic tutoring, and (iv) diverse texts.

Comprehension strategies occur in at least one of three segments of the instructional process, namely the introduction, the main body of instruction, and/or the concluding segment. Teachers who improve student

Table 8.5 Examples of explicit comprehension instruction

Before	During	After
Clarify objective or purpose	Present/expose to information/skills	Provide/elicit summary
Tie to previous learning	Examine concepts	Clarify problem areas
Use advanced organizers	Graphic organizers	Evaluate learning
Discuss expectations	Provide and guide practice	After-lesson assignments
Pose/elicit questions		Review
Model learning	Guide questions for text	Compare with expectations
Discuss and problem solve	Students write examination questions	Reflection
	Cooperative groups—share, discuss, and report	

comprehension examine each segment to determine the effectiveness of their lesson. Table 8.5 includes instructional strategies that have been determined to be most effective in one of the three segments (Guerin, 2004).

In addition to examining each segment separately, there are methods of instruction that provide a more strategic approach to comprehension instruction. For instance, both SQ3R (survey, question, read, recite, review) and KWL (what do you know, what do you want to know, and what have you learned) provide a process for achieving comprehension. Methods such as direct instruction, constructivism, thematic instruction, and problem-based instruction offer contexts that address comprehension or in which various comprehension strategies can be applied.

SPEAKING/DISCOURSE

Classroom content-focused listening and focused speaking are activities that can improve both student literacy and understanding in subject areas. The key to success is to create student conversations and oral reporting that result in near perfect student expressions. The activities listed in Table 8.6 are designed to improve listening and speaking skills within content areas.

PROJECTS AND SKILL DEMONSTRATION

Once a student with poor reading and writing skills has access to information, the student may still have problems demonstrating his or her understanding and skill. There is an assortment of non-written methods for measuring levels of student understanding including construction

Table 8.6 Examples of activities to improve listening and speaking skills

- Focus students on listening and encourage them to practice making thoughtful oral responses to the oral reports or comments of other students
- Read to the class and have students verbally summarize or critique the information
- Have students predict the content of a selection and, after reading, have them review their predictions
- Create small book, chapter, or assignment focus discussion groups and then allow student sharing, listening, and discussing
- Give students time to prepare oral reports or demonstrations and coach where necessary
- Have small groups of students demonstrate or dramatize a theme, hypotheses, piece of information, research study, etc.
- Encourage the use of content appropriate language, concepts, and demonstrations

projects, oral reports, demonstrations, dramatizations, and oral responses to oral questions. The challenge to the teacher is to determine alternative non-written response formats that allow for legitimate communication and evaluation within a content area.

Teachers have preferred activities where students demonstrate progress. Students need to be prepared to use those activities appropriately in the class. This means preparation that rises to a level where students can explain to other students what the project, reports, etc., should include in terms of general content, subdivisions, length, appearance, and style. Effective teachers provide examples of effective products/demonstrations and give students guided practice in report writing or oral presentations. Low-achieving students often need additional examples, guided practice, coaching, and feedback.

ACCESS

For poor readers, the lack of access to information is a critical barrier to school success. Even though these students may be able to understand, remember, and apply information, the inability to read denies them admittance to written knowledge. Improved reading is desirable and may eliminate the barrier, but reading improvement is a slow process and neither student nor teacher can afford to wait for improvement's arrival. Options to a written format, however, are available in all content areas. These options can include audio recordings or CDs of books, peer or adult readers, peer oral reports, cooperative learning groups, academic coaches, and visual presentations of material (e.g. videos, graphs, timelines, graphic organizers, and Venn diagrams) (Burke, 2002).

STANDARDS

The initial implementation of a standards-based curriculum requires a considerable investment in time and energy. Translating standards into effective classroom practice demands a careful analysis and alignment of standards, objectives, and activities. The analysis should include an identification of the unique literacy needs within the content area, the strategies to improve literacy, and the literacy needed to achieve proficiency on state mandated tests.

Teachers need to "unpackage" the standards and their objectives and to identify sub-objectives or sub-elements that will allow students with various entry skills in reading and literacy the opportunity to succeed. Teachers who follow a direct instruction or text-based model of teaching will tend to define the sub-objective in terms of a linear progression toward the standard and its objective(s). Those using a constructivist, problem-solving, or balanced model may view sub-elements as important concepts, process, or attitudes of the standard (Gagnon and Collay, 2006, p. xix). In practice, teachers operating from various instructional models can usually agree on sub-concepts or objectives, but will differ on methods of instruction.

Teachers can use Bloom's (1956) seminal work, *Taxonomy of Educational Objectives: The Classification of Educational Goals: Handbook 1. Cognitive Domain*, to determine the level of achievement required in standards and objectives. Bloom (1956) identified six levels of cognitive development and proposed them as a sequence that moves from the simplest to the most complex. The wording used in state or professional standards and objectives often includes words from the taxonomy and indicates the expected level of proficiency. The wording that teachers choose to use in their objectives, elements, or associated instructional activities should also reflect the cognitive level needed to move the student toward the standard. The six levels of Bloom's (1956) taxonomy are presented in Table 8.7.

The advent of mandated testing has been a stimulus to increased in-classroom assessment. Day-to-day and week-to-week assessment can measure the effect of changes in classroom instruction and suggest areas that need improvement. Classroom assessment, when aligned with the knowledge and skills required on state tests and exit examinations, can both measure growth toward proficiency and predict student weakness and strength. Test data can assist teachers to determine individual and group growth and to establish need for instructional modifications.

Typically, some students excel and others fall behind minimum expectations. This is no longer acceptable. Students who excel need support to continue to advance and those who barely achieve or those who fall behind require serious attention. It is not enough to gather evaluation information

Table 8.7 Bloom's (1956) cognitive taxonomy

- Knowledge (recall)
- Comprehension (general understanding)
- Application (transfer to practice)
- Analysis (relationship of parts)
- Synthesis (organizing into wholes or parts)
- Evaluation (judgments about effectiveness, usefulness)

at the midpoint and end of the semester. Data from frequent measurements can provide both the teacher and the student with ongoing evidence of progress or stagnation. If assessment indicates that growth has not occurred, new teaching strategies need to be employed quickly and evaluated promptly. Students should expect to receive appropriate and timely instruction. Frequent assessment can spur action, as acknowledged in the statement: "What gets measured gets done . . ." (McEwan, 2001, p. 110). Table 8.8 briefly describes an assessment process designed to support skillful literacy instruction and to implement a teaching culture that supports instructional improvement.

In other professions, practitioners act collaboratively when they need second opinions, new ideas and suggestions, more information, further training, outside expertise, etc. Case studies, student study teams, ongoing training, and consultation are but a few of the ways educational professionals can improve their instructional understanding and skill. To reach the goals in No Child Left Behind and other reform movements teachers need to undertake continual instructional improvement. New teaching concepts, such as differentiated instruction and universal design, require teaching staffs that are open to examine new strategies in instructional

Table 8.8 Use of assessment data to improve teaching effectiveness in literacy instruction

- Entry assessment establishes student skill levels as they enter high school and determines the need to improve content and literacy instruction in feeder schools
- Ongoing assessment is designed to align skill levels, content objectives, and standards and to lead to appropriate and timely instruction
- Basic, alternative, differentiated and response to intervention instruction provide targeted responses to group and individual assessment data
- Prompt reassessment measures effects of new instruction and identifies needs for additional modifications in instruction
- Teachers seek expertise, coaching, peer assistance, or other staff development to improve instruction in the face of evidence of continued low student performance

delivery. Such openness requires staff development to achieve desired teacher proficiency (Nunley, 2006). This is especially true in literacy instruction because teachers often have had insufficient pre-service preparation in the literacy instruction required in their content areas.

Curriculum and school reform, however, require more than alignment with standards, improved strategies of instruction, and frequent student assessment. Student progress is also determined by the class, school, and community context in which instruction occurs. The critical elements of student attitudes and motivation are often more important than specific instructional strategies, attractive materials, and school structure. Teacher behaviors can impede or foster student motivation and growth (listed in Table 8.9).

Motivation

Extrinsic and Intrinsic

Motivation is one of the vexing problems for high school teachers. Negative peer pressure is often stronger than the influence of a teacher and a history of mediocre student performance or school failure does not inspire student confidence or commitment. A positive learning culture is one way to improve individual student performance in both the classroom and the school. The need for motivation in the area of literacy improvement is equal or greater to the need in the academic subject because of the history of previous literacy failures.

Student motivation is usually responsive to either reinforcement outside the content of instruction and/or to intrinsic rewards for success in learning a subject. Teachers remain a most powerful motivator when they inspire confidence, pride, belonging, and success. Peers, while many times detractors, can also act as positive models and support success. This occurs in classrooms where students feel a sense of personal satisfaction and responsibility for others. Cooperative learning, service learning, class projects, and class celebrations can create an instructive and rewarding environment. An example of a highly motivating, respectful, and organized classroom is provided in Table 8.9. This example is based on thirty-five full period observations in the classroom of a highly successful high school teacher (Appendix A, from Spaulding, 1992).

Intrinsic rewards are generally more desirable than extrinsic rewards because they arise from the satisfaction of accomplishment. The adage "We persist in what we do well" describes intrinsic motivation. It means that activities that interest, challenge, and engage students in successful learning result in self-sustaining behavior. Students with a history of school failure do not easily achieve this experience. The challenge to the teacher is to

Table 8.9 Effective high school classroom procedure for literacy instruction

- Teacher quietly and personally greets each student individually upon entering the class or near the start of class
- Calendars of weekly assignments by time periods and with notes on assignments that are to be tested are posted and all students know what is expected even in periods of absences
- Students take assigned seats where their personal folders are waiting
- The first assignment is 15 minutes of quiet seatwork that requires no teacher assistance: the teacher moves quietly around speaking to each student
- Housekeeping is handled in first 15 minutes; no papers are collected or passed out during class but are put in student folders
- The teacher has high student expectation and the instructional support is designed to reach those expectations
- The following activities follow the quiet period: common instruction, demonstration, and practice assignments—assignments are highly individualized to fit level/need/skill of students
- The teacher moves around the room checking and assisting each student for brief moments
- The teacher positively accepts and supports all student contributions and participation
- Students monitor, self-correct, and participate in active learning
- The teacher's conversation is always quiet, positive, and respectful
- The teacher moves to vicinity of noise or distractions and attends to a nearby student who exhibits appropriate behavior and seemingly ignores mild misbehavior
- After a time, the teacher speaks positively with the student who was misbehaving
- Each week was culminated by the turn in of individual folders

provide sequenced learning tasks that can be easily achieved and provide the foundation for achieving more difficult tasks. It is expected that the initial stage of each new and difficult task will require external motivators, which will be needed until the student is successful and ready to move forward.

Typically, students who excel in school look to graduation as a step toward post-secondary education or training. For these students, the future may not be clear but the future does have a direction and high school graduation is a part of that direction. For low-achieving students, school can be a painful experience with no foreseeable purpose. These students often "count the days" until the end of schooling. Antidotes for negative feelings about school include the following: success in class, a teacher who cares, peers who support student success, supportive parents and family, and long-term goals that include graduation. Other sources of motivation are listed in Table 8.10.

Table 8.10 Sources of educational motivation and goal setting

- Teachers who students like, respect, or value achieve higher student motivation and performance
- Student successes, even small successes, can increase motivation within a subject area and across subject areas
- Opportunities for students to make classroom decisions, to exercise options, and to be self-determined can increase motivation
- Activities that involve student participation in the classroom or in the subject can increase motivation
- Teacher enthusiasm for a subject, topic, or activity can increase student motivation
- Subjects that have relevance to students' lives or that have a direct application outside the class can be motivating
- Student long-term goals, e.g. college or a skilled trade can sustain student motivation
- The methods of presentation and the attractiveness of a lesson can increase student motivation
- External rewards that are valued by the student can increase motivation

Student engagement is difficult to achieve and maintain in low-performing schools, and yet it is fundamental to successful instruction. Teacher enthusiasm can engage students in a topic of instruction but only student success can maintain student commitment. Table 8.11 provides examples of activities that can enhance student engagement.

Student involvement and motivation are serious considerations when planning for literacy improvement. Reading, writing, and speaking are basic to learning and student failures discourage further participation. By the time poor readers reach high school they have had years of public failure and have, doubtlessly, been subjected to many unsuccessful attempts to

Table 8.11 Students engaged in effective literacy instruction

- Create an atmosphere where students are acknowledged, accepted, and successful
- Reduce time in lecture mode and increase activities that require student participation
- Provide students with options and choices in assignments and/or reporting formats
- Tie learning to relevant experiences outside the classroom
- Link class instruction to student projects, service learning, or internships
- Provide for frequent, successful assessment experiences
- Provide instruction in the literacy skills needed in content area texts and tests
- Provide assistance that is timely and helpful, either individually or in small groups

remediate their problems. Content area teachers have the opportunity to renew student optimism about learning academic subjects. By increasing access to information, involving students in active learning, accommodating for differences, and renewing the excitement around literacy teachers can improve the achievement level of a full range of students.

Level 2: The Department: Assessment, Instruction, and Motivation

Grossman and Stodolsky (1995) observed that "For too long, research and policy in the United States have treated teaching as a generic activity, and teachers as more or less interchangeable parts within a school system" (p. 5). They went on to point out that, in high schools, "subject matter permeates the professional identity," "creates a conceptual context," "gives rise to distinct subject subcultures," and "underpins the organizational structure" (p. 5). The authors' research highlighted the important role that subject matter departments play in school change or reform. This section examines some of the actions that departments can take in support of components of literacy improvement (Table 8.12).

Assessment

ANALYSIS OF TEST SCORES AND SELECTION OF ADDITIONAL TESTS

School department members can provide both the content expertise and the subject context from which to analyze group test results. Subject matter knowledge allows them to interpret strengths and weaknesses as revealed on the test(s) and match those results to existing course content. Department members, in collaboration with their testing office or with test publishers, often can obtain more definitive test item or content analysis. They can also supplement testing to corroborate earlier results or increase their understanding of areas of interest.

Table 8.12 Department level: assessment, instruction, and motivation

Assessment	Instruction	Motivation
Analysis of test scores and select additional tests	Support collaboration	Determine student needs
	Determine course needs	Sponsor activities and incentives
Courses and modifications	Align with standards	
Monitor progress	Professional development	Support culture of literacy

Because group tests are used for a number of purposes and are sanctioned at different school and governmental levels, a department's ability to influence test selection will vary. The closer teachers are to the decision makers, the greater the teachers' influence on text selection. Optional or supplementary tests are left to the discretion of the department or school and can be chosen to focus on a specific area, such as literacy, or to more accurately reflect growth toward standards. The faculty often has no local influence on the selection of "High Stakes" or "Exit Exams", yet these can be very important to the lives of young people. Student preparation for these examinations is critically important to the student and the literacy requirements on these examinations should be clearly understood by content area teachers.

All members of a department should take an interest in group test scores. Even when test items do not seem to reflect teaching goals in some courses, important content knowledge and skills, such as content literacy, may be strengthened in non-test related courses.

COURSES AND MODIFICATIONS

Some group test results identify subsets of students who fail certain groups of items. This information can point to the need for targeted instruction or a strengthened curriculum. Large numbers of failures on subtests can be a clear indication that there is a curriculum weakness within a course or a series of courses.

Decisions to add courses, modify courses, and overlap courses are examples of changes that can result from test analysis and can affect a department as a whole. Infusion of information into courses can also have an impact on an entire department faculty. A successful focus on literacy improvement usually requires a consensus among department members. The specifics on literacy content, placement, sequence, strategies, and evaluation require collective wisdom.

MONITOR PROGRESS

Progress monitoring is a part of effective instruction. It can take many forms, such as a sequence of short tests, systematic probes of skill, logs of interactions, evaluation of products, and records of constructed knowledge. The elements of effective teaching generally include a purpose, topic, goal, instruction or guide, activity, and assessment. Frequent assessment has consistently produced greater learning than occasional assessment. Literacy improvement requires the same diligence as other learning. The challenge to content teachers is to identify the literacy level necessary to support student learning and the demonstration of that learning.

Instruction

SUPPORT COLLABORATION

Collaboration is an essential purpose of high school departments. The department is usually a cohort of teachers who, in common, have expertise in a content area. The title of the article by Grossman and Stodolsky (1995) identified "Content as Context . . ." The nature of the subject area determines a context in which communication and work is accomplished. Each subject area, to some extent, has its own language, its own way of thinking, and its own literacy. Effective teachers recognize and assist students to develop both the generic literacy of reading, writing, and speaking and to learn the specific literacy of the content area. Because developing student "literacy" is not specifically taught in teacher preparation, it takes content area teachers talking and planning together to bring a literacy focus into their subject area.

DETERMINE COURSE NEEDS

Within an academic department there are commonalties in vocabulary, language structure, textbook organization, report formats, and test content. In departments where course sequences are hierarchical any improvement in the literacy at one level will affect student success at subsequent levels. It is in the best interest of both students and teachers that a department adopts an explicit plan to assist students recognize and understand the literacy required within the discipline. Table 8.13 provides examples of literacy differences between school subjects.

Table 8.13 Examples of common discipline-specific literacy features

Feature	Examples
Vocabulary	Proper nouns in history versus technical words in science
Language structure	Narrative form in English literature versus expository form in social science
Text book organization	Time periods in history versus functions in mathematics
Report formats	Written reports in social science versus problem solving in mathematics and science
Test content	Identification of facts and/or narrative statements in history versus problem solving in mathematics and science
Ways of thinking	Scientific inquiry in science versus creative imagination in writing

ALIGN WITH STANDARDS

Departments with courses that share common responsibility in the preparation of students for particular standards require discussions and agreements among course instructors. A review of all existing course competencies will help in the alignment of courses with standards. A matrix of course competencies and standards can help determine if the learning needed to meet standards is covered within the coursework.

Implementing a standards-based curriculum is a daunting task for a teacher working in isolation. Together, teachers within a content area can determine the subsets of the standards in their subject and how they are distributed among courses. The actual writing of course content to meet standards is often best accomplished as a collaborative endeavor. Working together, teachers can come to understand the details of their department's curriculum, including overlapping instruction, problems in information/ skill sequencing, and "holes" in the program. Collaborative work in the alignment with standards can provide an opportunity for an in-depth review and modification of an entire departmental program.

PROFESSIONAL DEVELOPMENT

Instructional strategies, programs, resources, and assessment are relevant to improving literacy and require support from departments and schools. Teachers who are in the process of implementing new strategies and programs require resources to support these changes and departments need to advocate for this support. Traditional staff development activities such as workshops, seminars, and college courses, may need to be supplemented by more direct procedures like peer coaching and class observations. A change in instructional content also means new instructional materials. New assessment approaches may require both teacher-developed and published assessment systems and materials.

Motivation

Although the teachers' role is a key to student motivation, attitudes, and activities, the department and the school can both significantly contribute to increase students' commitment to performance. A school environment that fosters respect for all its students, provides opportunities for all to succeed, attends to student needs, and creates pride in school participation tends to build the context for committed and successful learners.

DETERMINE STUDENT NEEDS

A department can study student needs in much the same way that a teacher studies those needs. The department can access student test data and analyze it for the entire department. It can aggregate the data within the discipline and can determine needed improvements. A department can identify needs for staff development, course changes, feeder school improvements, student involvement (e.g. coaching, student fairs, and career orientations), collaborative cross-departmental programs, and community outreach.

SPONSOR ACTIVITIES AND INCENTIVES

A department can take steps to increase student motivation, engagement, production, and success. An effective activity can involve all the students within a class or program at some level of active participation. This takes teacher planning and foresight. A science fair, for instance, can have both individual and group entries with individual options as to the type of project in which to participate. Almost any activity that is appropriate for a single author/researcher/demonstrator can be designed to involve a team of participants. Cooperative learning, an effective strategy of instruction, provides various ways to engage individual students' in-group productions resulting in legitimate productive collaboration. Table 8.14 provides examples of department-sponsored motivating activities that provide students with opportunities to practice and demonstrate content area literacy.

Table 8.14 Examples of motivating activities involving literacy skills

- Science fairs
- Social science dramatization
- Mathematics and science demonstrations
- School, department, or class newspaper
- Class or team projects
- Field trip planning and student responsibilities
- Service learning reports
- Student field observations and internships
- Community fieldwork oral and written reports
- Presentations, demonstrations, and reports for other classes and parents

SUPPORTING A CULTURE OF LITERACY

It is difficult to understand a culture from within that culture. The four common ways to examine the culture of literacy within a content area are self-examination, peer review, outsider observations, and recent émigré (student) misunderstandings. The department structure allows teachers within the same discipline to examine and share their observations and understandings of content-focused literacy.

A template designed around the elements of content literacy can assist teachers to understand student needs. In general, culture is a set of shared beliefs, values, and behaviors. The culture of literacy in a content area includes the reading, writing, oral communication, practice, and comprehension common within specific levels of subject development. "Literate" is not synonymous with "expert," but does imply a minimum working knowledge and fluency in the subject. It means the correct application of skills in a given situation and ease with appropriate notations, formulas, applications, and understandings. Department discussions can help teachers identify appropriate levels of literacy at different stages of content development.

Level 3: The School: Assessment, Instruction, and Motivation

A schoolwide focus is essential to the improvement of literacy. The RAND Reading Study Group (Snow, 2002) identified issues in adolescent literacy and supported a need for literacy instruction across all subjects in the upper grades. Both the National Association of Secondary School Principals (2005), and the National Council of Teachers of English (2006) have developed positions and guides on the improvement of literacy in the schools, including literacy in content areas at the high school level.

The National Association of Secondary School Principals (2005) recommended that schools create an active literacy leadership team that includes motivated administrators, content teachers, resource teachers, a coach, a media specialist, and, possibly, a counselor. Because literacy instruction is often foreign to the traditional views of secondary curricula, teacher involvement and support needs to be solicited early in the process and teachers empowered to participate in the action plan. The commitment of the team is to improve the literacy of every student.

Table 8.15 identifies elements, within each literacy component, that are appropriate for high schools. The table is followed by a description of a sample of actions within each element.

Table 8.15 School level: assessment, instruction, and motivation

Assessment	Instruction	Motivation
Schedule testing	Provide texts/resources	Foster culture
Provide analysis	Professional development	Sponsor activities
Supplemental testing	Set focus and nourish schoolwide participation	Provide recognition and provide incentives
Department collaboration		

Assessment

SCHEDULE TESTING

The schedule of schoolwide testing is the prologue for other activities that are needed before actual testing begins. Schools can assist departments in preparing students for group tests and can support coordination between departments. Student preparation should include generic test-taking skills that are common across departments and content-specific test-taking skills for each content area. Examples of test items need to be available to teachers and students so that there is no mystery about how students are to be examined. School support and encouragement in preparation activities can lead to more confident and successful student performance.

PROVIDE ANALYSIS AND SUPPLEMENTAL TESTING

Publishers have become increasingly responsive to the need for comprehensive school, class, and individual test data reports. Teachers need to become testing experts who can prepare students, interpret results, and use test data to inform students and to design program improvements. These are skills that exceed most teachers' preparation and that need periodic updating as testing becomes more pervasive and sophisticated. Departments and schools share the responsibility for ongoing teacher support in test usage.

Group tests are best at recording the progress of groups of students at the class, program, and school levels. Classroom teachers also need information that they can use to differentiate and individualize instruction. Content area tests can supplement the standard group tests and provide more accurate and detailed information on subsets of students and individual students. Some tests are designed to provide for periodic testing and can help measure progress throughout a semester. Good teacher-made tests can also help monitor progress. School support in training and resources can help teachers become more effective teachers.

DEPARTMENT COLLABORATION

At the school level, departments can be engaged in dialogues around (i) how literacy is promoted within the classes of each department, (ii) how literacy can be promoted schoolwide, (iii) how students are prepared for the generic and content demands of test-taking, (iv) how progress is monitored, (v) how student literacy activities can be shared across disciplines, (vi) what types of staff development would improve literacy promotion and test-taking in all departments, and (vii) what literacy improvement strategies could be used effectively in multiple departments.

These and other cross-disciplinary staff development topics could help unify a school in its drive to improve student performance.

Instruction

PROVIDE TEXTS/RESOURCES/FACULTY DEVELOPMENT

Improving literacy instruction increases the need for alternative materials, new activities, progress monitoring, faculty development, and a clear, schoolwide action plan. With funding always in short supply, schools need to set new priorities, shift funding, and seek new funding. An examination of schoolwide activities that administrators might promote to improve school literacy can provide a guide for teachers' advocacy.

In *Creating a Culture of Literacy: A Guide for Middle and High School Principals,* the National Association of Secondary School Principals (2005) lists the steps that school leaders need to take to achieve the following: (i) become an effective literacy leader, (ii) put "assessment in the driver's seat," (iii) provide professional development, (iv) promote highly effective teaching, and (v) meet the needs of all students. The steps for each of the five areas are comprehensive and include six to nine activities for each area.

PROFESSIONAL DEVELOPMENT

The National Association of Secondary School Principals (2005) considered professional development a recipe for success in literacy improvement and the Carnegie Report (2004) listed it as a key element for success. The process of effective professional development is seen as long term and is characterized as collaborative, collegial, relevant, and job embedded. It should permeate the school and encourage discussion and shared experiences.

SET FOCUS AND NOURISH SCHOOLWIDE PARTICIPATION

Administrative support is essential to a schoolwide movement to improve literacy. Administration, through a literacy leadership team, can develop a teacher-supported schoolwide plan, determine school capacity for improvement, identify student needs, create a realistic budget, extend the time devoted to literacy, support schoolwide activities, and maintain teacher enthusiasm. These efforts are necessary to initiate, support, and sustain a comprehensive program of literacy improvement that incorporates the components of assessment, instruction, and motivation.

Motivation

FOSTER A CULTURE OF LITERACY

Although the teacher is the key to student motivation, the attitudes and activities of both the department and the school can have a significant

Table 8.16 Creating a literate college-bound or college-going school culture

---

- Include discussion and references to college as a natural part of the curriculum, K-12
- Maintain high, positive, reasonable, and supported expectations for individual achievement
- Provide sequences in course work that lead to entry and success in college, e.g. pre-algebra, algebra, and advanced mathematics and honors and advanced placement classes
- Provide academic assistance where needed
- Provide families with college-going information, potential financial resources, schedules, counseling, etc.
- Provide comprehensive student counseling including focus on course choices, available assistance, career planning, and post-high school goals
- Establish college partnerships including campus visits, aligned curriculum, on-campus courses, and advice
- Provide adequate testing and evaluation to guide instructional planning and supportive instruction, and inform students and their families of student progress

---

influence on students' commitment to performance. A school environment that fosters respect for all its students provides opportunities for all to succeed, attends to student needs, creates pride in school participation, and tends to build the context for committed and successful learners.

A cluster of strategies shows promise for improving attitudes toward school, reducing dropouts, and increasing college enrollments. These strategies are centered on creating college-going or college-bound school cultures (Oakes, 2002; Pathways to College Network, 2004; Moran *et al.*, 2005). Table 8.16 suggests activities designed to provide a comprehensive approach to creating a college-focused school climate in grades K-12. These strategies are designed to change attitudes of teachers, students, and families.

SPONSOR ACTIVITIES

Actions at the school level can have a significant impact on increasing the level of literacy among the student body; teachers can and should initiate, participate, and support school-level activities. A school that supports a culture that fosters improving literacy will support class-level improvements, provide a schoolwide focus on literacy development, and involve parents in the literacy emphasis. Table 8.17 provides but a few of the schoolwide activities that can enhance literacy.

Table 8.17 Examples of a schoolwide focus on literacy

- Fifteen minutes set aside daily when all students, teachers, and staff read quietly
- Students' written and graphic work is featured in daily bulletins or a school paper
- A broad spectrum of students' written work is featured in schoolwide fairs, within or across disciplines
- School-sponsored student entries in countywide written or oral competitions
- School performances designed to include a maximum number of student participants
- The school fosters and sponsors cross-age tutors, service learning, cooperative learning, family literacy projects, and career fairs
- School supports book groups or book talks with maximum student participation, decision-making, and discussion

PROVIDE RECOGNITION AND INCENTIVES

Aside from providing a direct focus on literacy, the school can create an atmosphere where all students are encouraged to set educational goals beyond graduation. Low-performing students often do not consider education after high school. Their parents often lack information about available financing and counseling. In addition to the lack of parent and student information, low-performing schools often neglect academic preparation that prepares students to succeed in advanced courses. For instance, pre-algebra may not be available to students in feeder schools or upon entry to high school, thereby limiting the students' mathematics options. Limited honors class offerings in low-performing schools also contribute to limiting student experiences and preparation.

Table 8.18 Developing post-graduate goals, resources, and support

- Orientation to post-graduate options
- "College talk" that starts in the early grades and continues through high school
- Career fairs open to all occupations, professions, and post-graduate schools
- Student counseling that is focused on career planning and support
- Parent counseling focused on post-graduate options and financial support
- An academic program that clearly articulates with 2- and 4-year post-graduate schools
- School partnerships with colleges that respond to student and system needs
- College courses open to high school students
- Internships that orient students to study and work after graduation

Increased student motivation to complete high school and continue education in the trades, business, or professions can improve student interest in all subject areas. Both young people and adults commonly acknowledge written and spoken literacy as the gateway to success in all occupations as well as "on the street." A school culture that fosters literacy uses strategies that enhance the value of education and the success of all students. Schoolwide and districtwide programs are described in Oakes (2002) and Pathways to College Network (2004).

Table 8.18 provides a sample of activities designed to improve student post-graduate planning and options with a focus on continued education.

Summary

Curriculum reform is highly dependent on improving literacy in all content areas. Change is needed if low-performing students and low-performing schools are to improve. Such improvements require strong teacher involvement at all levels of the school system, extending from the classroom to the board room. Each content area, because of its specialized language, test demands, and reporting formats, requires attention to its unique literacy demands. Informed, involved, and supportive teachers are essential to the successful implementation of literacy improvement.

Questions and Project

Questions and Actions

1. What is the distribution of reading skills in your class(es) by grade level or skill level and how do these influence your reading assignments? Determine the reading resources available to you that could be used to augment your basic test(s). Devise simple, teacher-made reading materials that can augment your instruction and identify other teachers in your department who might join you in developing/selecting these materials.

2. What accommodations are provided for poor readers in your classroom so that they have access to class-appropriate written materials? For instance, are materials read and discussed aloud in your class and are students taught to listen for critical information? Are tests provided in formats that allow poor readers to demonstrate their knowledge and are students prepared to understand the test formats and vocabularies in your subject area? What materials/strategies can you use to uphold the integrity of your subject and, at the same time, make your subject student friendly?

3. What action could you take in your department to improve the literacy skills of all students and how could you enlist other teachers/faculty in collaborative efforts to support effective teaching and learning? List the actions and determine which teachers might support you in these actions.

4. What reasonable action could you take to increase your school's focus on literacy in all subject areas and how could school literacy activities be translated into benefits for the young people who are enrolled in your classes? List schoolwide activities that might directly or indirectly benefit your students in your subject field.

Project

Review the group test(s) that your students take each year. Determine if they match the standards in your field and how they align with the high school exit examination related to your field. Determine the literacy skills needed (vocabulary and comprehension skills and test-taking skills) to successfully complete the test relevant to your subject area. Design a test preparation program that focuses on the literacy and subject matter skills needed to be successful on class, standardized, and exit examinations.

References

Allington, R. L. (2002). What I've learned about effective reading instruction. *Phi Delta Kappan, 85*, 740–747.

Blachowicz, C. L., Fisher, P. J., Ogle, D., & Watts-Taffe, S. (2006). Vocabulary: Questions from the classroom. *Reading Research Quarterly, 41*, 4, 524–539.

Bloom, B. (1956). *Taxonomy of educational objectives: The classification of educational goals: Handbook 1. Cognitive domain.* New York: McKay.

Brozo, W. G. & Hargis, C. H. (2003). Taking seriously the idea of reform: One high school's effort to make reading more responsive to all students. *Journal of Adolescent & Adult Literacy, 47*, 14–23.

Burke, J. (2002). *Tools for thought: Graphic organizers for your classroom.* Portsmouth, NH: Heinemann.

Carnegie Report. (2004). *Reading next: A vision for action and research in middle and high school literacy* (a report to Carnegie Corporation of New York). Washington, DC: Alliance for Excellent Education.

Donahue, D. (2003). Reading across the great divide: English and math teachers apprentice one another as readers and discipline insiders. *Journal of Adolescent & Adult Literacy, 47*, 24–37.

Draper, R. J. & Siebert, D. (2004). Different goals, similar practices: Making sense of the mathematics and literacy instruction in a standards-based mathematics classroom. *American Educational Research Journal, 41*, 927–962.

Gagnon, G. W. & Collay, M. (2006). *Constructivist learning design.* Thousand Oaks, CA: Corwin Press.

Gates-MacGinitie Reading Test (2000/2006). Meadows, IL: Riverside Publishing.

Grossman, P. L. & Stodolsky, S. S. (1995). Content as context: The role of school subjects in secondary school teaching. *Educational Researcher, 24*, 5–11, 23.

Guerin, G. R. (2004). *Module 1. Adolescent Reading Development.* Available at http://alternativeed. sjsu.edu (retrieved on February 20, 2007).

McEwan, E. K. (2001). *Raising reading achievement in middle vs high schools.* Thousand Oaks, CA: Corwin Press.

Moran, C. E., Roa, J. M., Goza, B. K., & Cooper, C. R. (2005). *Success by design: Creating college-bound communities.* Santa Cruz, CA: UC Santa Cruz Educational Partnership.

National Association of Secondary School Principals (2005). *Creating a culture of literacy: A guide for middle and high school principals.* Reston, VA: National Association of Secondary School Principals.

National Council of Teachers of English (2007). Adolescent Literacy. What is unique about adolescent literacy? Available at www.ncte.org/collections/adolescentliteracy (retrieved August 30, 2007).

Nelson-Denny Reading Test (1993). Rolling Meadows, IL: Riverside Publishing.

Nunley, K. (2006). *Differentiating the high school classroom.* Thousand Oaks, CA: Corwin Press.

Oakes, J. (2002). *Ensuring Equity in College Preparation: What K-16 Partnerships Can Do.* Online journal of Individuals with Disabilities Education Act, UCLA's Institute for Democracy, Education, & Access. Available at http://tcla.gseis.ucla.edu/reportcard/college/1/oakes.html (retrieved March 27, 2007).

Pathways to College Network (2004). *A shared agenda.* Boston, MA: The Education Resources Network.

Snow, C. E. (2002). *Reading for understanding. Toward an R&D program in reading comprehension.* Santa Monica, CA: RAND Reading Study Group.

Spaulding, C. (1992). *Motivation in the classroom.* New York: McGraw-Hill.

Vacca, R. T. & Vacca, J. A. (2005). *Content area reading: Literacy and learning across the curriculum.* Boston: Pearson.

Willoughby, J. (2005). *High stakes science tests: Will your students be ready?* New York: Glencoe/McGraw-Hill.

CHAPTER 9

The Impact of Response to Intervention on Secondary Literacy

MARCIA DAVIDSON

> The ability to read awoke inside me some long dormant craving
> to be mentally alive.
>
> (*The Autobiography of Malcolm X*, 1964)

Introduction

Providing support for adolescents who struggle to read has emerged as a salient topic of interest nationwide. This chapter examines the efficacy of the response to intervention model in stemming the tide of poor reading and literacy skills for students in secondary schools. The response to intervention model is defined and implementation strategies and programs for students who struggle to read are explicated. The chapter offers suggestions for systemic change at the middle and high school level using the response to intervention model.

Reading Instruction in Secondary Schools

According to conventional views, students attending high school are supposed to know how to read, so that secondary teachers focus on teaching the content of the course and not how to read, understand, and analyze large amounts of printed information. The reading demands become increasingly complex during the high school years so that those who are struggling with reading skills fall farther and farther behind. Adolescents who lack critical literacy skills need intensive explicit instruction in order for them to catch up with their peers. Yet middle and high schools are not prepared to provide this support. For example, many high school teachers are simply not trained to provide basic reading instruction and they do not see it as their responsibility. In fact, many take the position that teaching basic literacy skills is a complex endeavor and they do not have the training to provide the necessary reading instruction. There have been no broad-scale initiatives to make certain that teachers are prepared to use instructional practices that are scientifically based. Even if teachers were better trained in how to teach essential literacy skills, most schools are not organized to provide well-coordinated instruction across the content areas. Finally, many adolescents have lost confidence in their academic abilities and are no longer motivated to commit time and effort to learning the skills they need to be successful in school.

Students in secondary schools who have been identified as having reading skills that are significantly below grade level rarely get the support they need to learn to read successfully. In fact, many adolescents who are in special education as having a learning disability in reading have individual education plans that do not address the improvement of reading skills (Catone and Brady, 2005). Instead, these students are provided tutoring and support to pass tests and classes with no opportunity to learn how to read more proficiently. This practice seems to be part of a *Catch 22* scenario in which students need to pass classes in order to earn a diploma, so special educators are pressured to ensure that students obtain passing grades. Meanwhile, there is no instruction in the very skills that are the basis for their lack of success in the content classes. At the secondary level, both special education and general education courses typically focus on content and not basic skills like how to read. Demands of high school graduates have increased over the years and job skills are increasingly complex. Students who do not acquire sufficient literacy skills while in high school will not be able to compete in the job market. While there is a movement to "raise the bar" for high school graduates, that goal is unlikely to be achieved when there are so many students entering high school with very low reading skills.

Response to Intervention: A New Approach to Providing Reading Support for Struggling Adolescents

The Response to Intervention Initiative Signifies a Paradigm Shift in Thinking, Intervention, and Support for Struggling Readers at the Secondary Level

The response to intervention initiative is found in the 2004 reauthorization of the Individuals with Disabilities Education Improvement Act (U.S.

Department of Education, 2005). It is defined and described in special education law, but its focus is on building support and improved instruction in the general education classrooms. Response to intervention is the process of discovering what each student needs in order to learn and what instructional strategies work best. It incorporates research-based approaches, highly trained staff delivering the instruction, regular assessment and the use of data derived from assessments, which then are used to determine the best instructional next steps (Special Edge, 2007, p. 8). The common method of providing response to intervention is a multitiered approach with increasing intensity of services provided to students according to the results of data from screening and progress monitoring measures. The response to intervention model includes the following components.

- valid and reliable screening and progress monitoring measures
- scientific research-based interventions
- decisions based upon data from screening and progress monitoring
- powerful professional development for teachers in valid interventions
- resource allocation that ensures that interventions are appropriate and allow for the maximum student participation in the general education setting.

Operationalizing the response to intervention components requires that schools and teachers begin to incorporate ongoing assessment (data) into instruction to continually monitor progress. However it must be noted that in secondary settings, other than high stakes tests and course-related mastery examinations, there is often little schoolwide formative assessment conducted to determine which students in the general education classes are struggling with reading skills. Thus, it is difficult to determine the most appropriate intervention. For example, without data one cannot know whether poor achievement is due to a lack of skill or a lack of motivation or attendance or other problems. To pinpoint these students response to intervention uses schoolwide screening with valid instruments in order to identify which students are struggling due to poor reading skills. Once identified, students need to be grouped according to their specific reading needs (response to intervention multitiered approach) and then provided an appropriate intervention that will result in improved reading. Learning rate and level of performance are the guides in determining the effectiveness of the intervention. Learning rate refers to a student's rate of progress over time compared with initial levels of performance and compared with peers. The level of performance refers to an individual's relative standing on a reading measure compared to the expected performance. Decisions about the use of interventions are made based upon the information collected on the learning rate and performance of individual students (National Association of State Directors of Special Education, 2005). Progress monitoring, a key and critical component of a response to intervention model, ensures that students who receive an intervention be monitored in order to gauge whether the intervention is effective.

Response to Intervention in the Context of Effective Adolescent Literacy Programs

Instructional and infrastructure improvements are both integral features of an effective response to intervention model. For example, in response to intervention, there are mechanisms that address student achievement at the school level and at the individual student level with evidence-based interventions. Table 9.1 provides an example of how an adolescent literacy program can be integrated into the key components of a response to intervention model.

Table 9.1 includes all of the key elements identified by Biancarosa and Snow (2004) as well as the key components of a response to intervention model. It is important to focus on the professional development component identified in this table as it includes a number of elements that require knowledge and skills in how to teach reading. This is a cornerstone of any response to intervention model. Teachers must know how to use assessments to inform instruction and know the skills and strategies required to teach their students effectively the reading skills they need to be successful. The following questions provide an important foundation for framing the tasks that secondary schools must successfully complete in order to implement an effective response to intervention model.

1. What assessments are currently used to identify good and struggling readers?
2. What assessments are used to identify specific needs of individual struggling readers? What reading instruction is already taking place in content classrooms and what professional development do content teachers need to effectively address all reading components?
3. What reading interventions and supplemental reading programs are currently offered for struggling readers?
4. What information and professional development do the teachers of struggling readers need?
5. Is the scheduling process flexible enough to accommodate different grouping patterns for struggling readers? (Sedita, 2004, p. 3).

Table 9.1 Instructional and infrastructure improvements

Response to intervention	Instruction	Infrastructure
Valid screening and progress monitoring measures	Provide data to identify students in need of support in improving reading skills	Schoolwide screening and progress monitoring across all grades
Scientific research-based interventions	Interventions that align with content area instruction with specific strategies taught in all classes	Schoolwide process to identify key strategies and interventions that will improve reading skills across all content areas
Decisions based upon data from screening and progress monitoring	Use ongoing data to determine when students have achieved benchmark skills in reading and when interventions need to be modified	School has developed a data system so that screening and progress monitoring data are easily entered, summarized and interpreted to provide timely information to teachers and administrators
Professional development for teachers in valid interventions	Teachers learn effective ways to teach reading skills in the context of their content area. Professional development includes focus on the following elements: • decoding/word recognition skills • language processing • vocabulary development • background knowledge • comprehension/meta-cognition • study strategies • motivation • text-based collaborative learning • strategic tutoring • using diverse texts • the use of technology in building literacy competence	The school provides time and support for teachers, including teacher teams, to learn new strategies/ interventions and to confer with colleagues and experts on the fidelity of implementation of these strategies/ interventions. Identified strategies are components of a comprehensive and coordinated literacy program
Resource allocation that ensures that interventions are appropriate and allows for the maximum student participation in the general education setting	Teachers build capacity through effective professional development to provide reading and writing support for struggling students in their classes	The school has allocated sufficient resources to obtain appropriate materials and professional development for teachers and staff

Implementation of Response to Intervention at the Student Level: The Problem-solving Process

Full implementation of a response to intervention model at the secondary school level requires that the school considers tiers of support for students. Following the initial screening measure, there is likely to be a range of student scores suggesting that needs are varied and range from minimal support and accommodations to a need to provide direct instruction in aspects of the structure of the English language such as orthography and morphology. How can a school design an intervention system that provides appropriate support for a wide range of student needs?

The Three-tier Model

At the secondary level, the response to intervention model will look different because it is not linked with a schoolwide core reading program. Instead, the core at the secondary level is the focus on the critical literacy skills that all teachers agree are an integral aspect of their content area curriculum. Tier 1 includes the core content curriculum classes. The identified literacy strategies are integrated into each subject and taught by all teachers. Tier 2 is a class that provides more intense instruction in the literacy strategies that increase comprehension and vocabulary skills and can be applied by students in their core content area classes. Schools identify the schoolwide strategies that they determine best reflect the needs across all of the content areas. Tier 3 is the most intense level of support and tier 3 classes provide a more comprehensive core reading curriculum that includes phonological, orthographic, morphemic, semantic, and syntactic components.

Tier 3 students are typically unable to decode text efficiently. The school response to intervention team engages in a problem-solving process for those students who score at the 20 percent point (or other established cut-off point) on the screening measures. This process is required for those students who are struggling and not identified as in need of specially designed instruction. The response to intervention process is intended to provide tiers of support to ensure that students are provided support as soon as they are identified. In the elementary classrooms, this process is a response to the traditional "wait to fail" model. However, at the secondary level, it is assumed that most students with disabilities have been identified prior to entrance into high school. That, of course, is not necessarily the case and a system to address those students who need intensive interventions in middle and high school but are not identified as students with disabilities is essential. A comprehensive problem-solving process provides the framework for identifying the most appropriate intervention for individual students who are significantly at risk in the area of literacy.

The Problem-Solving Process

DEFINE THE PROBLEM

Defining Problem/Directly Measuring Behavior This includes collecting screening assessment and any diagnostic assessment information to help define specifically the student's instructional needs in terms of the extent to which reading skills are delayed.

PROBLEM ANALYSIS

Validating Problem The RIOT (review, interview, observe, test) approach is very helpful in validating the problem.

- review student records
- interview teachers and others familiar with the student to determine in which classes the problem is affecting performance
- observe the student in the contexts in which the reading problem is most apparent
- test the student with appropriate diagnostic measures when additional information about the problem is needed

Variables that Contribute to the Problem It is likely that, after the RIOT process is completed, additional factors/variables may be identified. For example, the student may struggle in classrooms that are noisy or do not offer outlines, peer support, or study guides to scaffold learning.

Develop Plan Following the completion of the RIOT process, the response to intervention team develops a plan to support the student. This is the point at which resources become critical. The plan needs to include instruction in the skills the student needs to acquire in order to be successful. That means that some teachers will have to know how to instruct students in the essential components of learning to read—helping students pass courses will not be sufficient.

IMPLEMENT PLAN

Implement as Intended A response to intervention team member will observe and consult with the teacher or teachers who is (are) implementing the plan to see how the implementation process is working. It is not useful to develop a plan, assign a teacher to implement it, and then never check to see if the implementation is going well. Fidelity of implementation is a critical component of response to intervention.

Progress Monitor   The progress monitoring measures described earlier can provide the evidence that the plan is working or that it needs revision. After eight data points, the response to intervention team can make a decision about the efficacy of the plan.

Modify as Necessary   When the data points are not demonstrating sufficient progress, the plan needs to be modified. The teacher implementing the plan meets with the response to intervention team to review and revise the plan and then continues to monitor progress.

EVALUATE

After several weeks or months of implementation, the team meets to determine whether the intervention is effective and whether the student continues to need support. Sometimes, when the intervention requires substantial resources and time, the response to intervention team may consider whether the student has a disability and will require even more intense support and remediation through special education.

For those students who are most at risk, the response to intervention process can provide a data-driven approach to ensure that the intervention meets the needs of the individual. In high school, there is little time to waste and each intervention decision must have a strong research base to ensure instructional efficacy.

Implementing a Response to Intervention Model in Secondary Schools

The response to intervention model can serve as a catalyst for change. With a focus on improving reading and literacy for all students the culture of the school radically shifts from content specialists to literacy generalists. Literacy and reading improvement become the foundation and centerpiece of the school driven by the tenets of response to intervention. To truly embrace this change the teacher must embrace the notion of schoolwide screening and progress monitoring. The following addresses some of the literacy measures for screening and progress monitoring that have been found to work well at the secondary level.

Screening and Progress Monitoring Measures for Middle and High School Students

There is some promising research on the relation of adolescent fluency, decoding, and verbal reasoning skills to high-stakes assessments. In a

Florida study (Torgesen, 2006), fluency, decoding and verbal reasoning scores of seventh and tenth graders on curriculum-based measures were compared with the students' performance on the Florida state examination. At the seventh grade, fluency and decoding deficiencies correlated strongly with level 1 and level 2 scores on the Florida state examination. For tenth grade students, verbal reasoning and fluency deficiencies were strongly related to scores obtained by students at levels 1 and 2. These findings suggest that, in general, oral reading rate and accuracy measures produce predictable growth rates for students in the elementary grades, but this stability decreases somewhat for older students (Fuchs, 2006). The Florida Center for Reading Research has developed two very promising progress monitoring tools for middle and high school students.

THE FLORIDA ORAL READING FLUENCY

This measure consists of grade-level passages that students read for one minute. During each of the assessment benchmark periods, students read two different passages with the scores averaged in order to obtain a score of words read correctly per minute. The averaged score represents a student's rate and accuracy, a necessary although not sufficient component of proficient reading (see data on Florida Oral Reading Fluency and the Florida Comprehensive Assessment Test) (Torgesen, 2006). A research team at the Florida Center for Reading Research (2007) developed charts identifying risk levels to assist schools in identifying appropriate levels of instruction for students. The oral fluency measure is administered individually to students (Florida Center for Reading Research, 2007).

MAZE PASSAGES

These include a variety of passages from diverse texts. The passages begin with a complete sentence. The rest of the sentences have the seventh word replaced with a word choice. The word choice option includes three choices: the correct word and two distractors. The distractors must be within one letter in length of the correct word and cannot place high demands on comprehension. Nevertheless, students have to be monitoring comprehension in order to select the correct word. Students have three minutes to read each passage. They read two passages at each benchmark assessment and the two scores are averaged. A chart similar to that developed for the oral reading fluency measure is used to determine the level of instruction indicated by the score on the maze measure. The maze measure taps fluency skills, comprehension and vocabulary and the measure is group administered (Florida Center for Reading Research, 2007).

CURRICULUM-BASED VOCABULARY MEASURE

Another assessment tool for progress monitoring for adolescents is a vocabulary curriculum-based measure developed at the University of Minnesota (Espin *et al.*, 2001, 2005). Content classroom teachers select the vocabulary terms for this measure since it is important that the vocabulary reflect the actual curriculum being taught. The procedures for developing vocabulary probes are as follows:

1. Teachers develop a pool of key vocabulary terms from the content they are teaching. They can select from content over the year or during a semester. These terms can be selected from textbooks, teacher notes and lectures, or both.
2. Definitions for each term need to be developed. The definitions need to be short and the easiest method is to use the glossary in the textbook. Try to limit the definition to fifteen words or less.
3. Create weekly measures by randomly selecting twenty terms and definitions from the item pool already developed. Also select two definitions that do not match any of the terms. Each probe will have a total of twenty terms and twenty-two definitions.

One suggestion is to write each vocabulary term on the front of an index card with the definition on the back of the card. Shuffle all the cards and place the terms on the left and the definitions in random order on the right. Number the terms and leave a blank space by each term. Put letters by each definition. The students write the letter for the corresponding definition in the blank next to each term (from www.teachingld.org/expert_connection/).

Scientifically Based Reading Interventions: Examples of Evidence-based Approaches

The school must also search for and use an evidenced-based program or approach that meets the idiosyncratic nature of the particular school. Scientifically based reading intervention aimed at building skills across content areas undergirds the response to intervention model. Evidence-based approaches should include the following elements to meet the instructional needs of adolescents who are reading below grade level.

1. Motivation to read.
2. Decoding skills and fluency.
3. Language comprehension skills including linguistic knowledge, morphemic, semantic, and syntactic knowledge.

4. Text comprehension skills including skills that teach students how to activate prior knowledge and engage with a variety of types of text (Diamond, 2004).

Content classes may address the need to motivate students, but it is unlikely that they provide the skill support many students need in phonics, fluency, vocabulary, and comprehension. In the elementary grades, these skills are addressed systematically and explicitly in effective core reading programs. However, core reading programs in secondary schools are rarely implemented outside of special education classes. A majority of struggling adolescent readers are not in special education and they are expected to be able to read and understand text across the content areas. Thus, reading support for these students requires a much more flexible and generalizable approach. The following programs have been implemented with success in both special education and general education classrooms and are based upon scientific research findings.

STRATEGIC READING MODEL (JOHNS HOPKINS UNIVERSITY, 2001)

This ninth grade curriculum is designed for students who are reading at least two grade levels below expectancy. It includes a 90-minute schedule geared to provide students with many opportunities to engage in reading texts of all types. The emphasis is on teaching specific strategies that support comprehension by providing the following opportunities.

1. Multiple chances to read text that is written at their difficulty level.
2. An instructional model that includes systematic instruction in strategies and skills and engages students in meaningful conversations about what they read.
3. A classroom that is filled with print materials that are organized for accessibility by students.
4. Ongoing assessment of student performance.

Strategic reading is included in the Talent Development High Schools, a project developed by Johns Hopkins University. More information on this model can be found at www.csos.jhu.edu/tdhs/pdf/SR_Awareness Brochure.pdf.

STRATEGIC INSTRUCTION MODEL (DESHLER, UNIVERSITY OF KANSAS)

The strategic instruction model developed by the University of Kansas is designed to support low-achieving adolescents by providing teachers with interventions that are presented in a "learner friendly" fashion and provide students with the skills and strategies they need to learn the content. The strategic instruction model addresses the challenge of linking core content courses with literacy instruction and suggests that secondary schools shift from a focus on covering content to one of promoting literacy by focusing on critical content with skills and strategies embedded naturally during instruction. While secondary teachers may question whether their responsibility includes improving the literacy skills of their students, they are responsible for aligning the curriculum with standards and then ensuring that their students meet those standards. The content curriculum in middle and high schools is where students apply their literacy skills and strategies and they need opportunities to practice these skills across their courses. This integration of content course curriculum with literacy instruction requires powerful professional development and allocation of sufficient resources.

More about the strategic instruction model can be found at www.ku-crl.org/sim/index.html.

SRA-McGraw Hill (1999) Corrective Reading

SRA-McGraw Hill (1999) Corrective Reading is a comprehensive intervention program for students in grades four to twelve who read one or more years below grade level. The goals of the program are to increase decoding skills, develop reading fluency, and build comprehension skills. The program can be implemented in small groups or in a whole class format. The two focused intervention strands are decoding and comprehension. A review of the program can be found at the Florida Center for Reading Research website at www.fcrr.org and at the SRA website at www. sraonline.com/di_home.html.

Language! (Greene, 2000)

Language! (Greene, 2000) is a comprehensive literacy curriculum that integrates writing, reading, spelling and other literacy related skills. This program is designed for students who are performing at least two years below grade expectancy. More specifically, *Language!* is for students who would benefit from a structured language curriculum. The program is highly individualized and can be taught in flexible, small instructional groups. There are three levels of the curriculum and each level takes approximately one year. More information is available at the following websites: www.fcrr.org/fcrrreports/PDF/Language.pdf or www.language-usa.net.

While traditional interventions at the secondary level have focused primarily on comprehension skills, they have often fallen short of expectations because the short-term gains from these interventions did not often transfer (Kulik *et al.*, 1990). Thus, there are new efforts to broaden the focus and content of secondary literacy interventions so that they include more than simple comprehension skills.

Instructional decisions require schoolwide commitment and a coordinated data system. It is important that school administrators consider who will coordinate the schoolwide screening and progress monitoring and how the results can quickly be shared with teachers. Further, these data can provide important school-level information such as progress toward meeting annual yearly progress goals and the effects of the literacy interventions in place. The benchmark scores for the literacy measures selected need to be understood and valued by the teachers in order to be useful in changing practice. Building capacity at the school and district level requires thoughtful and comprehensive professional development for teachers, staff, and administrators.

An Example of How Response to Intervention Might Work

In Lincoln High School, a committee was formed to examine the research on reading programs that are most effective for struggling students. This committee met with all teachers and administrators to provide a summary of their findings and recommendations for a new schoolwide intervention/support program for struggling readers. The faculty then selected a response to intervention team with a designated data coordinator and they began the response to intervention process by screening all students using a reading maze screening measure in order to determine which students were at risk for reading failure. Departments met and decided to restructure classes in order that an additional strategic reading course could be added to the schedule for those students who were at the 20 percent point or below on the maze measure. In that class, students were taught to read using *Corrective Reading* (SRA-McGraw Hill, 1999) and their progress was monitored weekly. Students scoring between the 20 percent point and the 35 percent point were provided a class in strategic reading in which they were taught strategies such as those in the strategic instruction model (University of Kansas, 2004).

All teachers in the content classes agreed to use a content enhancement routine (Bulgren *et al.*, 2007) to scaffold learning so that all students were taught how to utilize the strategy. These changes to schedule and to how courses are taught required substantial interdepartmental communication and collaboration as well as professional development for teachers and administrators in the new strategies and programs to be implemented and in how to effectively use the data from assessments and the decision rules in the response to intervention model.

Professional Development and Resource Needs for Response to Intervention Implementation

The content of professional development for teachers in implementing literacy instruction into all content area courses is of paramount importance. It must provide teachers with a systematic and connected approach to addressing the literacy needs of struggling adolescents, while maintaining the rigor and challenge that more skilled learners require. There needs to be cross-content area consensus regarding the literacy strategies that are taught in all classrooms and these strategies must be flexible enough to be relevant to all content area classes. There also must be common expectations for student performance and an understanding of how to use the data to make decisions about how much intervention to provide, for how long, and to whom. All of these decisions require that secondary teachers develop unique expertise in the response to intervention model in order that the process is consistently and powerfully implemented across the curriculum. Powerful professional development is a key to providing the in-depth knowledge and skills to ensure that interventions will result in substantive improvements in student learning. One program that exemplifies the rich and substantive knowledge and skills so important for teaching students the critical skills they need to be successful readers is *Language Essentials for Teachers of Reading and Spelling* (Moats, 2003).

Finally, considerable time must be allocated to this effort and the school and district must find ways to provide support for teachers as they begin the process of implementing literacy interventions across the curriculum. Over time, teacher leaders will take charge of the response to intervention implementation, but initially, experts will need to provide the core content and guide the implementation process.

Response to Intervention: Building Capacity to Meet the Needs of All Students

With its emphasis on data-driven decisions and powerful research-based interventions, response to intervention can provide an instructional model that supports both students and teachers in a coherent and effective manner. The model is flexible so that students can move in and out of tiers according to their needs. Students see the evidence of their skill improvement by being directly involved in their own progress monitoring so that motivation is a key component of their intervention.

The response to intervention model provides an opportunity to provide systematic reading support for all adolescents. Their need has never been greater and now, more than ever, there are resources and opportunities to meet the challenge of improving the reading skills of all students.

Questions

1. What would be the first steps to implementing response to intervention in your school? Jot down the barriers on one side of your paper and then on the other side the builders. Discuss in small cooperative groups. Decide on one barrier and then in your small group jot down the steps to overcome the barrier.

2. Review the five components of the response to intervention model and then using Table 9.2 begin to address the instructional and infrastructure changes that you might make at your respective secondary school. Write a one-page summary of what you are currently doing at your school site and the areas that need to be addressed to make response to intervention a reality at your school.

3. The process of screening students and monitoring the progress of those identified at risk is important in developing an effective response to intervention model. Consider the following steps to implementing a schoolwide screening process and explain how you would implement them in your school. Who would be responsible for determining the process of screening and progress monitoring? How would you organize the steps (e.g. by grade level, by content area, by program)?

    (i)   selecting appropriate instruments
    (ii) determining who is responsible for managing the data
    (iii) identifying students who are at risk based upon screening results
    (iv) grouping students and determining appropriate interventions based upon the screening data
    (v)   providing teachers with the skills to monitor the progress of students receiving interventions.

4. As you begin the process of implementing a response to intervention approach to supporting students, describe the current procedures at your school for identifying students needing reading interventions. Consider the following questions:

    (i)   How are students placed in reading intervention classes in your school now? Is there a problem-solving procedure being implemented?
    (ii) How is their progress monitored?
    (iii) What are the performance benchmarks that are tied to schoolwide reading expectations for all students?

    How could a response to intervention model at your school improve the learning outcomes for a greater number of students who are struggling in reading?

Website Resources

www.teachingld.org/expert_connection/
www.fcrr.org/fcrrreports/PDF/Language.pdf
www.language-usa.net

References

Biancarosa, G. & Snow, C. D. (2004). *Reading next – A vision for action and research in middle and high school literacy (A report from Carnegie Corporation of New York).* New York: Alliance for Excellent Education.

Bulgren, J., Deshler, D. D., & Lenz, K. B. (2007). Engaging adolescents with LD in higher order thinking about history concepts using integrated content enhancement routines. *Journal of Learning Disabilities, 40* (2), 121–133.

Catone, W. V. & Brady, S. A. (2005). The inadequacy of Individual Education Program (IEP) goals for high school students with word level reading difficulties. *Annals of Dyslexia, Vol. 55* (1), 53–78.

Diamond, L. (2004). Implementing and sustaining a middle and high school reading and intervention program. Consortium on Reading Excellence, Institute for Education Reform. Sacramento, CA: California State University.

Espin, C. A., Busch, T. W., & Shin, J. (2001). Curriculum-based measurement in the content areas: Validity of vocabulary-matching as an indicator of performance in social studies. *Learning Disabilities Research and Practice, 16* (3), 142–151.

Espin, C. A., Shin, J. & Busch, T. W. (2005). Curriculum-based measurement in the content areas: Vocabulary matching as an indicator of progress in social studies learning. *Journal of Learning Disabilities, 38* (4), 353–363.

Florida Center for Reading Research (2007). Retrieved on August 28, 2007 from www.fcrr.org/ assessmentMiddleHighSchool.htm.

Fuchs, D. & Fuchs, L. S. (2006). Introduction to responsiveness-to-intervention: What, why, and how valid is it? *Reading Research Quarterly, 41,* 92–99.

Greene, J. F. (2000). *Language!* Longmont, CO: Sopris West.

Kulik, C. L., Kulik, J. A., & Bangert-Downs, R. L. (1990). Effectiveness of mastery-learning programs: A meta-analysis. *Review of Educational Research, 60* (2), 265–299.

Moats, L. C. (2003). *Language Essentials for Teachers of Reading and Spelling.* Longmont, CO: Sopris West.

National Association of State Directors of Special Education (2005). *Response to intervention: Policy considerations and implementation.* Alexandria, VA: National Association of State Directors of Special Education.

National Reading Panel (2000). *Report of the National Reading Panel. Teaching children to read: An evidence-based assessment of the scientific research literature on reading and its implications for reading instruction* (NIH Publication No. 00-4754). Washington, DC: U.S. Government Printing Office.

SRA-McGraw Hill (1999). *Corrective reading.* New York: SRA-McGraw Hill.

Sedita, J. (2004). *Middle and high school reading achievement: A School-wide approach.* Retrieved November 15, 2006: www.seditalearning.com.

Special Edge (2007). Homegrown efforts prefigure national trends. Sonoma, CA: Special Edge.

Torgesen, J. K. (2006, August). *Improving Adolescent Literacy: Suggestions from Research.* Presented to the Florida Adolescent Literacy Work Group, Orlando.

U.S. Department of Education (2002). No Child Left Behind Act of 2002.

CHAPTER 10

Action Planning for Struggling Students to Improve Literacy and Content Area Achievement

LINDA CARNINE AND BONNIE GROSSEN

Introduction

If politicians could see inside the walls of our middle and high schools across America, they would be so alarmed that immediately they would make education the top national priority. In the large inner-city schools, politicians would see a majority of students who are so weak in basic skills that they cannot write a complete sentence, cannot spell correctly half the words they write, cannot read above a third grade level, and do not know that one-half is 50 percent. For these reasons in part, one-third of our nation's students drop out before completing high school (Bridgeland *et al.*, 2006).

This is not a recent problem. Since 1980 the National Assessment of Educational Progress Long-Term Trend reading data has remained relatively constant, with approximately 70 percent of students in grades four and eight performing below proficient levels. National Assessment of Educational Progress 2003 statistics indicated that big cities in these states experience failure rates of 57–73 percent for Blacks and 53–71 percent for Hispanics at fourth grade, dropping to 44–59 percent for Blacks and 43–59 percent for Hispanics at eighth grade (National Assessment of Educational Progress, 1999; National Center for Education Statistics, 2003). The current national high school graduation rate is 70 percent (Greene *et al.*, 2006). High school graduation rates are lower than 50 percent for African-Americans and Hispanics and as low as 28 percent in Cleveland City (Greene, 2002).

Failure is concentrated among students living in poverty. One-half of the children in our most populated states (California, Texas, Florida, and New York) live in poverty and, by the year 2010, one-third of the nation's children will be living in these states (Hodgkinson, 1992). This means that, if the pattern of failure among students living in poverty does not change, more than the current 30 percent of our nation's children will be leaving school without a high school diploma and, worse, without the basic skills to work at McDonalds. These high numbers of poorly educated youths will have a detrimental impact on the nation's economy and, ultimately, on our status as a world power. The picture of our future created by a close look inside our secondary schools would be one of large numbers of young adults so poorly educated and with such poor work habits, they are nearly unemployable.

As large numbers of students fail to thrive academically in our public schools and drop out or muddle along with minimal literacy skills, we pay for the social consequences of these students' illiteracy. This illiteracy accounts for the following: 75 percent of the unemployed, 85 percent of juveniles who appear in court, 60 percent of prison inmates, 40 percent of minority young people, and 33 percent of mothers receiving some kind of welfare (Orton Dyslexia Society, cited in Adams, 1990).

Research work conducted over the last 30 years has demonstrated that children of poverty do not have to fail. The direct instruction model can make a dramatic difference. Elementary children from high-poverty areas in the inner cities can perform above the 50th percentile (e.g. over twenty elementary schools in Houston, City Springs Elementary and other schools in inner-city Baltimore). Low-performing middle schools serving high-poverty communities can cut their bottom quartile by one-third to one-half each year (e.g. Santa Barbara County, Sacramento County, Riverside County, Los Angeles County, Ventura County, Imperial Valley, and the Bay area in California) (see Grossen, 2002a, 2004).

However, setting up a low-performing school for a turnaround is not simple. A school with 40–60 percent of its students performing more than two years below grade level in the far below basic or below basic performance bands must plan on a drastic restructuring of the daily schedule. Structuring the school environment for success, scheduling students into curriculum appropriate for their needs, securing training and support for teaching, using data to monitor progress, and identifying problems are all challenging parts of a successful turnaround.

Studies of successful literacy interventions have identified five pillars of successful early intervention with high-risk populations.

1. Providing leadership with focus.
2. Using literacy interventions with scientific evidence of effectiveness.

3. Scheduling enough instructional time and intensity to get the job done in a timely manner.
4. Providing sufficient high-quality professional development to ensure implementation fidelity.
5. Making data-based decisions using efficient assessment and ongoing progress monitoring tools (Crawford and Torgesen, 2006).

This chapter directly addresses the five pillars so needed to successfully implement a quality reading and literacy program at the secondary level. By providing guidelines for schools' action planning improved literacy outcomes and success in content area instruction are realizable. However, it must be noted that key administrators must determine a clear course of action and find a match between evidence-based programs, professional development, and the ongoing needs of the school. This chapter encourages secondary school leaders to adopt a model and, in this case, *The REACH System*, to support the five pillars of successful implementation for young people at risk of school failure. The chapter argues for direct instruction and related programs and practices that are (i) designed to raise literacy levels of struggling students (including special education and English-language learing), and (ii) based on scientific reading research. Many of these programs are captured in *The REACH System*, which describes different levels of instructional intensity designed to meet a wide range of struggling students' needs, i.e. interventions differ depending on how far below grade level students are performing. For students near grade level, content area recommendations are included using the big idea analysis and other strategies to enhance content area access for struggling students. The chapter also includes descriptions of assessment tools for placement, progress monitoring, and continued action planning with focus and prioritization.

Leadership

Strong, visionary, focused instructional leadership is quintessentially critical for schools to accomplish and sustain a turnaround in student performance. The building principal remains the critical leader in empowering staff to improve academic outcomes for students. Without a strong leader, schools may see spurts in academic gains, but they quickly vanish. When building leadership is frequently changed, a new principal every year or two, a school typically loses its focus and academic practices drift back to "business as usual" with high proportions of students failing to meet standards or make substantive progress. So far, no reports of sustained educational improvements exist without strong leadership driving the change.

The instructional leader, whether it is the principal, assistant principal or designee, needs to know how to:

- establish a vision with buy-in from staff to drastically improve student literacy;
- interpret and communicate about the student performance data for the school (using disaggregated data to target different groups of students);
- identify with staff and acquire in a timely manner necessary literacy curriculum that has a research base or at least incorporates research-based elements;
- provide staff with relevant and timely professional development experiences to allow them to effectively deliver the instruction;
- allocate enough time and staffing necessary to bring students somewhat and significantly below grade level to grade level literacy performance;
- orchestrate a schoolwide positive behavioral support system;
- monitor student progress in their literacy skill development and adjust the school program if certain individuals or groups of students are not making progress.

Effective change begins with identifying and acknowledging that there is a problem. In the not-so-distant past, when no statewide tests identified failure among vulnerable subgroups, schools could ignore the fact that their African-American students were not learning as much as their White students. The old paradigm where reading inputs were more standard and reading outcomes allowed to vary is being replaced with a new paradigm where inputs vary and outcomes are more standard (Paine, 2005). The standards and accountability movement with high-stakes testing, publicized school report cards, comparisons of schools with similar demographics, and disaggregated data by student subgroups have all helped schools see exactly where their problems lie.

Problems without workable solutions will not motivate change. Hand in hand with acknowledging a student-performance problem is acknowledging that effective, manageable solutions exist for solving the problem. A firm belief that students do not have to fail and that schools and teachers can make the difference is crucial to establishing a vision of what can be accomplished with a school's struggling students.

Many building leaders have found it useful to locate and share evidence from effective interventions where schools have "beat the odds" by bringing high numbers of struggling students to near grade-level performance in a relatively short amount of time. Often school staff will try to explain away strong results with comments such as "they do not have as many __type of students or the socioeconomic status of their students is much higher than ours." Therefore finding schools with the same or similar demographics that have dramatically improved student performance is the first step in creating a vision that "it can be done." Allowing staff to visit comparable schools, talk to their staff, and then return to share ideas and plan together is key to transforming "it can be done" into "we can do it."

The building leader must keep the discussion focused on using research-based interventions to develop a plan. The plan for making fluent readers out of struggling students will include using research-based literacy interventions, scheduling enough time and differentiated grouping, providing high-quality professional development, and making data-based decisions. (See the Appendix for leadership resources, tips on communication, dealing with resistant teachers, etc.)

Once teachers are on board with plans, the leader must be willing to commit the time and resources needed to follow through in implementing the interventions. This means stepping outside of the typical school-scheduling box and creatively addressing regular academic requirements, so that more time and staffing can be devoted to addressing the instructional needs of the most needy students.

Fundamental to good leadership is providing positive feedback and encouragement, giving reassurance and credit to all. The building leader needs to constantly acknowledge even the smallest accomplishment of the staff in the effort to improve academic success for struggling students. Celebrations of success are part of the necessary diet of academic improvement efforts, which will starve and die out without them. The school leader is the key to making this happen.

Another ingredient in sustained academic improvements is data-driven decision making. Granted, many educators are responding to new accountability requirements with vacuous increases in testing just for testing's sake, without using the data to adjust instruction. But where struggling students are making improvements, leaders and teacher teams are looking at the progress data to regroup students and modify interventions based on what the student progress monitoring information implies. This process of data-driven academic decision making is captured in what the authors will call the action planning process.

Most U.S. schools have been unwilling or unable to commit the necessary resources that are needed to ensure success for struggling students. Struggling students will make no long-term progress without intensive interventions using instructional materials that demonstrate effectiveness through scientific research. Nonetheless, a growing body of research suggests that all but a very small percentage of students can be taught functional literacy (National Institute of Child Health and Human Development, 2000; Torgesen, 2002; Shaywitz, 2003; McCardle and Chhabra, 2004).

Selection of Evidence-based Interventions

Making fluent readers out of struggling adolescent readers takes about five times the effort that it takes to teach a beginning reader to read, but *it can be done.* Giving each citizen the ability to read is more important than any other learning we can provide. Doing so means that the school must be willing to dedicate significant time, energy, and focus to making fluent readers out of struggling readers. One often hears among secondary educators that "remedial education does not work." If it has not worked it is because it has been poorly designed, poorly delivered, and has received too little focus (i.e. treated as unimportant). Catching adolescent struggling readers up requires a coordinated, systematic approach that hinges on the effective use of evidence-based interventions. Evidence-based interventions might be more easily accepted in the field if practitioners more clearly understood what good reading requires.

The Requirements for Good Reading

To make a reader out of a struggling reader, one must appreciate what good reading requires of the reader. Reading is a multifaceted skill involving highly accurate decoding, language comprehension, fluency, and interest and motivation.

Decoding

One cannot be a good reader unless one can read with a very high level of accuracy, at least 98 percent. For example, below is a passage representing the information a reader would get with 85 percent decoding accuracy, generally accepted as an adequate level of performance.

> He had never seen dogs fight as these w__ish c___ f___t, and his
> first ex_____ t____t him an unf_____able l____n. It is true,
> it was a vi____ ex_____, else he would not have lived to
> pr_____it by it. Curly was the v_____. They were camped near
> the log store, where she, in her friend__ way, made ad_____ to
> a husky dog the size of a full-_____ wolf, th____ not half so large
> as _he. __ere was no w____ing, only a leap in like a flash, a
> met____ clip of teeth, a leap out equal__ swift, and Curly's face
> was ripped open from eye to jaw.

It was the wolf manner of fight___, to st___ and leap away; but there was more to it than this. Th__ or forty huskies ran _o the spot and not com_____d that s_____t circle. But did not com_____d that s_____t in_____, not the e___ way with which they were licking their chops. Curly rushed her ant_____, who struck again and leaped aside. He met her next rush with his chest, in a p_____ fash___ that tum__ed her off her feet. She never re_____ed them. This was ___at the on_____ing huskies had w_____ for.

Clearly, comprehension presents a serious problem for a reader with only 85 percent accuracy. A fluent reader with good comprehension must read with almost perfect decoding accuracy. If a reader makes only one or two errors, those errors will often involve less frequent words that are critical to the meaning of the text.

Language Comprehension

One cannot be a good reader unless one also has the language skills to understand the words used in the text. This can present a special problem for English-language learners and for students with limited vocabulary. Language development and background knowledge will limit the extent that a reader is capable of comprehension.

Fluency

Often times a student with good language skills and acceptable accuracy will still have difficulty with reading comprehension. This can be the case with a reader who does not decode with automaticity. The reader without automaticity uses his/her mental space to figure out the words, so that s/he has no mental space left for very much comprehension. The solution for this student is to build automaticity in reading so that no mental space is required for the decoding task. It is similar to driving a car. When one first learns to drive a car, all one's mental space is occupied with managing the driving process. For an experienced driver, these skills are largely automatic in many contexts and a driver has time to have a conversation with a passenger or let their mind wander to things other than the driving process. For a budding reader, a similar thing happens. When the decoding process becomes automatic, the reader's mind can wander from decoding to understanding the text. The reader's mind can also wander other places.

Interest and Motivation

When a simple lack of concentration on the meaning of the passage is the only problem a reader has, s/he is no longer a struggling reader. At this point, interest and motivation are major determiners of good reading and these can be the problems of any reader.

Additional Problems Presented by Older Struggling Readers

Most commonly, struggling readers have developed many bad decoding habits that require extra instructional time to unlearn. For example, many struggling readers have a habit of guessing a word based on only a couple of the letters in the word, instead of seeing all the letters in left-to-right order. Or they may read and reread phrases, guessing a word, coming back to correct the word based on context, and, finally, reading with considerably less than 98 percent accuracy.

Evidence: Is There a Pay-off?

Francis *et al.* (1996) found that 74 percent of children identified as disabled readers in grade three remain disabled readers in grade nine. One possible explanation for this permanence of reading disabilities is that most schools do not provide the kind of instruction struggling readers need to become good readers.

In middle schools serving grades seven and eight, we have brought all subgroups, including students with disabilities, to meet the annual yearly progress (AYP) goals of 2006. Will Rogers Middle School in Lawndale, CA, raised proficiency levels for challenging subgroups (students with disabilities, African-Americans, and Hispanics) by 50–350 percent, but failed to meet proficiency goals by half a percentage point. Another school, after implementing *The REACH System*, failed to meet their AYP because of only one subgroup, English-language learners. This school followed the common recommendation to place only English-language learners scoring level three or higher on the California English Language Development Test and scoring far below basic or below basic on the California Standards Test into the Direct Instruction intervention. The English-language learner students receiving Direct Instruction made substantial gains: 77 percent of the students scoring far below basic moved up at least one achievement level, while only 53 percent of the students in the standard English-language learners program moved out of the far below basic category.

With few exceptions, failing middle schools in California under program improvement and state takeover have met their AYP goals for standards-based assessments as set forth by No Child Left Behind after years of frustration and failure. In our work with struggling high school students in San Francisco, we have been able to turn a 44 percent pass rate on the California High School Exit Examination into an 85 percent pass rate through intensive, focused intervention that requires 150–250 hours.

To achieve these outcomes, we use *The REACH System*, a specific comprehensive system of professional development, curriculum, and instruction specially designed to close the educational gaps faced by adolescent at-risk students.

The REACH System

The REACH System addresses typical program limitations by providing explicit, systematic instruction built around three previously published programs: *Corrective Reading, Spelling Through Morphographs,* and *Reasoning and Writing.* These three instructional program series are combined to provide sufficient literacy instruction (at least two to three periods per day) to reverse the failure trajectory of struggling readers. These series of programs are both research based and research validated (see Grossen (1996) for more information about the steps in research validation). Each program incorporates the principles of instructional design that have been shown to meet the needs of students with diverse characteristics (Kame'enui and Carnine 2001) and has been further validated with controlled experimental studies evaluating the programs' effects on student achievement. Highlights from these studies follow.

The *Corrective Reading Program* (Engelmann *et al.*, in press a, b) was designed to remediate basic literacy skills for older struggling readers. The original decoding track published in 1974 (Engelmann *et al.*, in press a) was followed by a comprehension track (Engelmann *et al.*, in press b) several years later. The *Corrective Reading Program* is a direct instruction program that has over 30 years of data indicating that it can be used to accelerate the reading acquisition of older students with reading problems. These studies generally show that, when implemented consistently (at least four days a week) by well-trained teachers, the growth rate in reading increases to two or three times the normal rate, making it possible for many students to catch up in one year of instruction (see Grossen (1988) for a review of the research).

This pattern of effectiveness has been replicated with remedial readers in England, Australia, and North America (Maggs and Murdoch, 1979; Gregory *et al.*, 1982; Campbell, 1988; Clunies-Ross, 1990; Vitale *et al.*, 1993; Hempenstall, 2001), with students with limited English (Gersten *et al.*, 1983; Grossen, 2002a, 2004), non-categorical implementations with special education and regular education struggling readers (Lee County School District, 1977; Holdsworth, 1984–1985; Kasendorf and McQuaid, 1987; Sommers, 1991, 1995; Ross, 1998; Grossen *et al.*, 2000; Grossen 2002a, 2004), and in special education classes (Thorne, 1978; Polloway *et al.*, 1986; Arthur, 1988; Edlund and Ogle, 1988; Glang *et al.*, 1991; Thomson, 1992).

The *Corrective Reading Program* was designed specifically for older non-reading or struggling readers, covering the five critical elements of initial reading instruction (i.e. phonemic awareness, phonics, vocabulary, fluency, and comprehension), as well as addressing other deficits of struggling readers. In the initial levels of the decoding strand, students are taught phonemic awareness and phonics skills, as well as the vocabulary necessary to follow directions and understand what they read.

The *Corrective Reading Program* sound–symbol system, mastery of which is the key to fluent reading, includes only fifty-seven sound–symbol relationships, substantially fewer sound–symbols than the Orton–Gillingham system. The sounds students learn for the symbols were analyzed for maximum generalizability, so that students are able to read more by learning fewer rules. For example, the sound taught for the letter y is "yee," which works both at the beginning and end of words: yellow (yee-ellow) and puppy (pupp-yee). And it works in the middle of words: gym (g-yee-m). For many words the sound–symbol system produces close approximations to the real word. Students learn to use context to "make it a real word" for correct word identification.

Spelling Through Morphographs (Engelmann and Dixon, 2007) complements the decoding instruction in the *Corrective Reading Program* with a carefully engineered program for encoding instruction. *Spelling Through Morphographs* teaches a morphemic analysis for understanding meaning and spelling words. Students learn 600 basic morphemes and three major rules for combining them (when to drop the e, when to double the consonant, and when to change y to i). With these tools students can spell 12,000 words and have a general strategy for getting meaning from the words by analyzing the Latin-based components.

Fluency building receives heavy emphasis in the decoding strand after students have the gained necessary skills accurately to read words in both lists and contextual passages. Fluent word identification is not the only consideration. The comprehension strand in the *Corrective Reading Program* was designed to teach students critical thinking skills (e.g. analogies and inductive and deductive reasoning) and content knowledge (e.g. systems knowledge applied to body systems and economics). In addition, the *Reasoning and Writing* programs, particularly levels E and F, were designed to teach grade-level reasoning and writing skills and parts of speech and usage content in a manner that enables at-risk middle school students, who normally do not experience success in more cognitively complex content, also to succeed.

Reasoning & Writing E & F (Engelmann and Grossen, 2001) teaches students writing skills beginning with narrative writing, then moving into expository, particularly persuasive, and critique writing. Students learn critical reasoning skills, such as identifying inconsistencies and contradictions and learn to write critiques of false-cause arguments, arguments with misleading claims, arguments lacking specificity, and so on. Students also learn to write sophisticated compare-and-contrast essays.

The teaching strategies used in *Reasoning & Writing E & F* (Engelmann and Grossen, 2001) were experimentally tested before the program was published. These innovative strategies demonstrated powerful effects in bridging the gap between the performance of low-achieving students and high- or normally achieving students in cognitively complex content.

1. On a variety of measures of argument construction and critiquing, high school students with learning disabilities scored as high as high school students in an honors English class and higher than college students enrolled in a teacher certification program (Grossen and Carnine, 1990).

2. In constructing arguments, high school students with disabilities scored significantly higher than college students enrolled in a teacher certification program and scored at the same level as a group of college students enrolled in a logic class (Collins and Carnine, 1988).

The above studies represent controlled, experimental research using random assignment of students to control and treatment groups. Well-trained teachers in smaller scale, tightly controlled settings delivered the instruction with high fidelity. More recently studies have demonstrated how this level of fidelity in implementation could be maintained when bringing the instruction to scale in schoolwide implementations in high-need schools (Grossen *et al.*, 2000; Grossen, 2002a, 2004). The Goethe Middle School Research Project was the first step in bringing the middle school direct instruction research to scale in a replicable Direct Instruction Model for Secondary Schools. *The REACH System* (Grossen, 2002b) represents the knowledge base developed from the Goethe Research Project (Grossen *et al.*, 2000) and the knowledge base from the subsequent replications —failures and successes—that have also been published (Grossen, 2002a, 2004). (See www.higherscores.org for further details of *The REACH System*.)

General Characteristics of an Effective Intervention

Practice will not improve reading for a student who makes lots of errors in decoding accuracy. The poor decoder will just continue to guess and reread in all reading contexts. To improve reading, this struggling reader needs constant error correction feedback. When this reader makes a lot of errors, constant correction feedback can be irritating, punishing, unmanageable, and, ultimately, unproductive. So the struggling reader who makes lots of errors also needs a controlled text so that the error rate is reduced. Furthermore, the text needs to be controlled so that the struggling reader can focus on a manageable subset of the types of decoding errors s/he makes and get the needed practice to unlearn the bad habit of guessing.

In a typical middle school grade-level passage, the struggling reader might make errors on forty-seven different letter combinations and error types. A struggling reader will not remember any of the information presented in so many corrections occurring in random order. But if the passage is *controlled*, as in the *Corrective Reading Program*, so that only three types of errors could potentially occur, then the struggling reader might begin to learn to avoid making this error through intensive, focused practice. Without a controlled learning environment, the chances for the struggling reader to overcome the reading problem are quite slim.

A second feature of the controlled text is that it must be *unpredictable*. Struggling readers rely more on the context to figure out words, thus they reread a great deal, as they study the context. Initially to teach them to rely on the letters in the word, the text should be unpredictable—with very few context clues. If context will not work, the reader must start depending more on the letters in the words.

Below is a sample text that controls the error types that can occur and presents unpredictable text. The error type that is controlled here is the confusion of short and long sound of "o" based on the presence of a double or single consonant and/or the presence of a silent "e" at the end of a word: Tom was moping all day about mopping the slop on the slope. Or in the following example, the controlled error type is the pronunciation of the letters "ow": How do you know who made the tower horn blow. The following passage would be for struggling readers who are firm on all their consonant sounds, but have not mastered all vowel digraphs. This passage focuses on the "ai" digraph and r-controlled vowels:

> Bert had a job in a sailing shop. He was a clerk and he didn't like his job. Every day without fail, he went to the shop and waited for people to buy things. Then people came to the shop. They picked up paint and nails and containers for bailing. But every day Bert said to himself, "I'm tired of this job."

With an intensive focus on decoding using appropriately controlled text aligned to the level and the difficulties that the struggling reader experiences, struggling readers can become fluent readers. The learning curve will look something like the one in Figure 10.1.

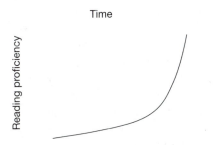

Figure 10.1 Improvement in reading proficiency over time

Initially, progress may seem slow, but as students begin to correct many of their problems, progress accelerates. It may take a semester to move a student from approximately first grade reading to second grade reading and another semester to move them from second grade reading to fourth grade reading and another semester to move them from fourth grade reading to seventh grade reading.

The key to success in all content areas beyond the necessary decoding skills, comprehension skills, and basic understanding of syntactic structures in English is vocabulary. Students will have mastered considerable vocabulary skills upon completion of *The REACH System*. This includes instruction in many tier two words, those occurring with moderate frequency (Beck *et al.*, 2002). These are systematically and explicitly introduced and reviewed in the contextual passages in the decoding track of the *Corrective Reading Program*. Students learn a dozen or more high-frequency affixes such as re, pre, un, ly, ness. Students also are taught an explicit strategy for figuring out multisyllabic words with ample practice in the strategy's use.

In decoding B2 and C particularly succinct, pithy definitions are pre-taught for words students will then read in narrative and expository passages. Students then practice substituting the new word in sentences containing the definition. For example, "Roamed is another word for wandered. Everybody, what's another way of saying 'He wandered around the parking lot'?"; "Taut means stretched tight. Everybody, what's another way of saying 'The sail was stretched tight'?". This same technique is used in the comprehension track level A, where many more high-utility words are introduced. Students are given short, kid-friendly definitions and then an example of the word's use in context. Students then practice substituting the word in a sentence.

In the comprehension level B program at least thirty to forty high-utility word families are introduced. The word family includes the verb, noun, and adjective, for example "construct," "construction," and "constructive."

Once students have learned the word family they use the word family in a wide variety of contextual activities. Every word family that is introduced repeats in exercises throughout the program's duration. All introduced words are presented in at least three more contexts. This cumulative review builds the long-term retention, as the word is committed to "deep understanding."

In the comprehension C program new vocabulary words are clustered in "memory sentences," a sentence that students memorize and utilize in distributed practice. For example, "By hesitating she lost her opportunity" is a memory sentence for recalling the meaning of *hesitate* and *opportunity*. This clustering of words with attached sentiment is a useful strategy for vocabulary retention highlighted by Beck *et al.* (2002) in *Bringing Words to Life*. The *REACH System* vocabulary instruction emphasizes explicit instruction in definitions with extensive practice in a variety of contexts and exercises.

If any additional time is available in the literacy schedule for the significantly below and below grade-level students, we strongly recommend schools use the *REWARDS Plus* (reading excellence: word attack and rate development strategies) and *REWARDS Intermediate* programs as well (Archer *et al.*, 2004). These programs provide students additional instruction on decoding and practicing multisyllabic words in sentences, content area passages and other reading materials.

Master Schedule and Student Placement

Once staff have committed to a specific, research-based intervention model, the next step is to analyze existing student performance data to outline a school plan for improving student performance using that model. Using these data, students will be grouped into three groups: (i) "significantly below grade level," students performing below the fortieth percentile or in the far below basic and below basic performance bands, (ii) "somewhat below level," students performing at the basic level, and (iii) "grade level," students who are performing at the "proficient" or "advanced" level. Student performance on high stakes measures used by the school, such as the Standford Achievement Test Level 10, Iowa Test of Basic Skills, or state tests of standards, will provide the most important evaluation data.

Classify Students Broadly According to Their Needs

Significantly Below Level Students

Students scoring below basic (below approximately the fortieth percentile or far below basic and below basic) on a statewide measure require intensive intervention in language arts in order to be brought to proficient levels in a reasonably short amount of time. Students who are performing significantly below grade level (i.e. more than two years below grade level) need three or four periods dedicated to catching them up. The goal of this intervention is to bring them up to a minimum of sixth grade level performance in no more than two years. This translates into making at least three years of academic growth each year in middle school.

Many far below basic students may have been identified for special education. Unfortunately, special education status has often been license to leave students significantly behind "with an excuse." Studies show that with the appropriate instruction, no more than 2 percent of the total student population should fail to reach average levels of performance due to a real learning disability. All other students should be expected to reach normal levels of literacy performance if given appropriate instruction (Lyon *et al.,,* 2001).

Think of intensive intervention students as if their issues were medical in nature. These students are severely at risk for dying academically. They are hemorrhaging. The school should declare a state of emergency for them.

Somewhat Below Level Students

Students scoring at the "basic" level (approximately the fortieth to forty-ninth percentile) are students who do not require an intensive intervention to be brought to proficient levels, but who could reach proficiency with a more strategic intervention. They have some of the strategies to become successful academically, but lack the mastery to make learning enjoyable, painless. They need medical attention for their broken collar bone and bruises, but they will heal with the right support.

Grade Level and Above Students

Students who are at grade level or above are those performing at a "proficient" or "advanced" level (above the fiftieth percentile) on standardized, norm-referenced measures. They need no medical treatment at the moment, but are exposed to all the germs and accident risks in daily life, so they also need safe, healthy support and nurturance.

Identify Student Placement Needs

Intensive intervention students need opportunities for intensive practice with controlled texts in an environment that provides constant corrective feedback that is not available in traditional middle and high school coursework. These opportunities have to be scheduled separately from the regular school coursework and should occur daily. Because an older struggling reader can perform at a wide range of levels, struggling readers should be placed in instruction that fits with their needs. Individualized instruction can be provided in groups if the students are placement tested and placed accordingly. At the middle and high school level, the authors place students in five different levels for intensive intervention.

Scheduling different levels of reading into the master schedule requires major effort on the part of the school administration. But if instruction does not fit the needs of the student, behavior problems usually occur. Students can become resentful of instruction that is well below their needs or frustrated with instruction that is beyond their ability to perform with success. When students are appropriately placed in reading instruction, we always find that behavior problems decrease as the struggling reader begins to experience success.

Place Students into *The REACH System*

The REACH System, like most intervention programs, has its own program-specific placement tests. Figure 10.2 graphically displays the relationship between *The REACH System* entry points, the program components, and approximate grade level equivalents. Students placing in the lowest level are essentially non-readers. They learn initial reading skills, including phonemic awareness, phonics, decoding, and language/vocabulary development with comprehension. The lowest level students of *The REACH System* are so far behind, they should receive four periods (60 percent) of their school day in language arts courses. Students placing at the second level read and write very poorly, guessing wrong most of the time. Second-level students should receive three periods of literacy instruction to address their deficits. Students placing at the third level need more fluency and comprehension as they improve their decoding, requiring at least two periods in language arts courses. Students placing at the fourth level require more vocabulary and comprehension development as well as decoding accuracy and fluency building. Students placing at the fifth level have no decoding weakness, but need writing development, comprehension and vocabulary building. They need only one additional period of language arts instruction.

Strategic level students can be placed in the fifth level of *The REACH System* without placement testing in the program. These students should receive the same support that students completing *The REACH System* sequence receive. Figure 10.1 shows the schedule for a middle school where 80 percent of the students have been performing significantly below grade level. For the lowest level students, four periods of *The REACH Program* are scheduled. Students who score at the fifth entry point will get *The*

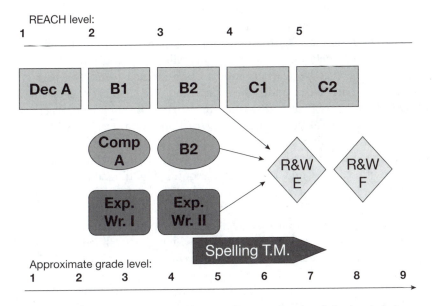

Figure 10.2 Alignment of entry points with program components and grade level equivalent estimates, of *The REACH System*

REACH Program in their regular language arts class. Students entering at the third and fourth entry points get an additional two periods of support in decoding and comprehension (vocabulary development).

A separate literacy intervention may not be necessary for proficient or advanced students. They likely need advanced literacy challenges to maintain their accelerated rate of academic growth. One means for addressing the various literacy levels is through differentiated instruction in an added literacy period. By creating a "zero" period at the beginning of the day, schools have been able to address this need. For students who are proficient/advanced, this can be a creative writing class, advanced novel study, or literature/talented and gifted-like course.

Restructure the School Day

Once a school has administered screening/placement measures and thoroughly analyzed their achievement data, it is time for action planning (Carnine and Silverstein, 2006). Providing more instructional time for the significantly below grade-level students means dropping many electives. Some middle schools have added a zero period for an additional language arts period for all students. If the students are already identified for special education services, they may receive much of this intensive instruction in their special education block classes.

This is not simple to schedule. Schools with larger groups of students in the significantly below grade-level category will require much more school restructuring. Elective teachers need to be retrained to teach a part of the language arts block under the supervision of a language arts teacher. You can anticipate that mathematics, music and PE, and science teachers will typically make outstanding direct instruction reading teachers with adequate initial training and supportive follow-up. Building instructional leaders need to involve the entire staff in collaborative planning for this literacy effort. No Child Left Behind requires highly qualified teachers and defines them as teachers with certification in the areas they teach. Teachers of other subjects can become highly qualified through a district-level training program designed specifically to prepare teachers to teach *The REACH Program.* They can also be paired with highly qualified teachers to make a teaching team, which meets the requirements of No Child Left Behind.

Dedicating instructional time commensurate with students' strengths and weaknesses in language arts is one of the critical pillars of a successful implementation. There are only a few alterable variables available for schools to use for bringing struggling students up to an adequate literacy level: *time,* additional *highly effective instructional materials* increasing response opportunities, i.e. positive instructional interactions (Torgesen, 2005) and *appropriate grouping* at a student's instructional level. Torgesen's (2005) intervention studies indicate that, for many older students with word level reading skills around the thirtieth percentile, a relatively smaller dose of appropriate group instruction can bring their skills in phonemic decoding, word and text reading accuracy, fluency, and comprehension into the solid average range. Yet for many older students with word level reading skills around the tenth percentile, much more intensive instruction involving double and possibly triple dosing each day will be required to bring them to the average range. Even with this instructional intensity, reading fluency is likely to remain substantially impaired. For students with word reading skills around the second percentile, much more instructional time will be needed to reduce their fluency gap and, thus, their ability to access text meaning (Torgesen, 2004).

Provide High-quality Professional Development

Successful implementation requires high-quality professional development with experienced implementers. Language arts teachers and elective teachers who teach the significantly below grade-level students will require at least three days of initial training and five in-class coaching visits by highly trained specialists in the specific intervention program. Teachers who do not specialize in a part of the intensive intervention model, but teach all parts, will need at least five days of initial training to deliver the program adequately.

Follow-up coaching visits are essential to ensure that skills learned in initial training transfer to the classroom. Coaches also help schools problem solve as the implementation progresses through the school year. Coaches can help schools learn how to respond efficiently and effectively to the on-going progress data.

Ongoing Data-driven Decision Making

Data-driven decision making is based on three factors.

1. A big look at outcome reading achievement data.
2. Screening and diagnostic assessment for students who fall into the basic and below basic categories on outcome measures of reading achievement.
3. Frequent progress monitoring, i.e. at least biweekly for significantly below grade-level students to monthly for somewhat below grade-level students.

Set Up a Progress Monitoring System

Progress monitoring measures should be implemented so that problems can be identified early and solved before the high-stakes, year-end tests. Two types of progress monitoring measures are important: (i) program-independent measures of progress and (ii) in-program measures of content mastery.

Program-independent measures should be quick, reliable measures of progress that correlate well with standardized measures of reading comprehension and content understanding (as measured by the district's adopted standardized testing program).

For intensive students, a measure of oral reading fluency on graded passages is generally sensitive to growth and correlates well with more comprehensive, time-consuming reading comprehension measures (for example, Dynamic Indicators of Basic Early Literacy and AIMsweb). Maze measures (a cloze procedure with multiple-choice options) are also quick and reliable to administer and are predictive of performance on accepted reading comprehension measures. Maze measures can be developed locally using research-validated procedures (Espin and Foegen, 1996) or published maze measures are available for purchase (the Multilevel Academic Survey Test by Howell *et al.* (1994)).

In-program mastery checks should also be a part of a progress monitoring system. Students who meet the program goals by passing the mastery checks should also show progress on the independent progress monitoring measures. If they do not, there is a possibility that the adopted program is not teaching the skills required to do better on the high-stakes, year-end measures. Teachers will need to turn in weekly reports indicating content coverage and group mastery data.

Operationalize the Set-up Process

Schools need to begin the program set-up process generally before the results of the current year's high-stakes tests are received. This means they must use year-old data for their first step in categorizing students. As Figure 10.3 indicates, students are first grouped into those students scoring below proficiency and those who do not, using the previous year's data. Students who were not proficient are given the REACH placement tests, found in *The REACH System*. Once the numbers of students at each intervention level have been estimated, the school can develop the master schedule and determine personnel and professional development needs and curriculum ordering information.

Independent fluency, vocabulary, and comprehension measures of progress, such as the San Diego Quick Assessment, oral reading fluency measures, and maze measures, should be scheduled to occur three times a year. In-program mastery tests are scheduled into the programs. Data collection times and subsequent teacher team meetings to analyze the data should be scheduled prior to the beginning of the school year and noted in everyone's calendar.

Grouping needs to remain flexible. This implies that a student who improves much more rapidly than others in his/her literacy group may be moved to a more advanced group during the quarter. The student may be required to do some additional catch-up and literacy homework and additional work in science and social studies to make this move. But the option should always remain available.

Teachers meeting regularly (monthly) to analyze progress data and adjust grouping can greatly enhance student success by tailoring instructional plans to meet individual student needs. These meetings should always be scheduled to follow the early, mid-year and end of year data collections as well as monthly. Team meeting discussions typically address the following.

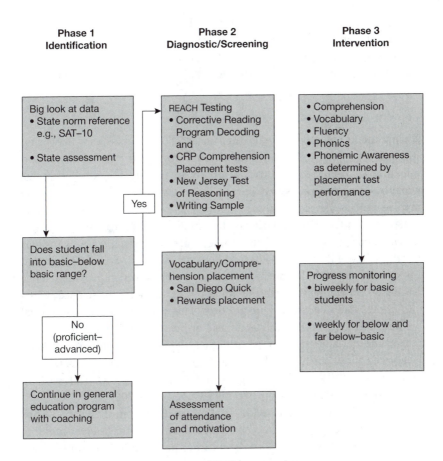

Phase 1
Identification

Phase 2
Diagnostic/Screening

Phase 3
Intervention

Big look at data
• State norm reference
  e.g., SAT–10

• State assessment

REACH Testing
• Corrective Reading
  Program Decoding
  and
• CRP Comprehension
  Placement tests
• New Jersey Test
  of Reasoning
• Writing Sample

• Comprehension
• Vocabulary
• Fluency
• Phonics
• Phonemic Awareness
  as determined by
  placement test
  performance

Yes

Does student fall
into basic–below
basic range?

Vocabulary/Compre-
hension placement
• San Diego Quick
• Rewards placement

Progress monitoring
• biweekly for basic
  students

• weekly for below and
  far below–basic

No
(proficient–
advanced)

Continue in general
education program
with coaching

Assessment
of attendance
and motivation

Figure 10.3 Flowchart showing steps in the REACH program set-up process

1. Reviewing lesson progress to ensure that an adequate number of lessons are taught to meet mid- and end of year goals.
2. Build in re-teaching sessions for groups not at mastery and determine skipping schedules for groups that are at high levels of mastery.
3. Determine particular needs for additional professional development at mid-year sessions.
4. Review student data to determine whether any students can be better served by regrouping (see Figure 10.3).

Those students not making progress require individual instructional planning with more frequent progress monitoring. Their instructional plan may include a behavioral plan, double dosing, in other words re-teaching content at a later period in the day until progress resumes, or additional fluency-building practice provided daily. For identified special education students, the individual plan will be a part of the individual education plan, but others, including students with bilingual issues and/or behavioral needs may also require individual instructional plans.

Content Area Access

Once students have completed REACH level 2 literacy goals, they may begin content area instruction with additional vocabulary and background information preparation. Procedures for increasing science knowledge while building the necessary literacy skills (Carnine and Carnine, 2004) involve both a *big idea* analysis of core science content, as well as daily vocabulary and background information building exercises. The McDougal Littell Science program combines these two instructional features in their middle school Life Science, Physical Science and Earth Science programs. These curricula include enormous Science Toolkits, which provide science teachers with extensive strategies for teaching decoding of science words and critical daily vocabulary instruction. This scaffolding proves essential for most students performing at a basic or below basic literacy level.

For additional content preparation, all higher needs students (REACH level 4 and above) including those who are English-language learners should complete the *REWARDS Plus: Application to Science* and *REWARDS Plus: Application to Social Studies* programs (Archer *et al.*, 2004).

These programs will provide students with the multisyllabic word reading strategies germane to each content area, as well as fluency-building exercises. Each REWARDS Plus Application program focuses on teaching affixes and word families critical for reading social studies and science content. In addition to building accurate word reading strategies, each program contains extensive vocabulary and comprehension building exercises. Students build fluency with background-building passages. They also practice expository writing assignments, learn how to complete various comprehension activities reflecting common test-taking formats, and build meta-cognitive strategies for reviewing written work (rubric summaries) for their own or a partner's work.

For more advanced strategies for accessing content area texts, Deshler and Schumaker (2006) consolidated all the major research findings in the field and provided documentedly effective strategies for optimizing curriculum access. They cited Kame'enui and Carnine's (1998) six principles for developing curricula to maximize learning of struggling secondary students. These design principles include (i) focusing instruction on *big ideas*, (ii) using *conspicuous strategies* to show the steps involved in solving problems, (iii) preteaching *background knowledge,* (iv) providing personalized guidance, assistance and support through *mediated scaffolding,* (v) regularly reviewing previously learned critical information through *judicious review,* and (vi) ensuring that new knowledge is linked to old knowledge through *strategic integration.* Grossen *et al.* (1997) defined these concepts in the following ways.

1. Big ideas: highly selected concepts, principles, rules, strategies, or heuristics that facilitate the most efficient and broadest acquisition of knowledge.
2. Conspicuous strategies: sequence of teaching events and teacher actions that make explicit the steps in learning. They are made conspicuous by the use of visual maps or models, verbal directions, full and clear explanations, etc.
3. Mediated scaffolding: temporary support for students to learn new material. Scaffolding is faded over time.
4. Strategic integration: planful consideration and sequencing of instruction in ways that show the commonalities and differences between old and new knowledge.
5. Primed background knowledge: related knowledge, placed effectively in sequence, that students must already possess in order to learn new knowledge.
6. Judicious review: sequence and schedule of opportunities learners have to apply and develop facility with new knowledge. The review must be adequate, distributed, cumulative, and varied.

A big idea analysis and application of the above design features was utilized in *Understanding U.S. History* (Carnine *et al.,* 1999). Big ideas are concepts or principles, which enable learners to organize, interrelate and apply information so meaningful connections can be made between historical content and their own lives. Volumes 1 (through 1914) and 2 (1914 to the present) follow a careful progression to lead students to an understanding of big ideas in history.

Examples of the curriculum's big ideas are summarized below.

1. The problem–solution–effect big idea structure helps students understand that people and governments tend to encounter problems related to either economic or human rights issues.
2. Economic problems are associated with the need for people to acquire or keep things such as food, clothing, and shelter.
3. Human rights problems are associated with the need for people to achieve religious freedom, freedom of speech, and equal protection

under the law, equal rights for women, minorities, different social classes, and so forth.

4. Another big idea in history is that the success of group efforts, such as wars or the establishment of colonies, is frequently associated with four factors: motivation, leadership, resources, and capability.

5. Other important big ideas taught in the curriculum include how the environment influences how people live and four stages in developing group cooperation.

Considerable research was conducted on these materials at the University of Oregon, where the text is available.

Summary

This chapter highlights multifaceted curricula (*The REACH System*) designed to address struggling students' literacy needs, and effective assessments for placement and monitoring progress. *The REACH System* addresses typical program limitations by providing explicit, systematic instruction built around three previously published programs: *Corrective Reading, Spelling Through Morphographs,* and *Reasoning & Writing.* These three instructional program series, which are both research-based and validated, are combined to provide sufficient literacy instruction (at least two to three periods per day) to reverse the failure trajectory of struggling readers. The most essential component for successful implementations is the commitment of enough time and intensity of instruction to make the difference with these students. The golden rule is the farther behind the student, the more time and intensity in literacy instruction needed to bring students to grade-level performance standards. Without grade-level reading performance, these students will likely never access content from other disciplines, such as science, social studies, health, or mathematics.

Questions

1. What are the three or four most important ideas you would share with a principal or other literacy leader in a middle or high school who was in the planning stages to improve literacy outcomes in their school? Assume that the principal or leader has general buy-in from the teachers about the necessity of improving their instruction and support for improved literacy in their students and that s/he is asking you for advice specifically about improvements in instruction.

2. Please comment on the following statements. To avoid as much as possible separating students who need intervention instruction in the

missing elementary-level pre-skills from students who are perform-ing near or above grade level, provide mainstream instruction that is designed to allow access for students who are struggling readers. To provide mainstream instruction that is exclusive (i.e. instruction designed specifically to meet the needs of only those students per-forming near or above grade level) is an elitist, discriminatory approach to education.

3. If you could change the way instruction is delivered in content area classes (history, social studies, and science) in middle and high school, what would be the three or four most important improve-ments you would recommend to improve overall literacy outcomes?

4. Develop an action plan based on current assessment data of student progress monitoring and end of year/outcome measures of read-ing achievement. Articulate goals for the upcoming year's reading achievement by class and group, such as English-language learning, special education, and Title I students. Apply available resources to provide students with high literacy needs with great instructional time to catch up to peers performing at grade level or near grade level. Allocate resources to provide professional development to staff in evidence-based intervention program materials.

5. Discussion items include the following. How can you intensify instruction within the literacy block to maximize interactive instruc-tion? Identify occasions where time is not used efficiently and make more efficient use of that time. Do teachers get the daily lesson started within two minutes of the period start? Does at least 80 percent of the period consist of interactive instruction with immediate corrective feedback? Do students spend no more than 10 percent of the period doing homework? Interactive instruction with immediate feedback accelerates learning. Long blocks of time for teaching skills are often poorly used.

6. The following is an action research assignment. If you were giving advice to a governor or commissioner of education of a state that was planning an initiative to improve adolescent literacy, what are the three or four most important ideas you would want to share? (These recommendations can be addressed to any aspect of the literacy challenge.)

Appendix: Leadership Resources

Communication lies key to visionary leadership. Several recent tradebooks may be useful. Scott (2004), in her book *Fierce Conversations: Achieving Success at Work and in Life, One Conversation at a Time*, points out that leaders need to engage in "powerful, strong, unbridled, unrestrained, robust" conversations "in which we come out from behind ourselves into the conversation and make it real." She provides guidelines for leading staff to a discussion of the bottom line. If you do not start dealing with the failure of a substantial number of your students, they will continue to fail in school and in life, requiring us all to carry them on our backs through taxes for social services.

Glaser and Glaser (2006) give us clear, simple steps to persuade in their *Be Quiet Be Heard, the Paradox of Persuasion*. Most importantly, this book provides a simple model for collaborative problem solving that will work in a school setting. Although Glaser and Glaser (2006) did considerable work in the private sector, they conducted many valuable workshops in schools dealing with conflict and needing improvements in communication. Their crib notes on "raising delicate issues" and "responding to criticism" are carried by educators far and wide who have attended their workshops and found their techniques essential for working in schools.

For more serious issues, for example dealing with resistant workers and staff with serious problems, McEwan's (2005) book *How to Deal with Teachers Who are Angry, Troubled, Exhausted, or Just Plain Confused* gives a set of commandments that are sound. McEwan's (2005) guidelines promote treating personnel with dignity and respect, while providing clear and definitive expectations about what needs to change. McEwan (2005) gives case studies and how tos for all types of situation that can and do arise in schools.

References

Adams, M. (1990). *Beginning to read: Thinking and comprehension skills.* Cambridge, MA: The MIT Press.

Archer, A., Gleason, M., & Vachon, V. (2004). *Rewards intermediate* (Sopris West Educational Services). Longmont, CO: A Cambium Learning Co.

Arthur, C. (1988). Progress in a high school learning disabilities class. *Direct Instruction News, 8,* 17–18.

Beck, I., McKeown, M., & Kucan, L. (2002). *Bringing Words to Life.* New York: The Guilford Press.

Bridgeland, J., DiIulio, J., & Morison, K. (2006). *The silent epidemic: Perspectives of high school dropouts.* Washington, DC: Civic Enterprises LLC.

Campbell, M. L. (1988). Corrective Reading Program evaluated in secondary students in San Diego. *ADI News, 7* (4), 15–17.

Carnine, D., Crawford, D., Harniss, M., Hollenbeck, K., & Steely, D. (1999). *Understanding U.S. history.* Eugene, OR: University of Oregon.

Carnine, L. & Carnine, D. (2004). The interaction of reading skills and science content knowledge when teaching struggling secondary students. *Reading & Writing Quarterly: Overcoming Learning Difficulties, 20* (2), 203–218.

Clunies-Ross, G. (1990). Some effects of direct instruction in comprehensive skills on intellectual performance. *Behavior Change, 7* (2).

Collins, M. & Carnine, D. (1988). Evaluating the field test revision process by comparing two versions of a reasoning skills CAI program. *Journal of Learning Disabilities, 21,* 375–379.

Crawford, E. & Torgesen, J. K. (2006). *Teaching all students to read: Practices from Reading First Schools with strong intervention outcomes.* The Florida Center for Reading Research (www.fcrr.org/science/sciencepresentations,Torgesen,htm).

Deshler, D. D. & Schumaker, J. B. (Eds.) (2006). *Teaching adolescents with disabilities: Accessing the general education curriculum.* Thousand Oaks, CA: Corwin Press.

Edlund, C. & Ogle, R. (1988). Amounts of training in DI and outcomes with secondary handicapped students. *Direct Instruction News,* 8, 14–15.

Engelmann, S. E. & Dixon, R. (2007). *Spelling through morphographs (SRA).* Columbus, OH: McGraw-Hill.

Engelmann, S. E. & Grossen, B. (2001). *Reasoning & Writing E & F.* Columbus, OH: SRA/McGraw-Hill.

Engelmann, S. E., Carnine, L., Becker, W. C., Johnson, G. L., Meyer, L., & Becker, J. (in press a). *Corrective Reading Program, Decoding Strand.* Columbus, OH: SRA/McGraw-Hill.

Engelmann, S. E., Hanner, S., Osborn, S., & Haddox, P. (in press b). *Corrective Reading Program, Comprehension Strand.* Columbus, OH: SRA/McGraw-Hill.

Espin, C. A. & Foegen, A. (1996). Validity of three general outcome measures for predicting secondary students' performance on content-area tasks. *Exceptional Children, 62,* 497–514.

Francis, D., Shaywitz, S., Steubing, K., Shaywitz, B., & Fletcher, J. (1996). Developmental lag versus deficit models of reading disability: A longitudinal, individual growth curves analysis. *Journal of Educational Psychology, 88* (1), 3–17.

Gersten, R., Brockway, M. A., & Henares, N. (1983). The Monterey DI program for students. *Direct Instruction News, 3,* 8–9.

Glang, A., Singer, G., Cooley, E., & Tish, N. (1991). Using Direct Instruction with brain injured students. *Direct Instruction News, 11* (1), 23–28.

Greene, J. (2002). *High school graduation rates in the United States.* (civic report) (pp. 1–22). New York: Manhattan Institute.

Greene, J., Winters, M., & Swanson, C. (2006). Missing the mark on graduation rates: A response to "the exaggerated dropout crisis." *Education Week,* March 29.

Gregory, R. P., Hackney, C., & Gregory, N. M. (1982). Corrective reading programme: An evaluation. *British Journal of Educational Psychology, 52,* 33–50.

Grossen, B. (1996). Making research serve the profession. *American Educator, 20* (3), 8–16.

Grossen, B. (2002a). The BIG accommodation model: The direct instruction model for secondary schools. *Journal for the Education of Students Placed at Risk, 7* (2), 241–263.

Grossen, B. (2002b). *The REACH system.* Columbus, OH: Science Research Associates.

Grossen, B. (2004). Success of the direct instruction model at a secondary level school with high-risk students. *Reading and Writing Quarterly, 20,* 161–178.

Grossen, B. & Carnine, D. (1990). Diagramming a logic strategy: Effects of difficult problem types and transfer. *Learning Disability Quarterly, 13* (2), 168–182.

Grossen, B., Romance, N., & Vitale, M. (2007). Effective strategies for teaching science. In E. Kame'enui & D. Carnine (Eds.), *Effective teaching strategies that accommodate diverse learners* (pp. 171–201). Columbus, OH: Merrill.

Grossen, B., Carnine, D., & Silbert, J. (2000). Direct instruction to accelerate cognitive growth. In J. Block, S. Everson, & T. Guskey (Eds.), *Comprehensive school reform: A program perspective* (pp. 111–130). DuBuque, IA: Scholastic.

Hempenstall, K. (2001). School-based reading assessment: Looking for vital signs. *Australian Journal of Learning Disabilities, 6,* 26–35.

Hodgkinson, H. L. (1992). *A demographic look at tomorrow.* Washington, DC: Institute for Educational Leadership.

Holdsworth, P. (1984–1985). Corrective Reading tested in U.K. *Direct Instruction News, 4,* 1–4.

Howell, K. W., Zucker, S. H., & Morehead, M. K. (1994). *Multi-level academic skills inventory (MASI).* Paradise Valley, AZ: H & Z Publications.

Kame'enui, E. J. & Carnine, D. (1998). *Effective teaching strategies that accommodate diverse learners.* Columbus, OH: Prentice Hall.

Kame'enui, E. J. & Carnine, D. (Eds.) (2001). *Educational tools for diverse learners.* Columbus, OH: Merrill.

Kasendorf, S. J. & McQuaid, P. (1987). Corrective Reading evaluation study. *Direct Instruction News, 9,* 7–10.

Lee County School District (1997). *An evaluation of Corrective Reading.* Lee County, AL: Lee County School District.

Lyon, G. R., Fletcher, J. M., Shawitz, S. E., Shaywitz, B. A., Torgensen, J. K. *et al.* (2001). Rethinking learning disabilities. In C. E. Finn, Jr, A. J. Rotherham, & C. R. Hokanson, Jr (Eds.). *Rethinking special education for a new century* (pp. 259–287). Washington, DC: Thomas B. Fordham Foundation.

McCardle, P. & Chhabra, V. (Eds.) (2004). *The voice of evidence in reading research.* Baltimore, MD: Paul H. Brookes Publishing Co.

McEwan, E. K. (2005). *How to deal with teachers who are angry, troubled, exhausted or just plain confused.* Thousand Oaks, CA: Corwin Press.

Maggs, A. & Murdoch, R. (1979). Teaching low performers in upper primary and lower secondary to read by DI methods (research report). Sydney, Australia: Macquarie University.

National Assessment of Educational Progress (1999). *Trends in Academic Progress, 1999.* U.S. Department of Education, National Center for Education Statistics (http://nces.ed.gov/ nationsreportcard/reading/results2003/districtsnapshot.asp).

National Center for Educational Statistics (2003). U.S. Department of Education, National Center for Education Statistics (http://nces.ed.gov/nationsreportcard/reading/results2003/district snapshot).

National Reading Panel (2000). Teaching children to read: An evidence-based assessment of the scientific research literature on reading and its implications for reading instruction. National Institute of Child Health and Human Development: Washington, DC.

Paine, S. (2005). *When the principal leads, the school succeeds: Leadership for results in reading first.* National Reading First Conference, New Orleans, July 26–28.

Polloway, E. A., Epstein, M. H., Polloway, C. H., Patton, J. R., & Ball, D. W. (1986). Corrective Reading Program: An analysis of effectiveness with learning disabled and mentally retarded students. *Remedial and Special Education, 7* (4), 41–47.

Ross, D. (1998). *Competing theories: Teach comprehension or teach decoding to improve reading comprehension in older poor readers.* St Kitts: Berne University.

Scott, S. (2004). *Fierce conversations: Achieving success at work and in life, one conversation at a time.* New York: Berkley Books.

Shaywitz, S. (2003). *Overcoming dyslexia: A new and complete science-based program for reading problems at any level.* New York: Knopf.

Sommers, J. (1991). Direct instruction programs produce significant gains with at-risk middle school students. *Direct Instruction News, 11,* 7–13.

Sommers, J. (1995). Seven-year overview of direct instruction programs used in basic skills classes at Big Piney Middle School. *Effective School Practices, 4,* 29–32.

Thomson, B. (1992). A field report: Specific learning disabilities Corrective Reading pilot study 1989–90. *Direct Instruction News, 11,* 13.

Thorne, M. T. (1978). "Payment for reading": The use of the "Corrective Reading scheme" with junior maladjusted boys. *Remedial Education, 13* (2), 87–90.

Torgesen, J. K. (2002). The prevention of reading difficulties. *Journal of School Psychology, 40,* 7–26.

Torgesen, J. K. (2004). *Reading fluency: How does it develop, and how can we improve it in children with reading disabilities.* The Florida Center for Reading Research (www.fcrr.org/science/ sciencepresentations,Torgesen,htm).

Torgesen, J. K. (2006, October). Research Corner: Successful interventions always increase the intensity of instruction. www.fcrr.org/newsletter/Two-Column/newsletter4_3column.htm.

Vitale, M., Medland, M., Romance, N., & Weaver, H. P. (1993). Accelerating reading and thinking skills of low-achieving elementary students: Implications for curricular change. *Effective School Practices, 12* (1), 26–31.

Index